About the Author

Katrina Kirkwood, a former medical research scientist with a passion for stories, is Doctor Isabella Stenhouse's granddaughter. Equipped with two science degrees and an art degree, she spent many years helping people in the South Wales valleys turn their stories into mini-films before embarking on her quest to solve the mystery of Isabella and her beads.

Following features about Isabella on the *BBC Antiques Roadshow*, in national newspapers, and on local radio and television, Katrina has been invited to write about Isabella for the magazine of the Medical Women's Federation and for *Beyond the Trenches*, the blog of the Arts and Humanities Research Council.

D1494658

Reviews

A great deal has already been written on the Great War. Isabella's tale does not take us into the trenches but to the end of the casualty evacuation chain. It gives us an intimate and often emotional perspective of a woman doctor as she battles to succeed in her chosen profession. The narrative kept me captivated. I found myself unable to lay down the book until I reached the final full stop.
Col. Walter Bonnici L/RAMC (Ret'd)

Tonight I felt drawn to Isabella again and couldn't stop. I rarely re-read a book and even though I know this story I wanted to follow it through to the denouement – which I felt you gave me … An expert might disagree with me, but this reader feels you will entice other readers to follow the trail too.
Lila Haines, Director of Egino C.I.C.

The writing's great, and you come away with a very strong composite picture of Isabella and her context. Really enjoyed reading it.
Patrick Dillon, Author, architect and broadcaster

The Mystery
of Isabella
and the String
of Beads

A WOMAN DOCTOR IN
WORLD WAR I

Katrina Kirkwood

LPRESS
OKE

First Published in Great Britain in 2016 by Loke Press,

10, The Loke,

Norwich

NR4 6XA

www.lokepress.com

Copyright © Katrina Kirkwood 2016

Typeset by Loke Press

A CIP record for this title is available from the British Library

ISBN 978-0-9954893-0-1

eISBN 978-0-9954893-1-8

PROLOGUE

"There might be German blood on these," I warned as I placed the box on the table. From its battered cardboard top poked a rectangular, twill-covered object and a length of red rubber tubing. On the box's side, a red stamp postmarked 1972 partly hid its label, 'Flower Press'. Carefully, my friends drew out a couple of photographs. Then some forceps. A wooden box flipped open to disclose a set of scalpels. The twill cover unfastened to reveal an engraved metal canister clanking with surgical implements, while the red rubber tubes straightened into an ancient stethoscope.

But there was no flower press. The box had been the nearest container to hand when I had received this legacy from Isabella, my grandmother. I had always intended to do something with it, sometime. I did not know what, but definitely something, sometime, and until that sometime came, the precious legacy would have to continue masquerading as a flower press.

Tracy began to examine one object in more detail, turning it over and peering at an inscription. "It says, 'Leith' here," she deciphered.

"That makes sense," I replied, "That's where Isabella was brought up."

"This one says Aberdeen, so that's Scotland too," another voice added.

I had never taken the trouble to examine the collection closely. I had never noticed the inscriptions, but my friends' observations made sense. Family tradition held that Isabella had qualified as a doctor in Edinburgh and had served in France, Malta and Egypt during the First World War. And the things you have lived with since childhood seem normal. Lots of grandmothers must have worked as doctors during World War I. It was nothing special.

But people's reactions told me otherwise. "What, she was a doctor in the First World War? Really? There can't have been many of them. How fascinating ..."

That day and afterwards, the comments kept coming, and I began to realise how little I knew about the story that had been hiding in my flower press box. First of all, was it true? If it was that unusual, maybe it was not. But if it was true, how come nobody knew anything about that part of Isabella's life? Why had she never talked about it? What had she actually experienced?

And how did I square my perceptions of the First World War, with its trenches, explosions, mud and gore with my fun-loving and utterly affectionate Scottish granny? How does being a war doctor fit with jelly in a silver dish, cheese on a bright green platter and mince pies from Fortnum and Mason; with her huge four-poster bed and its damask curtains, frilled pillows and thick silky bolsters? I used to stare up at the big, round hat boxes balanced on top of her wardrobe. When she opened the cupboard, there was a curious, woody smell and I could reach in to stroke her fur coats, bury my nose in their softness and breathe in their strangeness. She would pass me the ornate silver hairbrushes from her high dressing table and I would press them against my hand. They were soft, so much softer and yellower than mine.

Sometimes she would lead us through the white door in the corner of her kitchen and up the rickety iron steps onto the roof. Just like in *Mary Poppins*, we ran and chased and hid among the chimney pots. We crept to the very edge and looked all around the city, proud to point out the landmarks. Then, terrified but intrigued, we peered dangerously down and watched. Far, far below were cars smaller than the ones my brothers played with. The people scurrying alongside were tinier than their toy soldiers. Visiting Isabella was fun.

Fun, that is, apart from the scary room where Grandpa had died. I hated going in there. But his photograph remained; he was the soldier staring down from the sideboard at the bald patch on the rug where his sword had slipped as he sliced the wedding cake. Or so the story went. The bald patch was real. But the sword? The First World War?

I shiver and bring myself back to the present. 'Sometime' has arrived. I must discover the story of my mysterious legacy. The final item in the box clinches my decision. To me, it has always been the heart of the collection, and I draw it out cautiously – Isabella's string of beads. Like a necklace with no clasp, intricately woven and scarily delicate, its crazy colours stretch for nearly a metre. It is as narrow as my little fingernail, and matches no jewellery or clothing that I have ever seen.

I remember Isabella telling me that these beads had been

given to her by a grateful German prisoner of war. As a teenager, I hoped I sniffed a clandestine romance. As an adult, I loved the way the gift transcended the barriers of gender and enmity. Today though, I notice that one of the linen threads has worn through. As a single, glassy bead drifts loose, I catch it in my hand. Scarcely larger than the grains of sand from which it came, it has the advantage of them. It possesses a hole. That hole has given it connections. That hole has joined it to its companions and together they have lived a story, a story in some way linked to Isabella's secret medical past. As I roll the bead in my palm, I know it is time to reconnect my inheritance with its history before it is too late.

SECTION 1

1

Isabella wears a long, white lacy dress and an over-sized academic gown. Her fur-trimmed university hood drapes heavily over one arm, its silk lining glinting. Posed with a dip-pen, she is leaning forward, gazing ahead. It has to be graduation day, but how has an Edwardian girl earned the right to wear that hood? Her expression is solemn, but is she masking an un-Edwardian smile? Quietly glowing with pride?

My mind flips to a recent graduation ceremony: gowned girls tottering in their newly purchased heels and elegantly tight skirts were jiggling their slippery hoods and laughing with the boys. Tweaking the angle of their mortar boards, they queued to use the studio backdrop that trumpeted the university name in bold, block capitals. Long, glossy black hair swishing, a willowy girl took her turn. Snap, flash went the cameras. Click-whirr went the smartphones. A tiny, sari-clad woman eagerly joined the girl, curving her arm around the thick graduation gown. Then I understood. This was a first. The family had a degree. Just like Isabella's family – I glance back at the photograph in my hand – how many years ago?

Will I ever be able to find out? Isabella never became famous, so there seems little chance of unearthing her online. I could start with general history and simply google 'women doctors WWI'. I could trawl through museums and archives, but what if something – anything – Isabella-specific is hiding in some deep and distant part of the internet, or lurking in some library simply waiting to be discovered? I need a starting point that gives me a fighting chance of levering my way into Isabella's story. As I look back at my enigmatic grandmother refusing to meet my gaze from the photograph, the penny drops. Could her degree ceremony be exactly what I need?

It proves ridiculously easy – Google tells me that the graduation took place at the University of Edinburgh on 11th July 1913. My friends were right – being a woman doctor at that time was unusual: Isabella was one of only five women receiving a degree in medicine alongside ninety-three men. When the university emails 'We have the records of all our students', I rush to visit.

Cautiously turning the pages of a huge and elderly tome, the archivist lays Isabella's university record before me. The looped black words take me aback. Are they the youthful precursor to the scrawled, 'Love from Granny' messages at the bottom of my birthday cards? Or were they written by a clerk? Gingerly, I leaf backwards a page or so and discover that each record is in a different hand. I am, indeed, looking at Isabella's own writing – dip-penned a century ago. Physics, anatomy, *materia medica*, practice of medicine, mental diseases, surgical clerkship … .

Isabella seems to have recorded every course that she studied – the subject, the number of lectures, the dates, the teacher's name, the name of the University and how much it cost, but as I sit marvelling, the archivist presents me with a book, *Memories of a Doctor in War and Peace*, by Isabel Emslie Hutton. As I start to read, its words weave colour and detail round the bald statements of the Curriculum Schedule. In no time, it is as if I am being lured onto 'Isabella's Medical Ghost Tour'. Foolishly, it gives me goose pimples. It is as if that anonymous veil 'Granny' has slipped and I am glimpsing a secret past. But even as I glimpse, I hesitate. Should I wait? Read this later? Will I understand it better if I first work out what made her want to become a doctor? What gave her the courage to become one of those heavily out-numbered females?

Hopeful of uncovering clues, I dig into censuses, certificates and directories to thread together the facts. Isabella was born in Leith on 30th July 1887. Her three sisters, Ena, Beth and Jan, all came along soon afterwards. Home was a newly built house in a sheltered crescent, but they needed more space. I track them on Google Earth. First they moved to overlook the open green space of Leith Links, but by 1901 they had moved again, sliding round the side of the Links to a much larger house, where they employed a cook and a housemaid. Isabella's father, William, worked as a merchant with his brother and their father. Corn, hay, potatoes – they traded them all. As the years went by, the family business expanded to three addresses, two in Leith and another, 11 Atholl Place, in the heart of Edinburgh.

Picturing the Stenhouses huddling in a bare and poky office, *Christmas Carol*-like, I decide to take a look. The building stuns me. Towering above a hectic junction, classical and curved, it somehow holds itself calmly detached from the hurly-burly of the twenty-first century. Keeping my aspirations small, I begin imagining Isabella's black-clad menfolk toiling up the stairs to the garret, passing the wealthier businesses on the lower floors, but a fact-check stops me. The records report that the Stenhouses were in charge of this whole magnificent establishment. They did not toil up to the attic, genuflecting to the masters below – they were the inhabitants of the capacious rooms downstairs. They were the wealthy businessmen who perhaps occasionally nodded to the passing minions trudging up the stairs. I ditch my Dickensian fantasy – white and elegant above the grunting traffic, this place oozes stability and success, but it offers no hint as to why a daughter of this establishment should choose to go her own way.

Hoping I will learn more by visiting Isabella's home, I catch a bus down Leith Walk. Through photographs from the turn of last century, I start to see this road as Isabella does: people in hats straggle freely, untroubled by cars; dusty workmen excavate cobbles with spades and pickaxes to create channels for the new tram-lines. Then the bus rounds a corner, chugs a few metres and I spot the Stenhouse's road across the green of Leith Links.

Sudden rain forces me into the shelter of a disused building and I seize the moment to study John's Place. It is a typical, Edinburgh Georgian terrace, each house rising three storeys high above its basement and stretching three crisp white windows wide. The grey slate roofs match the weather.

I find myself utterly unprepared for the world behind No 9's front door. The hall seems to have stepped straight out of a fairy tale. An oval staircase, edged by delicate white wrought-iron balusters, spirals upwards from a cushion of rich blue carpet. It is strangely bright, the light pouring through an oval skylight in the domed ceiling. Isabella and her family lived here? It is more like a stately home – a National Trust property.

The front rooms are airy and large, the old shutters folded back to give a clear view of the rain powering across the Links. Number 9 is no longer a family home – it now houses a media company. Every wall is white, and large, loud artworks celebrate successful advertising campaigns, but traces linger. Redundant fireplaces sit opposite IKEA conference tables and plastic chairs. Bells for summoning servants remain, painted silent behind graphic designers intent on their screens.

I let time slip. How do the Stenhouses use this building? With father, mother, four sisters and two servants, who sleeps where? What happens in each room? In my head, I darken the walls, install some heavy wooden furniture, plenty of thick drapery and a plethora of ornaments. With no internet, television or even radio, how do they spend their days?

Music? Definitely music. There has to be a piano. Even the poorest of families aim for a piano, and this room is so vast I can give them a grand. I place an elementary book of scales on its music rack, ready for the girls to practise. Beside it, I add some Beethoven for Isabella's mother and a couple of Scottish song books for family music-making.

And how about reading? Thinking that an understanding of current affairs might trigger Isabella's ambition, I begin laying out a newspaper, but a headline proclaiming a juicy murder makes me hurry to hide it away. I had forgotten – girls are not allowed to read the papers for fear that their innocent minds will be tainted. Instead, I resort to the latest of Andrew Lang's fairy books, *The Pink Fairy Book*.

What else? Work baskets are safe, they definitely need work baskets – what with samplers, knickers, pillow-cases and petticoats, there is plenty to sew. I am setting out five – one for each child and one for their mother – when a photograph catches my eye and I go over to examine it. The four sisters are posing amongst the cane furniture and painted prettiness of Pettigrew and Amos' studio on Leith Walk, not far away. Each girl wears a gorgeous dress, their hands are gloved, their huge hats steady

and every curl is in place as they wait, faces fixed, for the photographer to finish.

I am still studying the lace and frills when a bustling noise seeps in from the hall. I turn, hoping. Could that be the girls going out? Might they be wearing these very frocks for a party?

I remember Isabella's parties … Christmas, the yellow light and thick velvet curtains, the green carpet, voices booming above my head. The grown-ups suited and tall, twiddling their sherry glasses. Kilt-clad cousins playing with my brothers. Mrs White, the Scottish 'help', bustling platters to and from the kitchen. Later on, we would be stationed in front of Andy Stewart and *The White Heather Club* – the Scottish accents, skirling pipes and swirling kilts, forces invoked by Isabella to breathe some sort of Scottish identity into her very English grandchildren.

Echoes of age-old bagpipes set my feet tapping as I imagine Isabella and her sisters discussing their dance cards – but perhaps they are not off to a party this time. Maybe they are going to a play or a concert – even in Leith there are a number of theatres and concert-halls. Or they could be dressing up warmly for a visit to Grandfather Stenhouse's farm at Hilltown, only a few miles east from here.

The ideas flood in – are the girls loading up the luggage to go and stay at the farm on the other side of the Forth where their mother grew up? Or – now this would be exciting – could it be one of the occasions when Isabella is going to sea? Is her trunk at the foot of the stairs ready for her to voyage across the North Sea to Norway in one of her father's ships? But perhaps that piece of family tradition is only a myth …

Moving to the window, I push aside the thick net curtains to watch the girls' departure. If I had been a child here, I would have spent hours watching the Links with its changing seasons and comings and goings. I have seen an old postcard of the trees in blossom, so I people the paths with ladies in huge hats and children bowling hoops. I let music drift over from the band-stand and wonder about golf. The game is played on the Links until 1905 but are the young Stenhouses allowed to play?

Abruptly, I pull myself back – this is getting me no nearer to finding out why Isabella chose to study medicine. I stare at the empty road – it is almost Sunday-quiet. And suddenly, I wonder. Could religion have been Isabella's driver? I can see the family joining the throngs walking to worship, the girls trying to hold in their excitement – they meet friends at church.

I look back into the room. It needs a Bible – one of those huge black, leather-bound family bibles with gold tooling. Their father is an elder at Pilrig Chapel, an evangelical establishment on Leith Walk. Although it has taken the risk of installing electric light, it heartily disapproves of the council's decision to run trams on Sundays. Plumping a heavy bible onto the shiny mahogany sideboard beside the picture of the girls, I wonder how many of Pilrig's two services and two Sunday Schools these four have to attend each week, and whether chapel attendance equates with faith.

Archive images show the groups of bare-footed children, basket-carrying women and flat-capped men who live in Leith's poorer districts. Could it be that Isabella, like other middle-class Edinburgh girls, is sent on church missions to the sick and housebound? Along with philanthropy, they learn about the ailments and struggles of others. Occasionally, I have read, such visits prompt a girl to aim for the medical profession, but when I look again at Isabella, her face gives nothing away. How much is she allowed to know and understand? And how on earth am I going to get inside her mind?

Heaving a sigh, I move to the back of the house. The rooms here are smaller and darker. In the basement, the ceilings are low and there is no garden. Instead, a small yard cowers, sunless, between the surrounding buildings. Washing would not dry here, and plants would not grow. It is time to go, and as the stout front door closes behind me, I earnestly hope that I will receive more illumination about Isabella's motives for becoming a doctor from her school than I have from this place.

3

The address has me flummoxed, '11 Abercromby Place', three small words in Isabella's Matriculation Record that are my only clue to her pre-University education. It is hardly the name of a school, and all I can find out in the library is that the building was owned by a Miss Williamson – which is no help at all. Disheartened, I leave, and find myself trudging past soggy tourist tartans. Out of habit I drift into a bookshop and meander towards the local history shelf. Suddenly I spot it: *Crème de la Crème: Girls' Schools of Edinburgh.*

Grabbing the book, I fumble for the index. Will I find Miss Williamson? Yes! As quickly as the sticking of the new pages allows, I read enough to shove the book back on the shelf, rush out of the shop and hotfoot it to the National Library of Scotland where I digest *Crème's* Page 32, and start picturing scenes from *A Little Princess* – young ladies learning from inept governesses amidst opulent silks in fusty, panelled rooms. Could Isabella have been a pupil under Miss Williamson, learning Music and French from the resident governesses alongside boarders from far-flung places such as India and Devon and thirty-four other girls, yet somehow managing to change direction and become a medical student? I hurry to check the 1901 census for John's Place. Bingo! All four girls are described as 'Scholars'. A visit is essential.

Abercromby Place lies in Edinburgh's New Town, and as I approach, it is the trees that catch my eye. Opposite the houses, they dwarf the railings that enclose them. Grassy slopes create a secret valley between their trunks. They must easily be a century old. At a nearby school, one girl visited all the houses bordering a similar patch of greenery to get permission for the pupils to use it for exercise and play. Could Isabella and the girls of Miss Williamson's academy have done likewise? I can see them marching across the road in a crocodile, pausing while the teacher unlocks the gate, and running amongst these very trees when they are a fraction of their present size. I strain my ears to see if I can catch the echoes of girlish laughter, their joy on release from study, and their repressed giggles as they march back to school, their faces glowing discreetly, and I follow them.

The terrace of houses is a taller, smarter reflection of John's Place, with Miss Williamson's No. 11 standing militarily erect immediately opposite the locked garden gate. Black iron railings are throwing a cage of shadows down into its double depth basement, and I imagine pinafored Stenhouses pattering down the iron steps, laughing when the sun shines and shivering when it snows.

Inside, I am greeted by a clone of John's Place – a curving staircase, domed ceiling and immense wooden doors. The basement is gloomy, but when I spiral up to the top, I emerge into the light, high above the trees. Not only is Abercromby Place six storeys high, it is near the top of a steep hill. From the back of the building, nothing blocks the sight of Fife far away on the other side of the Firth of Forth. It is a magnificent place for day-dreaming, for imagining the world beyond the classroom, but I collect myself. I cannot allow Isabella up here to the top floor. There are boarders, resident governesses and servants to house, let alone Miss Williamson and her elderly aunt. Best bring in some bedsteads and get downstairs.

I want to find Miss Williamson's office. On the ground floor? At the back where she can enjoy the view, or at the front where she can keep an eye on all who come and go? In imagination, I picture the first time Isabella's parents visit the school.

The maid shows them in and Miss Williamson looks up from her leather-topped desk. She has been at this job for many years and knows that the key to gaining pupils is to give the fathers what they want. The mothers rarely matter. If the father says, "My daughter is delicate," she will reassure him that it is perfectly possible for the dear girl to have a complete education merely by attending classes in the morning. If he declares that all he wants for his daughter is that she should be ready for a good marriage, she will assure him that the preparation of girls for their unique profession as wives is her main aim and that lessons will be given in all the key subjects – music, dancing, languages, sewing, knitting, elocution and deportment.

But she has to be careful, alert to the possibility that he might be one of those few fathers who genuinely wants his daughter to be prepared for the University entrance exams. Most middle-class parents feel that girls who do not need to earn a living should not take jobs away from those who do. Most of them regard public exams as fit only for those poor unfortunates who will have to work – but it would not do to make a mistake in this instance. Overlooking the irony of her own position, she rises and greets them, "Good afternoon, Mr and Mrs Stenhouse."

I survey the building's high ceilings, ornate cornices and spacious rooms. What does Isabella learn here? What subjects does she pencil into her weekly timetable? And what happens here that makes her want to study medicine? On her matriculation form she will write that she took 'Edin. Med. Prelim.' aged 16 in April 1904, passing the compulsory papers in English, Latin and Mathematics, and choosing French for her fourth subject rather than Greek or German.

Wanting to know more, I choose a bland meeting-room overlooking the trees and allow it to develop into a classroom. The noise of cars humming over tarmac fades and a horse and cart clatters past on the cobbles. Clearing out the conference tables, I set up a blackboard and rows of solid wooden desks. Fumbling piano chords from a music lesson across the corridor clash with the rhythm of a waltz whispering its way up from a dancing lesson downstairs. I replace the IT equipment with sewing baskets, hardback French primers and German grammars. I avoid bunsen burners, test-tubes and similar laboratory paraphernalia – science is utterly unnecessary for girls who are preparing to become wives. Instead, I hang up a world map, spattered pink with the British Empire, and the girl who was born in India picks up a long wooden pointer to show where she used to live, many weeks away.

The clock hanging on the wall reads half past ten. Although the teacher's desk is comfortably near the remains of the coal fire, she wears a fur coat and hat, and when the door opens, I can almost hear the girls sigh with relief – a maid is bringing in a scuttle of fresh coal. The pupils are bulky with the layers they are wearing in their efforts to keep warm. The fire blazes, the teacher stands, issues a command and they begin chanting – one nine is nine, two nines are eighteen, three nines are … and the scene blurs, the girls grow. Isabella's pinafore is replaced by a skirt and blouse, the girls conjugate complex tenses of French verbs, recite poems, and stitch beautiful embroideries. Many of them leave the classroom. Is it only Isabella who remains?

The December sky is overcast but she settles herself at a desk with an exercise book and a pencil. In only four short months she will be sitting her Medical Prelim exams. Her parents must have agreed to let her take them, and Miss Williamson must have arranged tuition, but it is said that few middle-class girls take their academic work seriously, and fewer still want to go to university. Many are simply eager to catch a husband and start their careers as married women.

So what keeps Isabella at her books? Is it really religion, or could she be like one girl I read about who declared that she took up medicine simply to avoid the boredom of being rich? Perhaps Isabella, unlike her classmates, fervently longs *not* to become a middle-class lady. After all, who would want to engage in that never-ending bustle of purchasing, organising servants, socialising and philanthropic fund-raising? Who would want to risk being one of those who sink into sickness, drained not by the rigours of childbirth, but by the tedium of filling so many long hours with a very few trivial responsibilities.

I peer over Isabella's shoulder. Her page is full of Latin, but it is far more than *amo-amas-amat* – the whole thing looks like an advanced translation and gets me speculating. What if Miss Williamson is not the inept governess I have been picturing?

What if she is an inspirational teacher who fills her girls' heads with dreams of lives lived well beyond the confines of hearth and home. In which case she may come in at any moment to check up on Isabella and make sure her star pupil achieves the highest possible marks. It is time to go.

Bidding farewell to the classroom, I walk up the hill to Minto House on Chambers Street. This building used to be the medical school for women – the faded paintwork above the doorway still reads, 'SCHOOL OF MEDICINE, 1878'. It accepted girls as young as sixteen, so Isabella could start her training here the moment she passes her prelims in 1904 – but she does not.

She will not arrive here until 1908. Why? What can possibly hold her back for a whole four and a half years?

4

By autumn 1904, Isabella is seventeen. She has lived through the joy of Queen Victoria's Diamond Jubilee and the sadness of her death, the downs and ups of the Boer War and the official visit of the new King to Edinburgh.

She has seen technological advance – trams now run up and down Leith Walk, lights powered by electricity are beginning to appear, and last year reports came from America that some gentlemen had flown a powered airplane along a beach.

There has been sadness – her grandfather died last year, so her father and his brother now manage the family business. But while she may have passed her exams and left Miss Williamson behind, she has no job, no income, no prospects and is legally entitled to get married. I picture her standing at the door of John's Place, waving her sisters off to their first term at school without her. She goes inside and she …

Well, what does she do in this see-saw time before her future tilts into the certainty of medical school? She is on her own with Mother, cook and the maid. The silence is unusual, oppressive. She knows there will be bridge parties, tennis, golf and plenty of time for church work. In these pre-television days of home-brewed entertainment, she will probably continue her music lessons and take part in amateur theatricals. She will certainly go to balls.

Perhaps the younger girls watch her preparing, the John's Place stairwell dim in the evening gloom. Somebody lights the gas-lamps – or have the Stenhouses already installed electricity? Isabella descends the spiral staircase, her luscious dress swishing against the slender balusters. Her necklace is simple, her hair up, her neckline modestly *décolleté*. Does a length of tartan grace her shoulders, ready for a Scottish dance? At the foot of the stairs, her mother waits. A willing chaperone, she will sit with the other anxious mothers examining their daughters' popularity on the dance floor, an early warning of their desirability as wives.

As the carriage rattles off across the cobbles – traditional scenario beloved of costume dramas – the Edinburgh Medical College for Women lies only two miles away. Bitter disagreements have surrounded the training of female doctors in the city, with first Sophia Jex-Blake and then Elsie Inglis setting up medical schools for women.

The light from a gas lamp momentarily falls on Isabella's determined face and once more I wonder. Could her ambition to study medicine simply stem from the desire to earn a good income and hold a respected place in society? That is all some girls want and, if that is Isabella's motivation, medicine is her best choice. Teachers and nurses are poorly paid and low in the social pecking order. Banking, the diplomatic service and the law are closed to women and in the whole of Britain, there are only two female accountants, three female veterinary surgeons and six female architects. Not that there are all that many women doctors. In 1901 only 60 were practising in Scotland, another 140 were practising elsewhere in Britain and a third as many again were working overseas, usually as missionaries.

Yet, while the total numbers of women practising medicine may be small, relatively large numbers of them practise in this city – it makes the profession very tempting for an intelligent young woman – but with the carriage hurtling Isabella towards the marriage market, I imagine her forcing herself to pack away her dreams. Tonight is for dancing and she is sure to enjoy the evening – she is a cheerful girl and is looking forward to seeing her friends, but … this restless ambition insists on drifting constantly to the forefront of her mind. She opens her purse to distract herself with its contents.

Seated beside her daughter in the carriage, Janet too may be haunted by Isabella's ambition. She and her husband have spent long hours on the matter. They simply cannot believe that women have the physical stamina for the profession. They discuss the recent tragic incident when the strain of the job led an unfortunate young lady doctor to take her own life.

"Being a doctor would be so lonely," thinks Janet. "Why, Isabella would be most unlikely to find a man who would marry her, so she would never have children. It really would be such a dreadful waste. Come to that, it would be positively selfish when the Empire needs all the sons it can get. And as to the work she would be allowed to do, why, she might even have to leave Edinburgh. And she would only be able to treat other women. Of course it would all be so inappropriate – there are so many situations a young, unmarried woman should not be expected to encounter, let alone all that blood and appalling poverty. No, it really would not be suitable." And Janet's thoughts, too, divert to the dance, where her hopes are pinned on romance ousting Isabella's unacceptable ambition.

But perhaps romance is not winging itself Isabella's way. Perhaps the partners who fill her dance card do not inspire her as she swirls round the ballroom. Perhaps her mind is not on polite conversation with the eligible young men whose strong arms enfold her, but insists on reverting to the possibility of study. Without her father's funds, her dream cannot come true. By the end of the night, she has not fallen in love, she has concluded she must employ all her daughterly wiles to win her father round.

The days and the months pass. '04 becomes '05, '05 turns into '06, and in a small leather bound album bearing the words 'Beth Stenhouse, 1906' on the fly-leaf I come across a clue. The pages are filled with verses from unknown well-wishers, each signed and dated, but tucked away on an elusive page deep inside, I find Isabella.

The scene plays itself out in my head. Beth is fourteen, and on 28th January 1906, she decides to get out her autograph book. She has had it for a couple of years, but she has not yet collected many entries. Carefully, she divides a yellow page towards the back of the album into sections, one for each of the six people who are now sitting downstairs in the sleepy aftermath of a huge Sunday lunch. Presented with the book, her father signs his name. Her mother obliges. Her friends Ermintrude Godwin and Leila Stock make their marks. Ena is out, but twelve-year-old Jan is eager to please her big sister – it is a *dreich* day and this is something to do.

And while eighteen-year-old Isabella writes 'Bell Stenhouse, 28th January 1906' inside one of Beth's boxes, I clench my fist in frustration. Almost every other autograph in the book fills a whole page and is accompanied by a verse, but the divisions Beth has made on this particular page have left absolutely no space for Isabella to add her personal touch. Oh, if only Beth had not drawn those wretched sub-divisions! Isabella would then have been forced into penning a greeting, and I would have had a rare and precious clue as to her thoughts. As it is, I have nothing but a signature. Bother Beth!

Pulling myself together, I comfort myself with the fact that at least I now know that eighteen months after leaving school, Isabella is still at home with her family. As winter turns into spring and summer comes, perhaps William and Janet Stenhouse hesitate. They can marshall all the arguments against allowing their precious eldest daughter to turn herself into a doctor, but they can see how set she is on the idea, how restless she is within their home. I can see them engaging in endless discussions – publicly over the dinner table, cosily round the fire, privately in William's study. Sometimes Isabella feels she might win, sometimes she despairs, sometimes her parents' arguments almost begin to convince her, until one or another thing happens to remind her why she can never, under any circumstances, continue with this kind of life. By summer, Ena too is free from school. She is two years younger than Isabella, and tradition holds that the two of them are sent to Paris and Berlin to perfect their languages and learn *haute cuisine*. An appropriate way to complete the education of the daughters of a successful, upwardly mobile Edwardian merchant? Or a pleasant way to distract an aspiring medical student?

By the time Isabella returns to John's Place, her ambition has not faltered. Maybe her parents make a final, feeble attempt to dissuade her – Janet has recently met such an unhappy woman, a doctor who has been qualified for a decade, and upon whom the struggle to find work and the isolation of the job has brought serious ill-health, a woman who declares that if she were allowed another chance she would prefer to marry and have children.

Their pleadings do not convince their daughter. She knows that she is an odd one out – that her drive and desire for a professional life are unusual, freakish even, but I suspect that she also knows she is not a sideline in the tide of history. I suspect she believes she will be joining pioneers in washing away archaic barriers. I look again at Minto House. The women who arrive here are not like twenty-first-century kids escaping for three happy years at Uni, nor are they on a conveyor belt to a ready-made career. They have needed immense spirit and determination even to reach the threshold of this door. Their unorthodox life-choice will set them apart from their peers forever. They may be dooming themselves to a lifetime of struggle but they are up for the fight and, at 21 years old, sometime in October 1908, Isabella intends to join them.

SECTION 2

1

Am I at last ready to get started on Isabella's Medical Ghost Tour? I study another photograph. Half past two, reads Isabella's wristwatch – a large-faced, mannish timepiece. An afternoon appointment? I zoom out to look at her. She is on her own – on her own in a dark world in a white coat; a white coat with creases so sharp and stiff that I can almost smell the starch and feel the thick, heavy cotton. There is a blemish in one corner. When I zoom back in, it becomes the name of the studio where Isabella and her sisters posed so prettily as children. All that remains of that prettiness is a ruffled blouse peeking out above the tightly buttoned V-neck of the coat. The details in the studio's address date the photograph to 1908. Could this be her first white coat, purchased so that she can start her studies at Minto House? The idea excites me. Is this a companion to the graduation photo – the two pictures bookending Isabella's training as a doctor?

The solemnity of sending her out to the studio to be photographed sweeps me into the buzz of excitement that ripples through the family as Isabella, after all these years, begins her new career. I almost get goose pimples again. Her sisters shuffle excitedly at the foot of the stairs, her mother gives her a deep, clasping hug, the cook and the maid bob discreetly and cries of "Good luck!" follow her as she sets out on her first day. Perhaps her father accompanies her … Minto House is not far from the office … just to keep an eye on her … ?

But there is a problem. Minto House has been sold. The news

breaks in March. After the summer term, no more classes for women medical students can be held in the building. The Scottish Association for the Medical Education of Women, who have been renting Minto House for their Medical College, decide that new premises are not their first priority. Instead, they regard this as the perfect moment to challenge the University of Edinburgh.

"The place already awards medical degrees to women – it should teach them too."

"The university has always prided itself on the quality of the training it offers, but for medical women it is functioning purely as an examining body, a role it has always professed to despise."

"Now that medicine has become so scientific, medical students need practical training before they sit their examinations, and it is difficult for any organisation other than a university to provide such tuition, especially in anatomy and physiology."

The Association even offers the university a phased handover of the teaching to make it easier, but the debate drags on. I imagine the whispers reaching Isabella: 500 male medical students have begged the university to refuse to teach the women; 24 of the 25 women who sat the university's physiology examination have failed.

At some point the discussions end. In a flat statement that allows no room for appeal, the university rejects the Association's arguments: given that it cannot see its way to allowing mixed classes in the Faculty of Medicine, it does not have the resources to teach the women.

The debate in John's Place has to shift. It is no longer about whether Isabella should be allowed to study medicine, but whether she will have to give up her dream, or whether she can go further afield – to Glasgow, or Aberdeen, or St Andrews, or even over the border into England – anywhere that still trains women to be doctors.

But behind the scenes in the heart of Edinburgh, a new solution is reached. Ignoring the Association, the university gives individual recognition to the lecturers who have long taught the women students. Banding together, the men resurrect the name of Sophia Jex-Blake's original medical school to create a new 'Edinburgh School of Medicine for Women'. By October, just in time for Isabella to start the new academic year, it is set up and ready in Surgeons' Hall, just round the corner from Minto House.

Readying myself for the Ghost Tour now, I hesitate. I started this quest to unearth the story of the beads and the medical kit lying in the Flower Press box. As Isabella starts her studies, she will begin gathering these objects. She has to venture into specialist medical instrument shops unaccustomed to serving women. She has to brave the looks of the shop assistants – men? – behind the counter, and march her new kit home. For the umpteenth time, I pull out one of the tools she has just purchased. If I am to thread these objects back into her story, I need to understand them. I arrange to see an expert. A quick chat with him, I think, then Ghost Tour, I am all yours.

The historian is patient. The wooden box of scalpels is an anatomy dissection kit. Wood cannot be sterilised, so when the medical world discovered that sterilising the equipment used in operations reduced wound infection, they replaced their old wooden handled tools with solid metal implements. I unbutton the twill pouch to show him the surgical instrument set with its proud inscription, Dr Isabel Stenhouse, Leith NB.

"That khaki-style cover does not necessarily mean the instruments are military," he warns. He identifies a suture needle in a small, silvery case – it still rests on pink tissue. He goes through the miscellany of solid metal sterilisable surgical instruments she has kept: artery clamps, forceps, scalpels and more. How, why and when did Isabella use them, I muse as, at last, I allow the Ghost Tour to take charge.

Stop No. 1 is Surgeons' Hall itself. As Isabella walks towards its splendid façade on her first day, she is following in illustrious footsteps. In 1870, Sophia Jex-Blake and six other women came here to try and sit an anatomy exam. It was part of their battle to enter the medical profession, and it caused a public riot. Not that the violence broke their resolve, I muse, as I cross a courtyard and enter the museum near where Isabella and her fellow students have to dissect their way up the whole hierarchy of the animal kingdom. Starting with crayfish, they move on to earthworms, skate, frogs, pigeons and finish with rabbits, getting a thorough schooling in zoology before being let loose on the intricacies of human anatomy.

They are studying botany as well as zoology. Stop No. 2 should take me out to the Pentland Hills, where they hike miles on botany field-trips, the length of their walks destroying my preconceptions of how far young ladies can possibly trek in long skirts. But it is not a Saturday; they will not be there. Instead,

I follow Isabella to Stop No. 3, the George Square home of her physics lecturer, Dr Dawson Turner, a man so enthusiastic about his work that X-rays of his damaged hands will end up as specimens in the museum I have just left. His name will be inscribed on a memorial in Hamburg to pioneers whose work on X-rays damaged their own health, and his book will be of such interest that it will be re-issued in the twenty-first century. Not only that, as the vice-president of the Scottish Automobile Club, he owns two cars and, this evening, he and his wife are hosting a gathering for his students.

I watch mixed groups of jeans-clad students lounging across George Square and mentally replace them with segregated groups of men and women in Edwardian dress, self-consciously avoiding one another as they approach Dr Turner's house in the half-light. The door opens and they vanish inside. After a pause, the music of popular songs begins to spill from the windows. A piano, played sometimes skilfully, sometimes less so, accompanies different singers, different songs. There is occasional laughter, deep male amusement punctuated by demure feminine titters. By the time the students emerge from the house, it is dark, but although the icy distance between them has grown smaller, there are definitely no couples. The women walk purposefully, their hearts occupied solely by their work.

I, too, re-focus on their work, hurrying back to Surgeons' Hall for Stop No. 4. Isabella's Curriculum Schedule tells me that she learns human anatomy from a Dr Joseph Ryland Whitaker, another expert whose book is available online, while Isabel Hutton tells me how his wife had died in 1905, and that he is tall, slender and has mutton-chop whiskers. She brings alive how he talks non-stop, instructing and assisting every pair of girls, determined they will master the mysteries of the structure of the human body and how, if one mode of instruction fails, he just laughs and tries another. Mnemonics and rhymes are his speciality.

Suddenly I wonder. Could Isabella have been recalling Joe Whitaker when she passed her anatomy kit on to me, the anatomy kit the historian has so recently identified? In her second year, she has to attend one hundred anatomy lectures and start the long course in Practical Anatomy. Dissections take place here. The British Medical Journal informs me that their conditions are cramped, so I picture a small room crammed with body-length slate-topped deal tables.

Isla, a recent anatomy graduate, has explained to me how it feels to cut up a human body. "You think you know what it's going to be like from watching medical programmes and from text books, but it's nothing like that. After the initial shock of cutting into a human being, you face layers of yellow fat, and you don't really know what you're doing, what you're cutting through."

I open the anatomy kit and lift out one of Isabella's scalpels. It is surprisingly light; the handle rests easily in my palm. I can see Isabella tying on her ugly, red waterproof apron. She, too, opens the wooden box of her dissection kit. She picks out another scalpel. The scene becomes clearer. As if she were my daughter rather than my grandmother, I hold my breath, wondering how precise she will be as she slices through the tough tissue, lifts the yellow fat to one side and locates the delicate structures beneath.

"You have to use forceps to hold the skin back while you cut down and it's very heavy. Once it slipped from my forceps and splashed onto my friend's lip," Isla told me.

Mesmerised, I watch as Isabella explores while her companion reads from a large book. Something about it is eerily familiar and I twist my head to make out its title: *Cunningham's Manual of Practical Anatomy*. Oh, I know it so well – the soft furriness of its worn leather binding, its weight on my hands, the creamy stiffness of its thick pages and the hundreds of gorgeous, gruesome engravings. Isabella gave that book to me – years later, of course, when she no longer needed it. Somehow, I have managed to lose it – but now I desperately want to re-examine it – page by page, cut by cut, muscle by nerve by artery … but I cannot. It is over there, right beside the cadaver, getting as greasy and splattered as a well-used recipe book.

Squeezing between the other groups, I tiptoe nearer to Isabella's table. She has exposed the whole leg now and is probing at something. She and her companion bend their heads closer, frowning. Suddenly they draw back, blinking – the formalin is overpowering. Now they are referring to Cunningham. The other girl pokes something cautiously and they both look back at the book. Carefully, Isabella eases back a flap of muscle. Her hands are red and rough from formalin and coarse soap, not smooth like when she held little Jan's hand. I can imagine her mother lamenting their unladylike appearance, but now she and her companion are nodding enthusiastically, their faces beaming – they must have unearthed what they were looking for.

Mrs Meikle, the caretaker, is coming over and I strain my

ears to pick up their gossip. She is famed for her stories. Apparently she once found herself preparing the body of a well-known music-hall singer for dissection. She had been very eager to examine the voice-box that had given hours of pleasure to so many audiences.

"There may be pacemakers or scars from things that have happened in the person's life. That makes the body more like a person," Isla has warned me, "They don't look human, being yellow-brown from the fixative. Most of them are fairly old, and when one group had a young body, it was quite a shock to them. Sometimes it's easy to forget that they were somebody's daughter, father or sibling."

I get out of the way as Isabella bends to pick up a scrap of tissue from the floor. Mrs Meikle is gathering other scraps of body, placing them back with their corpses, making sure each body, each person, is kept together.

"The college made sure we respected the bodies. We were given no information about them but the relatives were able to hold a ceremony and have a cremation after the dissection was complete," Isla has explained.

A tour group breaks the spell, and I find myself standing with the scalpel in my hand. As I pack it away, I am jubilant. Now I know that a century ago, Isabella used this little kit to cut through Scottish flesh as she learned the layout of the human body. It is not yet German blood, but a little part of Isabella's legacy has become a little less mysterious.

2

From the tiered wooden benches of an old lecture theatre, students watch a huddle of people poring over a body on a wooden table. I zoom in – and draw back in shock. Those people at the foot of the lecture theatre seats are not simply examining a body, they are operating. It is so public that I am far from sure I like Stop No. 5, these photographs sent by Laura, a kindly archivist. Numerically, there are more surgical instruments than anything else in the miscellany Isabella has left behind, so I certainly need to find out how she began surgery, but surely it cannot have been like this? The patient has no privacy. The whole procedure is a spectacle. Let alone that the students are wearing their ordinary jackets, and half the operating team are in shirt-sleeves rather than properly gowned up. There is no sterility – these conditions are terrible! Has Laura sent me pictures from the wrong era?

The photos, Laura has explained, show the large lecture theatre of Edinburgh Royal Infirmary, where Joseph Lister lectured during the nineteenth century. It had remained unaltered for decades, but by the time Isabella begins her surgical training, small changes have been made. Easily cleanable metal tables have replaced the old wooden trolleys. The use of masks and gloves by operating theatre staff has been made compulsory, but Isabella and the other students will still be watching from the wooden lecture theatre benches.

I let the scene come to life. The Chief Surgeon, in line with his practice of grilling all his students, is summoning Isabella to the front to examine the patient. The women beside her shuffle to let her pass, she descends the steep steps of the theatre – as steep as Upper Circle seating in London's West End – and walks over to the table where the patient is lying. Rubbing her hands to warm them, she feels across the abdomen, trying to detect any abnormalities beneath the skin. The Chief barks a deeply Scottish question at her. How does she react? Hesitantly, quickly, accurately?

The Scotsman reports her exam results: she passed Systematic Surgery – as taught by Mr Lewis Beesly – with First Class Honours, 78 per cent. Many of the women scored high marks – 78 per cent was third in the class. Checking up on her lecturer, I begin to wonder if someone in Edinburgh has a vested interest in keeping the old school alive and prominent – as if to emphasise the quality of their tuition yet again, Mr Beesly's book, too, is available on Amazon.

The practical classes take place in the early morning, and I imagine Isabella leaving John's Place before most of the household is up in order to reach the Infirmary on time. Quickly she is immersed in the intricacies of bandaging, or the nuances of how to apply a plaster cast, or the details of how to prepare a patient for an operation, or whatever other essential everyday medical skill their clinical tutor has decided they need to assimilate that day. Her experience grows and soon she becomes a surgical dresser, assisting Mr Wade at operations.

Mr Wade is a little over thirty, energetic, humorous, unmarried and very attractive. A hero of the Boer War, he is engrossed in pioneering research into possible causes of cancer. He has taken the trouble to learn his students' names, but keeps them at arm's length. Privately, many of the women medical students are in love with him but the only safe way to express their feelings is to work even harder. For most of them, romance is not an option. Their devotion is to their training. Few can afford to give time and energy to frivolous matters, and few men are prepared to risk courting a woman as determined and independent as a 'Lady med'.

Could Mr Wade himself be the reason the women score such high exam marks, rather than the quality of their professional motivation or the tuition they are receiving, I ask myself, but since they have laid love aside, I do too. Isabella, like other lady medical students before her, stands opposite this heart-throb, passing him instruments, threaded needles, swabs and every bit and piece that each operation demands, for six months. She gets to know his individual preferences and is promoted to surgical clerk. Now, she has to examine the patient on the ward before the operation and take the history so the whole team know what is going on. She writes up the operation and records the patient's progress.

An email drops in. 'Is this of interest?' asks Laura. I download the image and 'Yes!' I shout ineffectually through the screen, clenching my fists with excitement. 'The Winter Session at Edinburgh Royal Infirmary, 1912–13' states its caption. Four men relax in chairs softened with tartan blankets. Behind them stand sixteen women. There is no question about it – Isabella is amongst the group. Not only do I recognise her, her name is inscribed on the frame. Thank you Laura, this is most certainly of interest!

Some of the women sport mannish ties or bow-ties, but Isabella has chosen a delicate, high-necked white blouse. I convince myself that the faces of the tie-wearers are fiercer and wonder how Isabella chose what she wore. I imagine her surveying her wardrobe near the start of the course. She fingers the frilly blouses that she loves but the older students have warned her that if she continues to wear them, she risks not being taken seriously. She reaches for a more severe jacket and shakes her head. No, she cannot bring herself to let go of her standards. She will have to work with male doctors but she decides she would prefer them to regard her as too pretty and agreeable to be training as a doctor than to have them laughing at her for being a frump who has abandoned her femininity and dresses like a man. And when there is to be a photograph ...

In the seat of honour in front of the women sits Mr Dowden, another of Isabella's Clinical Surgery teachers. He is thin and grey, taller and more erect than his juniors. A frightening tutor? An awesome Scottish wit? Used to being in command, decisive? How did he treat the women, how would Isabella have described him?

I imagine the men standing up and stretching when the photographer is satisfied. Do they discuss their cases, or their colleagues, or golf – it is Scotland, after all. They drift – or do they rush? – back to work. The girls flurry to the wards, quiet within earshot of their chiefs. No. Women like these who are determinedly making their way in a male world will not flurry. Instead they will ...

Oh how I wish a snapshot lasted more than an instant! I

want to see how Isabella and the others walk. I want to hear the tread of their shoes on the stones, I want to catch the mood of their gestures. More than anything else, I want to eavesdrop on their conversations. I want to know who these women are, where they have come from, and why. I want to dip into their friendships, and find out everything about them. It is the old, old story of a picture being worth a thousand words, but today this particular picture has raised far more questions than it has answered and all I can do is email a 'Thank you very much!' to Laura.

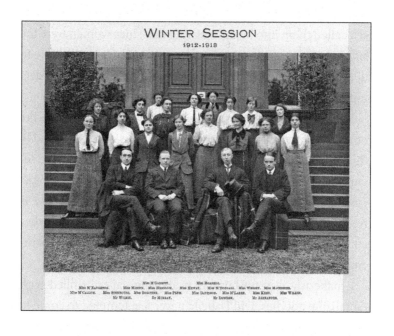

Passing new buildings housing departments of subjects that did not exist a century ago, I leave the university. The vehicles must be travelling twenty miles an hour faster than when Isabella came this way. Lamp posts flaunt loud advertisements for gigs. Cheap pubs and menu deals abound. Youngsters throng the streets, their iPods seeping beat, their phones leaking laughter and their lips OMGs. I dodge a blindly texting girl and emerge into the hurly burly that is Princes Street. Even a kilted piper's valiant efforts to make music are failing to dent the clamour of rerouted buses and jammed traffic.

Yet beside the windows of Jenners department store, the women stand silent. Over a hundred years ago Mr Jenner himself called them into being, insisting that since women were the support of the house, then female statues – caryatids – were to uphold the windows of his store. Appropriate really, considering the nature of Stop No. 6.

Rotating through the store's ornate doors, I luxuriate in the opulence of the antique decor, but find myself stopping dead in the Grand Hall. It is indeed so very 'grand', so very solid and secure. Exactly the spot for a comfortable, middle-class, Edwardian shopping experience. The sort of life my grandmother is rejecting. An elderly niece of Isabella's has recently let slip her aunt's complaints about how hard it had been to study medicine – the fitting in of the courses, the opposition.

I make my way upstairs, past alluring galleries filled with tantalising goodies. Did Isabella never feel tempted to come in here? To join her friends and give up the struggle? I settle into a window seat in the café. Before me are the Scott Monument and Princes Street Gardens, the rerouted buses and jammed traffic becoming a mere distant rumble through the thick glazing.

A century ago, photographers stationed themselves at windows along this same street, and I can almost feel the throng of spectators joining me. Their tweed jackets and thick stuff skirts press me forward as the casement opens and the excited hum of the crowd below comes rushing in. Leaning over the stonework, I marvel at the sheer numbers lining the road. Caps, straw hats and highly decorated female bonnets stretch ten deep in both directions. A similar crowd lines the opposite side of the street, where policemen stand, eagle-eyed for wrongdoing. Between them, no traffic is passing – no horses and carts, no trams, no carriages and no new-fangled motor cars.

A distant hint of music gets the hats swivelling in harmony to the right. Rather less harmoniously, they compete with one another, bobbing up and down in their determination not to miss whatever is about to appear. Soon, their attention is focused on the carefully styled tableaux parading before them on horse-drawn drays, on the bands marching past, and on the cohorts of women.

It is October 9th, 1909. The demonstrators, a few men among the women, pepper their protest with cries of 'Votes for Women!' This is not the first time the suffragists have processed along Princes Street. Two years ago, in 1907, 10,000 spectators watched 1,000 demonstrators march past.

Stately above the purple, green and white flags of the Women's Social and Political Union comes a huge, carefully embroidered banner bearing the image of a snake twined round a pole – the emblem of the medical profession since the days of ancient Greece. I watch it with interest. Last year, 1908, most of the women registered as doctors donated money to support the campaign for votes for women and, beneath me, women doctors are carrying this banner proudly along the street. Is there any chance Isabella is campaigning with them?

I scan left and right – is she down there now, unrecognisable beneath her hat? It would be risky. Even Mrs Pankhurst has acknowledged the peculiarly difficult choice that medical women face. Taking a visible part in the campaign for the vote could harm the prospects for winning their other battle – the fight for full acceptance by the men of the medical profession.

Daily, Isabella and her fellow students struggle to remain polite and patient in the face of the constant rudeness, criticism and patronising attitudes of the men teaching the medical courses, men who regard training women as a mere stepping stone to the much more important job of teaching male medical students. Taking part in suffrage activities could give such men just the ammunition they need to nip a young woman's career in the bud.

From my vantage point in Jenners, the sound of the demonstration gradually fades but, as time flashes forwards to 1911, the campaign for 'Votes for Women' becomes even louder. The census that year becomes a rallying point. "Since we do not count," the campaigners declare, "we will refuse to be counted." Planning to stay up all night to avoid inclusion in the census, they arrange parties and activities across the land. Extremely doubtful that Isabella will be tempted to take part in this almost invisible action, I log on to check the census return for 9 John's Place. To my astonishment, I find that William has included only his wife and Beth on the form. No Jan, no Ena, and – most importantly – no Isabella. None of the trio are snug at home on census night.

My hopes begin to rise. Could they actually, contrary to all my expectations, be census-dodging? When I extend my search to include every district of Edinburgh, the result is still, 'No matches', so I am holding my breath as I broaden my search one stage further. Bother! There they are – Isabella, Ena and one servant are at Hilltown, the family farm just outside the city. Isabella has recorded her occupation as Medical Student, Ena has none. Not that Jan has turned up, but then she is only 17. It seems more likely that she has followed her sisters to Europe than that she is census-dodging with older activists.

Another idea emerges. From Isabella's Curriculum Schedule, I know that in the summer of 1911 she will sit exams in Pathology, Practical Pathology, Materia Medica & Therapeutics, Forensic Medicine, Clinical Surgery, Vaccination, Mental Diseases and Post-Mortems – a group of exams which are said to be the most insurmountable obstacle of the whole course. Previous students declare that any woman who can manage these third year exams is sure to succeed in their finals. So what is the exact date of this census? Easter Sunday, 2nd April, I read, just when Isabella is likely to be entirely focused on revision.

Yet even as I adjust to the fact that there is no evidence that allows me to depict Isabella as a flag-waving suffragist, I notice something strange about her Curriculum Schedule, something that simply does not add up. For every non-hospital course, she has written 'Edinburgh' as the name of the university where she was taught. Which flies right in the face of all I have read and understood on the matter. She cannot be right! She cannot be the one woman student the University decides to accept, can she? I double-check my sources, but whichever source I examine, up comes the same answer: Isabella will be sitting for the University's exams, but she can only study for them on an extra-mural basis at the Edinburgh School of Medicine for Women.

Have other women students made the same claim, I wonder? Not the one I dig out. She has studied the same courses as Isabella, under the same tutors, but she has recorded the name of her university correctly as: 'Edinburgh School of Medicine for Women'. She has made no false claim to be studying at Edinburgh University. It is completely confusing. When Isabella is aiming for a high degree of accuracy in her exams, why is she being inaccurate here – well, more than inaccurate, lying? Is it simply the size of her sprawling hand-writing? Or because two words are quicker than six? I wonder. Is there any chance that she is indulging in a little aspirational form-filling, some harmless white lying? Arguing to herself that since Edinburgh University will award her degree, she deserves to belong? I let my latent suffragist dreams return, imagining her thumbing her nose at authority in a teeny-weeny, feminist gesture.

A couple of hugely pregnant women heaving themselves into seats nearby bring me back to Jenners and remind me of an ironic twist to Isabella's troubles as a female medical student. Trainee women doctors in Edinburgh are not allowed to deliver babies in their own city – the men reserve that privilege for themselves. But could I be detecting hints of professional rather than political ambition in Isabella? While most of the girls take themselves over to Glasgow, she chooses to go all the way down to Dr Annie McCall's Maternity Hospital in London.

Dr McCall, I learn, set up the unit in frustration at the number of women dying in childbirth. She is determined to discover ways of saving both mothers and babies, and has staffed the outfit entirely with women. Suffragism is everywhere. Many of Isabella's fellow students come from the London School of Medicine for Women. The founder's daughter, Dr Louisa Garrett Anderson, will be sentenced to six weeks in prison for breaking windows at much the same time as Isabella is delivering babies with Dr McCall.

Leaving the two mothers-to-be moaning about their varicose veins rather than calculating the odds on the likelihood of their own deaths as they give birth, I depart. From the far side of Princes Street, I turn to wave goodbye to the caryatids who witnessed it all, and who still support the house.

4

Soon, the Ghost Tour has me slipping past a painted advert so old that Isabella, too, may encounter it on her way into one of the tiny alleys that criss and cross behind the stateliness of the Royal Mile. Here, she treats the impoverished inhabitants of these tenements as part of her practical pharmacy and vaccination courses through the Cowgate Dispensary and the New Tron Pharmacy. Passing beneath an archway, I am greeted by a phalanx of festival balloons. I am sure there are many colours amongst them, but I notice only the suffragist purple. Even more purple hits me when I emerge from the tiny, stepped alleyways onto Lothian Street. In her wildest dreams or darkest nightmares, Isabella could never have imagined the purple of this huge, wild, Festival udder, and I turn from it. Across the road lies a place she knows well: Stop No. 7, Jericho House – an old Catholic church. Today, it is a refuge for the shuffling homeless men who cluster round its doorway dragging on their fags. One hundred years ago, women from the Faculty of Arts converted the top floor into a haven for female students. I picture small clusters of girls hurrying over there, long skirts billowing in the wind, one hand clasping books and the other, their hats. Isabella follows. She grips not books, but her medical bag. My thoughts drift …

There is a photograph of a wintry John's Place which Isabella has used as a postcard to her sister Beth, who, it seems, has been enjoying a few days away with Auntie. "Tell Auntie I only wish I could have had a weekend with her," writes Isabella. Is this simply courtesy, or do I detect a trace of mournfulness?

She and her colleagues are so single-minded, I read, and so thrilled to be able to study that they allow themselves almost no time off.

"The social side is still rough compared with other students – non-medics," interpolates Kate, a twenty-first-century junior doctor, determined not to be outdone. "We have to be more responsible than they do."

When Isabella does permit herself the luxury of a visit to this Union, it is the aroma of cock-a-leekie soup and the voice of the cook's daughter coaxing the ladies to come to the table that greets her as she tugs open the heavy wooden door and trudges upstairs. Wearily joining a trio of women, she tries to leave the memory of the tenements behind her. Another girl appears at the top of the stairs, tousled and out of breath. Glancing round the room, her eyes light as she spies Isabella and her friends. Hurrying between the tables, she begins her tale almost before she reaches them …

"Have you seen what is going on at the Mercat Cross? You would never believe the crowd – or the racket of suffragist speeches and cries for votes. I couldn't work out what was going on, but then I spied some auctioneers trying to sell some sticks of furniture – not that anyone was buying; there was too much noise, nobody could hear them. And then I saw her – Dr Cadell – Dr Grace Cadell who runs the Hospice – she was in the middle, leading them all! It turns out that the furniture belonged to her! Would you believe it? The bailiffs have confiscated it and are selling it off because she has refused to pay her house tax!"

She stops, out of puff, and looks round to see the effect of her news. "Good for her!" exclaims one girl.

"So much more fitting than breaking windows like Mrs Pankhurst's lot!" adds another.

"Dr Cadell's group draw the line at using violence, don't they?" queries a third.

"The old idea was always that rational argument and proving that we are as good as men would gain us the right to vote, but I'm beginning to wonder," comments somebody.

"There is no hope that we'll ever get there on that basis," agrees another. "Every instinct would like to go on hoping, but time and again Parliament has broken its promise and failed to pass a law that gives women the vote. One rather begins to wonder if it will ever happen … "

Sometimes, I imagine, the lady students are only too glad to lay the vexed matter aside – there are other subjects to debate than women's suffrage, are there not? German aggression? The Empire? Servants and the new national insurance payments?

"Oh, come, this is all far too serious. Did you go to that concert the other evening? The most exquisite music, a new young pianist – I can't recall his name, but he really was excellent. You really mustn't miss the next one, it was divine … "

Another girl suggests a visit to a theatre; she's heard that one simply must see the new show. Then someone else reminds them of the dance, and they compare notes about dresses and hair-styles and look forward to waltzing across the sprung floor of the debating hall – secretly wondering whether they will be in the arms of their favourite … for there's no harm in having a secret favourite, even if they have declared themselves unavailable for romance, is there?

And when they next gather here, they will, perhaps, be full of tales of how the male medical students had failed to recognise them in their gorgeous, frou-frou dresses, and how delightful it had been to observe the shock on the men's faces when they eventually realised that these beautiful girls were the severely clad women they had been working beside on the wards. The group of friends will laugh as joyously as any other young students as they talk over the fun of the evening and recall how the young, newly married chaperones had been so good about turning a blind eye …

The noise of festival contractors interrupts my thoughts. The homeless men who huddle round the door are only the latest in the procession of outsiders for whom Jericho House has been a refuge. Women arts students have gained a position of respect and hold a certain amount of power within the University. They have managed to set up this Union, for example. Yet the female medical students are still constantly having to remind themselves that they are lucky to be able to sit for the examinations at all. I read how they continually give thanks for their predecessors, women like Sophia Jex Blake who battered on the doors of the medical profession until they opened a chink. Yet Isabella's spirit does not seem to be breaking. One day, a photographer catches her unawares. She has been bent over playing with a dog, and her laughter almost ripples from the picture. At any moment that dog will spring back up and just carry on with his game. Isabella's plain dress and slick pompadour may be suitably discreet for an Edwardian lady medic, but her excited beam would suit twenty-first-century social media to a T.

5

I only have to turn round to see the final Stop of Isabella's Medical Ghost Tour, the McEwan Hall. Today it is partly shrouded by Festival paraphernalia, but it appears new and stylish to Isabella and her colleagues as they gaze at it from Jericho House. With its huge curved façade, corner towers, arched frieze and rooftop balustrade it is imposing enough to daunt the faintest heart. To go there, the lady medics do not just have to cross the road – they have to jump the awful hurdle of Finals.

As Isabella revises, suffragettes bomb the Edinburgh Royal Observatory. It is nine years since she passed her medical school preliminary exams, and perhaps a decade or more since she conceived the startling idea that she, Isabella, might actually become a doctor. Pale-faced from long hours of study, she and the other women wait in the same line as the men for their examinations. Desperate not to fail, desperate not to let down the pioneering women who have gone before them, they are fully aware of the rumours that many of the examiners still cannot abide the thought of women being doctors. They know they will not be allowed to get away with the slightest deficiency.

In the University archive, the men's and the women's curriculum schedules lie un-segregated, bound one to another in alphabetical order, exactly as their owners queued for finals and in direct contrast to the way in which each woman and each man had earned her or his right to queue for that examination. It is almost as if the whole struggle has been flattened.

Inside the McEwan Hall the new organ plays, and Isabella and the other graduands sit in rows awaiting their turn on the platform. Nothing has changed. Recent graduands would know what to do here. Isabella would feel at home with their ceremony. Today, 13th July 1913, twenty-three prizes are being presented. All but two are reserved for men, but at some point comes the stomach-clenching moment when the news comes out as to which of the five women graduands has gained the highest marks. That woman is the one who will be awarded the Dorothy Gilfillan Memorial Prize, the award for the most distinguished woman student at the Final Examination for the Degrees of M.B.,Ch.B. That woman is the one whose journey to the platform will honour her achievement. That woman is the one who will go home with about £13, a sum which one online calculator suggests would convert into a generous £850 in the twenty-first century.

A solemn voice announces the recipient of the award – and it is Isabella who is wriggling her way out of her seat and making her way to the dais. It is Isabella for whom applause is resounding. Her journey to the front may not be accompanied by the yells and cries that greet Facebook generation prize winners, but Isabella Stenhouse is the most distinguished of the women students …

I try to moderate my enthusiasm. It is not as if she is the most distinguished student of a hundred or more. Yet however much I reason with myself that there are only five women who could have won the prize, and however much she would want me to maintain my dignity, I still want to give my grandmother an excited, twenty-first century hug.

Music plays, the ceremony closes and I am back where I began, watching Isabella pose for her graduation photograph. Pensive, I click open a copy of that very photograph, intent on reflecting upon all I have discovered, but her hair-style distracts me. Peering forwards, frowning, I zoom in and out. Has she trimmed her pretty long hair? A few months earlier at the Edinburgh Royal Infirmary, it was pinned back, conventional, safe. Today I am beginning to suspect that she has taken the daring step of getting rid of her long curls. Zooming right in, I scan slowly round the perimeter of her head. Yes – the cut ends are flying free. Scissors have snipped, long tresses have fallen, and Isabella has emerged looking utterly modern. My mind tracks again to that twenty-first century graduation ceremony. Those graduands too, took time to style their hair, choose new shoes, new dresses, new everything for their big day. Not that Isabella has had complete choice in the matter. Regulations dictate that her dress must be white, although it hardly matters. Gowns are only made in men's sizes and hide the women's dresses well, but nothing can conceal Isabella's flagrantly modern hair-style.

6

"Five years have come to an end. It's all gone so quickly," reflects Junior Doctor Kate, newly fledged in her cap and gown. I agree. As the Ghost Tour has whirled me through Isabella's five years at medical school, other charms have strung themselves along the thread of Isabella's curriculum schedule beside Isabel Hutton's reverse crystal balls, but now I need to track down a connecting strand and a new supply of beads.

Logically, Isabella and her gowned colleagues first task is to straggle out of the Great Hall into the no-woman's land between student-hood and professional life. But where do they go from there? As a starting point, I head for the Medical Register. Kate will follow well-trodden training paths mapped out for her in NHS hospitals, but in 1913, I read, Isabella and her four fellow women graduates can only dream of the hospital appointments that are the ideal way of building up experience. If they can afford to wait, they may come across a hospital post which allows applications from women, but it is most likely to be in some marginal discipline that the male doctors, begrudgingly, share. The men usually reserve the most prestigious areas for themselves. Pulling the heavy, red, 1913 edition of the register off the shelf, I am well aware that Isabella and her peers may have to let their enthusiasm die down. They may have to settle for appointments outside hospitals where they will learn far less. However brilliant their skills, they will end up working with women and children, in dispensaries, poor houses and asylums, or in public health.

Laying the volume on a table, I start leafing through the

pages, intent on admiring 'Stenhouse, Isabella' in all her glory. But however hard I look, 'Stenhouse, Isabella' is not here. What has happened? Determined to solve the mystery, I grab the next volume. It is all right – she is in the 1914 edition. But – hang on – why is she not listed until 16th December? I check the companion book – the Medical Directory. She is not in that at all! What is she up to? The four women who graduated with her are, quite properly, listed in both the Register and the Directory for both 1913 and 1914, but Isabella, the most distinguished woman student, has only got herself listed in one of the four volumes, and that only at the last minute. Is there a problem?

It does not take long to find out that even while Isabella is sitting for her graduation photograph, disturbing events are taking place in Leith. The dockworkers came out on strike some days before the ceremony and countless other unions have joined them. Even as she poses, the port of Leith is at a halt – no goods are arriving, no goods are departing – nothing is moving.

The 16th, 17th and 18th bring three long nights of rioting. With the Stenhouses' livelihood relying on the smooth import and export of goods, and the docks being only a few minutes away from John's Place, I imagine them lying awake listening – anxious, silent. The thin panes of 9 John's Place allow every sound to spill through the house – the smash of glass, the furious chants and the angry cries. The arrival of naval gunboats sets the strikers marching angrily past the house onto Leith Links, union banners high, spectators lining the route. I picture the Stenhouses looking out at the strikers' desperate faces – hungry, angry and frightened for their families – violence on the brink, emotion as intense as that of the miners in 1984. The only people 'doing brisk business' in Leith, reports the local paper, are the glaziers. 'For a brief space of time, hell was let loose in Leith.'

When an even bigger march takes place two days later, the Stenhouses are tensed for disturbance and trouble. Perhaps they hold their breath for the full quarter of an hour it takes for nearly 13,000 people to process onto the Links. But they can relax. The mood has altered. The protest remains peaceful. When the strikers return to work a few days later, Isabella and her family can leave their vigil and assess the damage.

But was there damage? Exactly how had the strike affected them? Should I be suspicious? Only a few months later, on 13th November, Isabella's father dies at the age of 59. An obituary states that he died 'after a prolonged illness', but how prolonged? So prolonged that I have missed the fact that Isabella has been studying under its shadow, with every patient she sees reminding her of her father sick at home? Or only prolonged for three months, with the family blaming the stress of the strike for his condition?

Could this be why tenacious young Dr Isabella Stenhouse fails to get her name straight onto the Medical Register? Easing out of her intense focus on passing exams, does she perhaps even delay looking for work to take on the traditional role of unmarried daughters – caring for her father as he suffers from the pulmonary oedema and aphasia which will, ultimately, kill him?

She is certainly in the house when he passes away in the early morning. Later that day, she goes out to register his death, making sure she squeezes 'M.B.,Ch.B.' beside her signature on the death certificate. Perhaps it is even she who organises the announcement in the Scotsman that a service will take place in John's Place before the burial? I picture mourning-clad figures arriving at the door and gathering round the coffin in the front room – the room where the Stenhouses sang and sewed as children. The Pilrig pastor conducts the service. The bearers raise the coffin and carry it out through those paired porch doors. Horses decked with black feathers draw the carriage hearse to the cemetery at Corstorphine, on the other side of the city, where William's father, mother and other Stenhouses already lie. Some of his workers carry the body to the grave. Family and friends follow. At the graveside, do Isabella, her sisters and their mother toss their symbolic handfuls of earth onto the coffin before returning to their home?

With none of the girls married, William's brother is the only male Stenhouse left, but exactly six months later, he too dies. Suddenly. No prolonged illness this time, a stroke simply overwhelms him and he is gone in an instant. His death, too, happens in 9 John's Place. Again, Isabella is present as he passes away. Again, she is the one who goes to register his death and determinedly signs herself 'M.B.,Ch.B.'. A second funeral service is held in the house. The sisters and their mother follow yet another carriage hearse which carries the coffin of yet another beloved relative to Corstorphine. As they toss second handfuls of earth into this second grave, I imagine the raw memories of William's recent death magnifying their grief. I suspect it is

Isabella who takes on the role of head of the house. A month later, 24th June 1914, a notice in *The Scotsman* reveals that it is she, not her mother, who is helping to wind up the business.

My mind counts down – 24th June 1914. Isabella, her sisters and their mother do not know that, in Sarajevo, Gavrilo Princip is preparing to shoot Archduke Franz Ferdinand and his wife when they visit Sarajevo in four days' time. It makes me shudder. However bereft and grief-stricken my ancestors may be feeling at this moment, they have no idea that they are about to face something even more momentous than the loss of their two male breadwinners. I have to squeeze myself back into their innocent ignorance, and try to ignore the hindsight that assures me that, whatever Isabella's career plans, they will be derailed. Whatever her ambitions, they will be thwarted.

I leaf on through the Directories and Registers, wondering whether they give any hint of what she is planning. Bingo! Despite the huge upheaval her family has faced, Isabella manages to land herself one of those coveted hospital resident's posts. But it is not in Edinburgh. And it is not in one of the disciplines women doctors are usually forced to accept. Isabella will be heading to England. She is about to become a house surgeon at Liverpool Royal Infirmary.

My mind flies to all those surgical instruments she collected. Can she be hoping to become a surgeon? Caution, I warn myself. She will have to fight hard and show more than mere dogged determination if she wants to become a surgeon. Male doctors are firmly convinced that women are not physically strong enough to be surgeons. They declare the responsibility for making the bold and speedy decisions required by surgery is far too much for a woman, let alone that the whole job is utterly at odds with any semblance of femininity. Yet Isabella, medical bag in hand, catches the train to the port city, ready for her first day.

There are outpatient clinics, there are ward rounds. There are dressings, new admissions and, once or twice a week, there is Theatre. I visualise her scrubbing-up, pulling on her rubber gloves, adjusting her mask and walking over to assist the surgeon at the operating table. Then I read how it is considered more acceptable for women doctors to give anaesthetics than to operate, how anaesthesia is not yet a separate speciality, and how one of the house-surgeon's usual tasks is to get the patient safely to sleep. Dropping the idea of artery clamps, I re-direct Isabella towards the patient's head, where Danielle, an anaesthetist, helps me to picture her world.

Isabella has given chloroform before. She did a two-week placement during her training. She has learned that it is more dangerous to under-dose than to over-dose – if she does not give enough chloroform, the patient may die of shock. While she drips a generous amount of chloroform onto a mask and presses it tight over the patient's face, nurses and medical students hold the resistant patient down. Gradually, the struggles subside, and within a couple of minutes sleep has arrived and the surgeon can begin.

Now, her job is to monitor the patient. I discard images from television medical dramas. There are no bleeps. No cardiac wave forms race across monitors. That is not Isabella's world. She has only her eyes, her hands and her stethoscope. She is glad to be using one of the new light-weight metal masks which lets her see the colour of the patient's face and whether an unhealthy sweat is developing. She can check the conjunctival reflex and watch for the telltale sign of pupils flickering beneath the patient's eyelids while her fingers feel for the carotid pulse. She senses its rhythm and power, the signs of how fast and how strongly the patient's heart is beating. Someone else is monitoring the patient's wrist. Simultaneously, both of them notice a rise in heart rate and Isabella quickly increases the amount of chloroform dripping onto the mask. She certainly does not want the poor patient to wake up while the surgeon is still working on her.

At the end of the operation, I send Isabella out – slightly sleepy and stinking of chloroform. Scrubbing herself clean, she looks in on her patients and then … but before she leaves I read further. It seems that she may have a chance to use her scalpel after all. It depends on the surgeon, but some, just some, encourage their female house surgeons to take their turn at operating and do not tie them to the administration of chloroform.

So when Isabella does, at last, go off duty? There is a flourishing branch of the Association of Registered Medical Women in Liverpool. Set up with only nine women in 1879, the organisation has now become an important source of sisterly support. One very eminent woman doctor is part of the Liverpool group, Dr Frances Ivens. She holds several important, surgical posts and travels all over the North of England reading papers, encouraging junior doctors to aim high, and taking any action she can to help when the inevitable problems arise. Isabella may be away from home in her first job in a hostile professional environment but she is not entirely on her own.

Reaching into the Flower Press box, I untangle her stethoscope. It smells of rubber and age. When I put it on, its weight drags uncomfortably on my ears. The sound of the twenty-first century hushes, but I detect nothing. Isabella has become a professional, applying its bell to ailing bodies, interpreting the sounds she hears, and working out what needs to be done. It is emblematic of her medical authority. Where, I wonder, is she hoping to use it? Who is she hoping to tend? As I coil it back into the box, the beads brush against my fingers. I still know as little about them as when I began my quest, and with war imminent, I guess I should be preparing. I cannot afford to miss vital clues to Isabella's prisoner of war through simple ignorance.

7

It is easy to discover that since the end of last century, most glass beads have been made in the north of Bohemia, where beautiful quartz sand carpets the forests. Trees are felled to fuel the furnaces and melt the sand into tiny, translucent droplets. But if all beads come from the same place, I am no further ahead on understanding Isabella's particular set of beads. Does the design offer any clues?

Twenty individual motifs are linked by complex decorative sections. Each motif is nine tiny beads wide and about twenty-four beads long. They are all different. Twenty distinct patterns chase one another along the strand in shades of pink, white, green, gold, blue, silver and red. I compare the patterns with pictures of standard design motifs. There is a Greek key design – coppery coloured beads sparkling against their white background. Suddenly, I find myself narrowing my eyes at some gunmetal grey beads that lie, almost hidden, in a sea of deep, glassy blue, and I draw back very, very fast. I do not want to confirm what I think I can see. Bracing myself, I peer forward again, and I trace one grey leg, two grey legs, three grey legs, four grey legs spidering out from a single centre – a swastika, the obnoxious symbol of Naziism, is lurking menacingly near the end of this precious string of beads. It may give credence to the idea of the strand coming from Germany, but … what was my grandmother thinking?

Slowly the date dawns on me. These beads, this swastika, was woven before the Nazis came to power. Hurrying online, I learn that archaeologists had discovered the symbol during the excavation of Troy. They believed it to have been an ancient religious sign. By the start of the twentieth century it had become a popular symbol for good luck and success.

I breathe again. It makes complete sense for war beads to include a swastika. It makes just as much sense for a Thank You present to include best wishes; yet the whole strand is still an enigma. What, exactly, is it? With two ends but no fastening, it cannot be a necklace. Is it be a sampler, I wonder? Bead-weaving only needs simple tools – beads, string, a needle and a basic wooden loom. Will the prisoner himself thread the beads for Isabella, a kind of therapy to pass the long hours until the end of the war? To test the idea, I try making a replica. The smallest beads I can find are giants beside the little specimens threaded onto Isabella's strand, but they constantly dodge my fingers and obstinately refuse to cooperate. Threading them is so tedious and frustrating that one motif is quite enough for me. Putting the loom away in disgust, my admiration for the maker of Isabella's beads spirals. Whoever wove Isabella's beads had far more time and patience than I am prepared to give. They had either needle-sharp eyesight and glaringly bright lighting, or good lenses and a machine. There is no way it can have been made in a dingy prisoner-of-war camp – and anyway, how would the prisoner have got hold of all those beads? Rejecting the sampler idea I conclude that if there is any truth in Isabella's prisoner story, her grateful patient must already have been in possession of the beads when he is captured. Not, of course, that any prisoner of war is going to come her way just yet – but at least I am a little readier for him when he does.

SECTION 3

Hesdin, le 1er Mai 1915

LE GENERAL D.E.S. DE LA X° ARMEE

à Madame DOUGHSY WYLLIE,

Directrice de l'Ambulance Anglo-Ethiopienne

à FREVENT

1

Anglo-Ethiopian Ambulance is a strange name for a unit with a French address, I reflect, as I fail to find the name online. I am trying to fathom a two-page letter, written in French, that Isabella's daughter has lent to me. *Hesdin, le 1er Mai 1915,* states its header, *Le General D.E.S. de la X° Armée à Madame Doughsy Wyllie, Directrice de l'Ambulance Anglo-Ethiopienne à Frévent.*

Could it have been a hospital? The Anglo-Ethiopian Hospital? 'No results containing all your search terms were returned.' I get no more luck with 'Doughsy Wyllie'.

Still firmly convinced that nothing directly related to Isabella will exist, I head for the Women's Library. Presenting my request for material about women doctors serving in WWI, the archivist digs out a fascinating Master's thesis, apologising that there is not much else. I settle down to make notes, but the archivist is not satisfied – she is sure she can do better. After a while, she comes over and whispers news that thrills me. The Imperial War Museum holds the papers of one 'Mrs Doughty-Wylie', including the diary of the Anglo-Ethiopian Hospital in France! Getting there as fast as I can – as if it would vanish – I dig through two deep archive boxes and light on a brown envelope labelled '1915'. Three exercise books snuggle inside, one red, one green and one sky blue. They are corner shop quality, fuzzy with age and handling. Inside, ancient black words wiggle across the pages, smothering margins, headers and footers. I want to find Isabella's name quickly, but the script proves too illegible to pick much up by scan reading, and I have to plod through, word by word, until, at last – there she is 'Miss Stenhouse'. Trying to hurry on, I find 'Isabel', and then 'Belle'.

Overjoyed that the archivist has set me on the right track, I rummage deeper into the boxes. Soon, I find myself whooping out loud, shattering the academic silence. In my hands lies a photograph of Isabella. She is standing, un-uniformed, beside fourteen uniformed nurses and four mustachioed men in military dress. Above the group hang a trio of flags and a sign reading, 'Anglo-Ethiopian Hospital, Fondation Association des Dames Françaises'. Isabella looks well-satisfied and I *feel* well-satisfied. In 1915, Isabella, the Anglo-Ethiopian Hospital and Mrs Doughty-Wylie, go together.

Towards the bottom of the box, I am rewarded with another prize. When Britain declared war on Germany in 1914, explains Mrs Doughty-Wylie, she and her husband had been at the British Legation in Addis Ababa. Wanting to do their bit, they had arranged to set up a 100-bed hospital in France. Just as she was about to leave for Europe, the young Emperor-designate of Ethiopia, Lij Yasu, paid them a visit. He was not alone. With him came a herd of four hundred horned Ethiopian bulls, snuffling and shuffling under the blue Ethiopian sky. Lij Yasu presented them to her, explaining that they were for soup for the wounded soldiers. I picture the most minute muscles of her face twitching as she forces the etiquette of gratitude to hide her sheer consternation as to what to do with these beasts. Thankfully, she declares, one of the Prince's courtiers had a more practical turn of mind. There and then he bought the whole herd, leaving her a useful sum to turn into broth. In tribute to the royal soup-provider, they named the hospital the

'Anglo-Ethiopian' and flew the striped Ethiopian flag beside the Union Jack.

Picking up the photograph again, I chuckle – quietly. A striped flag does indeed hang beside the Union Jack. Somewhere in France a little bit of African sunshine was raised to thank Prince Lij Yasu for his gift. Whoever would have guessed? It would have made a cheering story on a wartime winter evening behind the Western Front – and it explains the strange address on Isabella's letter.

It takes many visits to transcribe the diary of the Anglo-Ethiopian Hospital. As I work, I become familiar with Mrs Doughty-Wylie's turn of phrase. She becomes a real character – an upper-class English lady who knows her place in the world and is determined to claim it. I resort, perhaps improperly, to calling her Mrs D-W.

Addis left behind, she wires, cajoles, criss-crosses France and calls in favours from all and sundry in single-minded determination that her Hospital will find a home to which the French Army will be happy to send their casualties. By 18th December 1914, she is jubilant. With the promise of casualties from the French Tenth Army, equipment is transported, staff arrive and the hospital sets up in Frévent, a town recently threatened by the German advance. On the 21st December comes her first mention of Isabella. Oh, it is a gem – but what a challenging gem! Coming from Mrs Doughty-Wylie's point of view as Directrice, it needs twisting and turning until, prism-like, it reveals Isabella's perspective and slides onto the thread of her story.

A telegram is winging its way across the Channel to Isabella. With every word costing, it is terse and to the point. Something like:

PLEASE SEND SURGEON STOP URGENT STOP.

It makes no sense as a first communication. Isabella must already have an inkling that the Hospital's whole mission is in jeopardy because the Army is unhappy about the number of staff and has threatened to stop the flow of wounded. A second surgeon is needed pronto.

Question piles upon question. What makes Mrs D-W think Isabella can find her a surgeon? How do they know one another? Or do they? Is Mrs D-W just contacting 'Miss Stenhouse' on the recommendation of a friend? What has Isabella been doing since the war began?

Everyone, male and female, old and young, is said to have been deliberating how best to help. Have the Stenhouse girls joined the frenzy of uniformed volunteering among middle-class women? I imagine it being hard to resist the hurricane of patriotic fervour that is whipping across the country.

The British Red Cross report that they have no record of Beth or Jan, and I have to remind myself that nursing is only one way of helping – there are a hundred and one other things that need doing: knitting, for example, or fundraising for a myriad different causes. Their news of Ena is different. She enrolled with the VAD (Voluntary Aid Detachment) in 1911 and since October, they tell me, she has been working as a VAD nurse in St Leonard's Convalescent Hospital, a mile or so from John's Place.

But Isabella is not Ena, Beth or Jan. Her training has set her apart from the bulk of middle-class women. As one of the 0.024 per cent of practising doctors in Britain who are women, she has specialised skills to offer. Ever since August, she has been facing a different dilemma as to where her own patriotic duty lies.

I bring up another photograph from her archive. Five male doctors stand in a hospital ward amongst half a dozen nurses. The War Office expects this war to be short. It does not want to take on more doctors than it thinks will be required to treat the number of casualties it predicts. It is confident that by enlisting only young men not yet tied down with practices and families, the need will be amply covered. Three such young doctors, men whose names Isabella knows, whose ambitions she understands, look back at me from Isabella's photograph. Are they, I wonder, like so many other young men, eager for the fray, envious of those who have already gone and fearful of missing out on the great adventure?

I imagine a call-up telegram arriving. The junior doctors gather round the youngest man, shaking his hand. The patients cheer him as he leaves the ward. But how will the older men behave? Senior doctors are said to be less than keen, arguing that this enlisting is totally unnecessary and wondering grumpily what all the rush is about. And what about the nurses? Will some of them go too? Do they yearn to be the romantically glamorous visions who tend the exhausted heroes arriving on the wards, still coated in filth and blood from the battlefield? No, these women are serious professionals. Such foolish fantasy is for untrained volunteers. These are career nurses. They may go, but they will go because they have a job to do – not because of some romantic nonsense.

But what is a *medical* woman to do? As she considers Mrs D-W's telegram, I imagine Isabella reliving the August buzz in Liverpool. Young male doctors are trying to leave as fast as they can. As Isabella leaves work, a colleague comes up to her, grabbing her arm.

"Have you heard," she gasps, "Miss Ivens has left!" Isabella stops, her eyes wide. What? When? Why? The questions remain unasked as her friend gabbles on. "She is going to Belgium. The poor Belgians need all the help they can get." The two women stand, staring at one another. Miss Ivens – gone? If she can go, then *anything* can happen.

Stunned, every woman doctor within reach makes sure she gets to the next Association meeting – where the news has all changed.

"Miss Ivens was unable to land. She was turned back at the port."

Somebody else brings other news, "Dr Inglis has had a meeting with the War Office. She went with the offer of a whole hospital staffed by women, and they have turned her right down! They told her to go home and sit still! Would you believe it?"

Frustration fizzes in the air. A young man can volunteer. A nurse can volunteer. A completely untrained woman can at least become a VAD or work in a factory, but qualified women doctors are prohibited from using their skills to help the soldiers of their nation.

As I look at the women who have gathered, I hazard a guess as to where each one works, settling some into private practices in the poorer districts of the city, and casting others as public health officials or school inspectors. Miss Ivens, with honorary appointments at two hospitals and a vast practice, would be the most distinguished of all. Few of these women work with male patients. Medical men do not want to share that part of their domain. Surgery, too, is work that the men keep for themselves. In being a surgeon, Miss Ivens is very exceptional.

The pre-event hubbub lulls as a call from the front gets the ladies filing into their seats. This is not what you would call a large gathering but the Chairwoman is clearly determined that everything will be done properly. Minutes are read, apologies given, the first couple of items on the agenda are covered and then comes the moment for which they have all been waiting – the speaker. She goes straight to the heart of the matter:

"Madam Chairwoman, Ladies, the advent of war has presented us with one of the biggest questions of our professional lives. How are we, as medical women, to do our best for our nation? Some, like Miss Ivens, have attempted to go directly to Belgium. Others, like Dr Inglis, have tried official channels, and have had their offers of assistance rejected by the War Office. Nevertheless, each and every one of us, quite rightly, wants to help our country in its hour of need. What are we to do? Mrs Fawcett has given us invaluable guidance," declares the doctor from the platform.

A divisive fidget rustles along the rows. Mrs Fawcett, the sister of one of their heroines, Dr Elizabeth Garrett Anderson. Mrs Fawcett, the President of the National Union of Women's Suffrage Societies, the NUWSS, who has not supported the militant action of the suffragettes. Mrs Fawcett, whose Union has already suspended all suffrage action for the duration of the conflict. They have read her letter to the papers. If this speaker is citing Mrs Fawcett, some of the assembly are not sure that they will like her advice.

"Our place is here at home," continues the voice from the platform. "With so many medical men crossing the Channel to treat the casualties of fighting, who will care for those on our own shores if we too flock to France? Our duty is to hold the fort, to fill the vacancies left by our male colleagues, to work harder than ever. For many years, we have been telling all who will listen how necessary we are. Now, more than ever, that is true. Trying to join the staff of a field hospital may appear to be more exciting, but now is not the moment to seek thrills. It is our patriotic duty to stay in our posts, to do all that is required of us and more. Diligence and moral duty must prevail."

She sits down to ambivalently polite applause.

"Any questions?" asks the Chairwoman. Hands fly upwards. She picks someone at random.

"I agree with our distinguished speaker," asserts the voice. "The departure of men leaves many of the population vulnerable and lacking in medical care. It is our duty to ensure that the health of the general population is maintained ready for the victory."

Another arm is flung up. "My friend and colleague is right," its owner announces, "but she misses the point. With the men absent, posts which have hitherto been closed to us will open. We will be able to enter areas from which we have hitherto been excluded. This is our chance to prove that we are more than capable of undertaking these roles. We have no need to go to France to pursue our professional and suffrage goals. Here at home, in the wards and clinics, we will prove ourselves as we carry out our duties quietly, calmly and efficiently. This war is giving us an open door to the full range of work offered by our profession. Mrs Fawcett is right – war medicine is men's work. Leave the battlefield for the men and we will – at long last – win our old battles in the wards of our island home!"

Another woman jumps up, incensed, "Listen to yourself: 'The war is men's work, leave the battlefield to the men,' " she mimics. "What have we been arguing all these years? Why, I thought we had been asserting that anything men could do, we could do too! I thought we all believed we were as capable as them – if not better! All of a sudden, it seems, we are not! All of a sudden we have found something we do not believe we can do! Something that now causes us to agree with our male foes that we are lesser, that we must take the poorer jobs, the inferior status! Come on ladies! This is no time to sit still as the War Office demands! This is the moment we have been waiting for all these years. We will show the world that we can protect the health of the nation as well as any man. Yet that is not enough. Far from it. There is so much more that we must achieve. We have to go. We must be there in Belgium, we must be there in France. We must greet the ambulance trains, the stretchers, the walking wounded. We must examine the most horrific of injuries, we must operate on the most mangled of bodies. We must not flinch from whatever we find, whatever we see. We must show ourselves as capable as the men on their own bloody battleground. Only then will people believe us. Only then shall our status as equals in the profession be assured. And if we do not, ladies, if we do not, we will be doing exactly what the men want. We will be agreeing to stay exactly where they want us to be, and ladies, I tell you, we will deserve neither the respect nor the jobs we desire."

She sits down. There is a stunned silence before the applause begins.

In December, when Isabella receives Mrs D-W's telegram, she can look back at how the debate has raged on. As summer turned into autumn, the papers may have been full of the German advance towards Paris and the Battles of Mons and the Marne, but the lady doctors had been following a different struggle. Nothing so insignificant as rejection by the War Office could have held back Dr Inglis and her supporters at the Scottish NUWSS. On discovering that the French Army's medical services were failing to cope with the astounding number of casualties, they had come up with a scheme to provide a hospital to care for wounded Frenchmen. Dr Ivens' wish to serve at the Front had been granted, for she had been placed in charge. Soon, the Serbs, too, had asked for help. And one hospital has grown into two hospitals, both staffed entirely by women ... The Scottish Women's Hospitals.

At the start of my investigation, librarians and archivists had assured me that if Isabella had served in the First World War, she must have been with the Scottish Women's Hospitals, the SWH. But if she was, I had argued back, why do her few papers bear the name of the Anglo-Ethiopian instead of the SWH? Now, I am puzzled in the other direction. If Isabella wants to go to the war, then why not with the SWH? They are local, after all, and it is more than likely that she knows some of the women involved. It seems so obvious. Has she been too slow off the mark? Is she still immersed in settling family affairs and completing her contract in Liverpool? Or is it that she is wary, as some women are, about allying herself to something that springs so directly from the suffrage movement?

But then it strikes me; perhaps the reluctance comes not from her, but from the SWH. I discover that it will be 1917 before the SWH risks taking on a doctor as young and inexperienced as Isabella is in 1914. Even then, the woman concerned will have to use almost super-human powers of persuasion to get them to accept her. If appointing such a junior doctor will be a risk in 1917 – when SWH has grown into an established organisation with three years of successful war service under its belt – how much more of a dangerous gamble would it be in 1914, when the organisers need to prove that their enterprise works? They can afford to take no risks. They will appoint only the best, most experienced women. Even if Isabella is not content with taking advantage of the highly desirable hospital residencies left vacant by the departure of almost one sixth of the doctors in Scotland for the war, even if patriotism, or the desire for professional advancement, or a spirit of adventure, or an idealistic dream of wanting to end war forever is making her want to go to war, is she, at the moment, too young and inexperienced for the Scottish Women's Hospitals?

As the arguments and memories course through Isabella's mind, I picture her shaking herself out of her reverie. The war will be over by Christmas, people had said. Now, it is almost Christmas, the war is not over, and she must hurry to find a surgeon for the Anglo-Ethiopian.

2

Christmas arrives. It is the Christmas of the Christmas truce, when football is played in no-man's land and German and British soldiers sing carols together before they return to their weapons. It is the Christmas when the Anglo-Ethiopian sends back its new autoclave because it bears a tiny label, 'Made in Germany'. It is the Christmas when, for the first time, thousands of soldiers lie wounded in British hospitals, and Isabella starts surgeon-hunting. When 1915 dawns, the situation is so grave that Christians and Jews pray together for God's blessing on the Allied cause – and Isabella is still urgently seeking a surgeon.

I plough on through Mrs D-W's diary. Here she is again, on the afternoon of the 19th, as guns boom through the cold French January air. Frustratingly, as I tease out that Isabella has written with the name of a possible surgeon and has asked Mrs D-W to wire a reply, the script in this crucial, Isabella-linked section scratches into illegibility. 'Dr Cockett, a friend of Isabella's', I make out. A friend … could romance be in the air? I make a note to look out for him as, gradually, I decode a significant new development.

The numbers of wounded reaching the hospital have increased to the point that the staff are desperate for more help. Until today, they had thought they would get away with a dresser (a medical student with a little surgical experience) but today something has crystallised the fact that a dresser will simply not be up to the job. They need the help of a fully qualified doctor. A fully qualified doctor like Isabella, I wonder, as the writing tangles into itself again. I think it is saying that Isabella will be joining them in March – but is it?

That same 19th January, Zeppelins cross the British coast and bomb Great Yarmouth. One hundred years on, it sounds almost bland, sadly normal, the sort of thing that happens somewhere in the world every day, but in 1915, it is a first. Never before have missiles from the air hurtled through the darkness, blasting their way into bedrooms and sitting rooms. Never before have ordinary British families suddenly had to choose where and how they are least likely to be killed. The news feeds into the countless other stories Isabella and her family, in fact the whole nation, are hearing about the atrocities the Germans are committing: the rape, the pillage, the pathetic orphans, the refugees tottering with loaded carts along pitted roads to escape the heinous Hun. War stories have become part of their lives, anything seems possible, believable. Or should that be impossible, unbelievable? These dreadful Germans simply *must* be stopped!

But has Isabella volunteered to help stop the Germans by serving at the Anglo-Ethiopian? I scour the diary; sometimes it feels like a fuzzy phone call where the signal drops in and out. Stories begin, then fail to disclose their middles. Endings lack beginnings or middles. And often, a middle sits solo. As I search for the next instalment of the story of Isabella and the need for an extra doctor, I hit 30th January – the last entry in Volume 1.

It is 6th March before the next exercise book, pale green this time, begins with, 'I've lost my diary. It's so sickening. Lord knows who's nicked it. It was in my writing case. I had it last night in the setting room.' Boom. With the 'sickening' loss of that diary go my chances of finding the middle and end of this critical story. But if Isabella is to be the Anglo-Ethiopian's new doctor, March would be a sensible time to arrive. Her sister, Jan, is about to marry Frank, an Australian doctor at present working just outside Liverpool.

"Is he somebody Isabella met at work," I ask myself, "an old friend?"

"Will he be a suitable spouse for my Jan?" I imagine the girls' mother asking herself. With no husband to protect her daughters from unsuitable marriages, I can see her feeling the weight of her responsibilities and quizzing Frank, measuring him up as he tells the tale of how his own father had been brought up in Ireland.

"A brewer by trade, he set sail for Australia in 1857. To begin with, he worked in the booming goldfield towns of Victoria: Bendigo, Ballarat, Jamieson. He became a Mayor, got married, and the children started coming." Frank laughs about that, "My father was so impressed by the Americans he met in Victoria that he and my mother called my oldest brother 'George Washington'!"

Janet loses track of how many brothers and sisters were born. Struggling to picture this other, antipodean, world, she holds onto the facts that seven of the children survived and that, for some reason, the family moved to Brisbane.

"I'm the baby of the family," continues Frank, "Kangaroo Point, Brisbane, 1882," Such strange names, thinks Janet, picturing bouncy mammals surrounding a perambulator. She tries to pay attention, but she is concentrating too hard on Frank himself to take in every detail of his story. His father seems to have become very suitable – a lawyer or politician – but he is now dead. The brother with the daft name is also dead. She watches her potential son-in-law as he describes enthusiastically how his brother had been a wise lawyer, a keen academic, and how he had died while he was helping to set up a university for Queensland.

"His wife and daughters are still at home in Brisbane," Frank concludes.

"As is your mother," thinks Janet to herself, "and for the time being there is war, and you will probably remain here to support Great Britain, but afterwards, you will go back. You will go back to your mother and, if you marry my Jan, she will go with you."

I know I would have cried, but perhaps Janet is made of tougher stuff. Britain controls an Empire. Letters may be the main means of keeping in touch, travel may be slow and arduous, but family after family has members scattered across the globe, and the Stenhouses join the ranks of these scattered families on 22nd February 1915, as Scottish Jan Stenhouse and Australian Frank Power are married in Edinburgh's Roman Catholic Cathedral – and Jan moves down to Frank's Lancashire home.

Plodding forwards in the diary, I discover that Isabella will arrive in Frévent on 20th March. So, with the wedding out of the way, she has to work fast. To begin with, she needs to tell her boss. Then there are the papers and passes.

"Such a nightmare – the rules keep changing – one never knows where one is."

"What about clothes, my dear, have you got anything suitable for a war? And will that old luggage do or do you need a Wolseley?"

On the other side of the Channel, the discovery that the Anglo-Ethiopian is arranging for Isabella to be shown the dressings on her very own ward the moment she arrives, perturbs me. Surely being responsible for a whole ward full of wounded from the word 'Go' is too much? Isabella has never seen a wounded man before. How will she know what to do? I panic, as I try to work out how much my grandmother knows about what she is in for.

I am sure Isabella has been as horrified as anybody as the lists of men killed and wounded in battle, and the awards for bravery, have stretched endlessly down the columns of the papers. I am certain she has devoured every article reporting medical developments in the care of the wounded. But that is not the same as hearing the shrieks and groans of wounded men echoing through the night. It is not the same as being covered in blood and pus from a messy amputation. Dr Frances Ivens prepared for war work by reading up about new surgical techniques and amputation procedures. Is Isabella spending hours in the University Library amongst the medical journals that are reporting the latest techniques for managing injuries? Does she dig out Cunningham to remind herself of the anatomy of the male body?

All too soon, Ena, Beth and Mother are bidding her farewell at Waverley Station. There are hugs and kisses. Promises to write are made many times over. So are the wishes for good luck. The porter stashes Isabella's luggage on board. The handkerchiefs first wave, then conceal tears. The same pattern is being echoed in almost every railway station across the world … soldiers, women, red eyes, trembling lips, brave faces, the laughter, the embraces, the words of advice, the tremulous determination to forbid the tears. Steam masks the failure of those tears to be stemmed as the hissing engine drags its nervous cargo out and far, far away, leaving emptiness, the journey home, the gap at the table, and the start of the never-ending fear of what news may arrive.

Aware of what Isabella's family are going through, Major Lizzie Hunt, RAMC, a woman doctor who has served with the Royal Army Medical Corps in Afghanistan explains, "It's much easier being the one who is going out."

If it really is harder for her family, what is Isabella feeling? She must be aware that she is about to see horrific sights; that she may face danger. As she passes the fields of northern England, does she consider how the work may be more taxing than anything she has ever faced? As the flatter land of the south approaches, does the possibility that she might not be up to it even cross her mind? Somehow, I doubt it. Funk is not an option. Funk is not what patriots do. It is not what women doctors do, but, "I was scared that I might find myself cowardly," comments Lizzie.

Perhaps Isabella battens down any fear with Edwardian iron discipline and chooses instead to press the peaceful countryside into her mind, noting the lambs, the primroses and the late daffodils, forcing herself to savour each sight for the times when she needs something comforting to bolster her over the next few months. And, of course, just in case – it will never happen – but just in case – she never sees it again.

At Victoria station, I imagine her watching the khaki figures around her bidding their farewells to the people who love them, observing their smiles and smelling their fear. Climbing aboard, she seats herself. Last-minute soldiers clatter along the platform, crashing packs and rifles into already full compartments. Doors bang, whistles sound, the train lurches and Isabella is on the way to France.

SECTION 4

1

With Isabella on her way to the Front, I resume my investigation of the beads. I must be prepared – who knows when her prisoner may turn up. I find myself queuing between a Kodak sign and some huge dolls at the Antiques Roadshow. "Try Miscellaneous first," the people at the ticket office had told me, "and if they can't help you, go to Jewellery." As I edge towards the front, I survey the camera set-ups and lighting rigs on the other side of the room. Even if they have decided these beads are too ordinary to film, I find them fascinating. At the front of the queue, I hand them to the expert.

"Hilary would like these," he declares, beckoning her over. Picking them up carefully, she explains, "These are a woman's belt. They are early twentieth century, German or Austrian. The story that they came from a prisoner of war is quite credible. He would have carried them in his pocket as a talisman or memento. Soldiers carried the most unexpected things."

Yes, Yes and a double Yay! On the journey home I dream of a romantic evening long ago. If I was planning to give my soldier lover a memento to take to war, I would not choose something as impractical as a string of beads. A card, a photograph, or maybe a lock of hair, a book or a poem, but not a straggle of tiny fragments of glass. It must have been an impulsive act …

It was the last night before he was leaving for the war. The sky was clear and the moon was full, of course. And they had been dancing. Strauss, maybe, or Lehar? As the music played, their eyes met as if for the first time. Did she take off her belt and give it to him? No, that would have been too forward. He must have gone down on bended knee, begging his beloved for a token to carry him through the ordeal to come. Promising to remember her every day, he had reached for her hands, and as she bent forward to accept his gesture of love, her loosely knotted belt had slipped off. He had snatched it up, kissed it and tucked it into his pocket before she could protest. Some time later, battered and hardened by war, he had been wounded and taken prisoner. At death's door, Isabella had been sent to tend him. Surprised by this beauty with a stethoscope, his heart had quickly succumbed. On his recovery, deeply grateful, he had presented her with his girl's beads.

No, that is no good! I cannot have him swept off his bed-bound feet by Isabella's charms – he has to remain loyal to his first love. His gratitude to Isabella has to be because she has made it possible for him to return to his beloved. After all, I do not really want to risk my grandmother falling in love with the enemy.

Not long after this flight of fancy, I notice that London's Victoria and Albert Museum occasionally offers advice about items owned by members of the public. Eagerly, I book my slot, arriving in plenty of time to be disappointed by the costume display. However carefully I study it, I get no sense of what Isabella and her colleagues wore. Disgruntled, I trek upstairs and mooch slowly past one display of glittering antique jewellery after another, until, unexpectedly, something catches my eye. It is only a necklace, but, just like Isabella's belt, it is made of tiny glass beads woven into a flat band. Hurriedly, I search for the label. Perfect! The piece, a '*sautoir*', was made in Vienna in the early twentieth century. That adds even more weight to the idea that Isabella's beads were a gift from the enemy – Austria was, after all, Germany's ally. But as I study the *sautoir* in more detail, I hesitate. Its construction is certainly identical, but unlike Isabella's beads, its two ends are woven firmly together into a narrow beaded tassle. I panic. Have Isabella's beads somehow come unthreaded over the years? Have I damaged them?

The minutes tick desperately slowly until, at last, I find myself seated opposite two experts at the back of the museum. Reference books before us, they explain how Isabella's beads are very much related to the *sautoir* in the gallery.

"These bead strands were called *sautoirs* from the French *sauter*, to jump, because their length and weight enabled them to bounce with their wearer's movements.

"No, Isabella's beads are not broken. Some *sautoirs* joined at the ends, others did not. Open-ended *sautoirs* like Isabella's were worn like a narrow scarf. They could be draped in countless different and attractive ways."

"Could the prisoner have made them?" I ask.

"No, they are much too fine to have been made in a prison camp, but that she was given them by a prisoner of war is quite credible."

As they talk on, I begin to get a feel for the woman who originally owned these beads.

"Their design is a product of the Secessionist movement, the

Austrian equivalent of Art Nouveau. In choosing to wear these beautifully crafted beads rather than precious stones set in gold or silver, their wearer was making a very definite statement. She would have been somebody who associated with men of officer class, not common soldiers."

On my way home, I revisit my earlier picture of this woman. A craft-loving person after my own heart, she has become a character in her own right, with her own place somewhere on the outskirts of Isabella's story – the outskirts, that is, so long as I am not about to uncover a love triangle.

2

Boarding the car ferry at Dover, I am haunted by my reading. A century ago, these cliffs back-dropped the paraphernalia of war. Now, the ferry is filling with laid-back holiday makers and off-duty lorry drivers. A myriad languages murmur. The scent of hot food and paper-cup coffee percolates the lounges, yet I find myself thinking of the countless warriors who have sailed this sea through the centuries. I imagine hostile naval ships creeping above the horizon, the sweat and smoke of sea battles, blood spilling into the Channel. I scare myself pretending to scan for torpedoes. Some families in 1915 are so nervous about their womenfolk crossing this sea that they make them promise to wear a lifejacket throughout the journey.

Grateful that torpedoes are not on today's menu, I conjure up decks filled with young, khaki-clad soldiers, smoking because they always do, smoking because they are excited, smoking because they are facing their fears, smoking because they are sure they will beat the 'Boche'. I imagine a white painted hospital ship passing, a green stripe and a Red Cross painted on its side. It is not long since the Battle of Neuve Chapelle where 7,000 British and 4,200 Indian soldiers have been killed or wounded. The men lining the sides of the ship are waving as cheerfully as their wounds permit, but below deck, nurses are tending other men – men too badly injured even to know that they are leaving the battle behind.

Isabella had seen this coast when she went to Europe before she began her training, but in March 1915 it is radically different. Even in bad weather passengers can see the military encampments standing proud above the cliff tops all the way from Calais to Normandy. Isabella lands in Boulogne, plumb in the middle of that line of encampments, but I land in Dunquerque, near the Belgian border. While I steer nervously out of the ferry terminal, the diary tells me that Isabella steers between the mothers and wives of men wounded in the recent battle. Surprised, I learn that the Army encourages visits from the relatives of men whose wounds are so serious that they cannot be brought home. It even pays the fares of those who cannot afford them. Every day, anxious relatives arrive at the French ports and make their way to the hospital where their son, or brother, or husband, lies in some critical state.

I picture Isabella taking in all she sees: the relatives, the stretchers bearing the wounded, the soldiers going in every direction, the military cargo being loaded and unloaded. She keeps an eye out for Lady Rosalind Northcote, the daughter of an Earl, and an expert on herbs. Neither a nurse nor a doctor, Lady Rosalind simply wants to do her bit by volunteering to help the Anglo-Ethiopian. Together, she and Isabella need to find their lift to Frévent.

Wanting to mimic Isabella's route, I take the slow road, but however hard I look out for sights she may have seen, I cannot possibly recreate the jolting she had on the bumpy road surfaces, nor her interminable waiting as jams of motor ambulances blocked the carriageway, nor the sounds and smells that engulfed her. The car carrying Isabella and Lady Rosalind, in the unreliable manner of all these new-fangled motor vehicles, breaks down three times before it reaches the Anglo-

Ethiopian. By the time they arrive it is late, and they are greeted with bedlam: bad news from the Front, hellishly irritating French Army bureaucracy, operations, dressings, anaesthetics and, oh, the staff! Lady Rosalind is bursting with the problems she has encountered in obtaining her permits, Miss Sandford is distraught for fear her brother has gone down in the sinking of the H.M.S. *Irresistible.* In twenty-first century serenity, I go to sleep to the sound of a babbling brook.

3

The next morning, I walk along sun-filled streets to the *Médiathèque Municipale* de Frévent. I am on a mission to find the building where Isabella worked – the one pictured in Mrs D-W's photograph, where Isabella stands with the other staff beneath the flags. All my attempts to discover its location in advance have come to nothing, so this is a long shot. Could that photograph have been taken here?

I am greeted by M. Jaques Crampon, who has a huge beard and a very deep voice. In no time he has me seated at a tiny table in the children's corner, leafing through books of old photos. In as little time I am up again, hardly believing that I have already found what I am looking for. Waving the book at him, I jab a finger at a group of photos. He seems unsurprised. Naturally it still stands. He knows the building well. *L'Hospice* is just round the corner. *L'Hospice*? I can hardly believe my ears. The word 'Hospice' has come up time and again in the diary, but in every case I have transcribed it as 'Hospital', assuming I must be mis-reading the scrawl. Could the 'Hospital' in the Imperial War Museum photograph really be '*L'Hospice*' in Frévent?

Heads together, eyes squinting, we compare the two pictures. Yes, the buildings are the same, er, no they aren't, er, *oui, non* … er?? Ah ha. Simultaneously we spot the drain-pipe. Unobtrusively from its corner, it convinces us. At last we grasp how the book photograph and the museum photograph match up and our doubts are quashed. *L'Hospice* is the building which housed the Anglo-Ethiopian. *L'Hospice* is the building where Isabella worked.

In M. Crampon's book, I read how, as the Germans advanced in 1914, the people of Frévent welcomed refugees into the town. They collected food for the families of men who had gone to fight. One midnight, an explosion resounded through the streets – the railway bridge was being blown up on the orders of General Joffre. When a few German soldiers reached the town, occupation loomed. In preparation, the townsfolk gave money to the bakers so they could feed the poor even if the Germans gained control. Flour began to run out and volunteers with hunting rifles stood guard over bridges and railway lines. I shudder – even amongst the colourful security of these children's books, I feel closer to World War One than I have ever felt, safely on the other side of the English Channel.

Following M. Crampon's directions, I set out for *L'Hospice*. Beside the *Médiathèque*, the river bridge is smothered in geraniums. I pause, haunted. Did huntsmen really stand guard here as the Fréventins feared for their lives a century ago, a few short months before my grandmother arrived? Walking pensively on, I round the corner, and the connections begin to flood in. There is the Hotel d'Amiens. I know it already. The staff had a meal there before Isabella came out. Can it really still be here? Now that I understand what Frévent has just been through, I feel ashamed at my fellow countrymen's complaints, 'Really,' writes Mrs D-W, 'dinner last night was too much for our nerves, it consisted of fried liver and as a second course liver stewed in small pieces.'

As I turn towards the market, I see the roof of the Hospice peeping above the stalls. I try to picture Isabella slipping out here for odds and ends, but I hesitate. Was the market held here a hundred years ago? Some friendly women reassure me, "But of course, Madame! The market has been here for centuries!" So I buy a memento, a souvenir of Isabella's odds and ends.

Four storeys high and brick-built, the Hospice eerily matches the photograph. Except for the adults with learning difficulties who smile trustingly at me as I walk through the green gates that pierce its tall boundary walls. *Accueil* is to one side. I press the bell. After a long delay, Madame answers.

"*Non, je regrette, je ... non.*" Madame assures me that she is the only one on duty and that I cannot visit. Her *Non* is very firm. Is anything old left inside? No, it seems nothing remains from a hundred years ago.

Secretly I am convinced I would find a trace, but Madame will not budge. I have to content myself with permission to take a photograph outside. The staff of the Anglo-Ethiopian may have vanished, but the drainpipe has not. I make sure I include that crucial piece of evidence in my viewfinder. As I press the shutter, it is hard to keep the camera steady. My hands want to punch the air, my whole being is singing. I have found the place where my grandmother worked in the war, the place she never mentioned.

4

The Hospice roof is pierced by a row of windows. Behind them, I understand from the diary, lay the staff dormitory. Letting the muttering of the twenty-first century and the daylight fade away, I imagine Isabella lying there a week after her arrival, restless in the moonlight. She can hear the groans of the aching French soldiers, *poilus*, downstairs. Sleep refuses to come. Her mind is far too full of all the week has held. Letters being the texts and social media of her era, she grabs her writing tools, tiptoes across the room and creeps downstairs.

From the diary, I try to work out what she might write:

The Anglo-Ethiopian Hospital, Frévent, 27th March 1915

Dear Mother, Ena and Beth,
It was late when I arrived here last Saturday, but first thing
on Sunday morning I was put to learning my patients'
dressings. How the men did stare when I walked in! They
had never seen a medical woman! Thankfully, they seem
to have recovered from their shock and already they accept
me.

Some of the wounds are very shocking

She pauses – how much should she say? She wants to keep in touch, but how is she to do that without causing anxiety?

Major Lizzie faced the same dilemma, "There were a lot of

things I couldn't say to my mother for fear of worrying her."

Sighing, Isabella wonders where the limits lie. What will up-set these people she loves?

The diaries of untrained volunteer nurses tell how, to start with, they retched and fainted at the bloodied, mangled bodies they were called upon to tend. As their experience grew, they record being unable to believe how they have adapted to cope with whatever the war throws at them. Isabella is coping. She knows she is coping … isn't she? She has certainly never seen worse, but … She picks up her pen, about to cross out the tell-tale phrase. But no, she cannot do that; it will show through and worry them all the more. She looks heaven-wards for in-spiration. Ah. Here is a way to shed an optimistic gloss:

Some of the wounds are very shocking but I believe this
hospital is doing well. A doctor who paid us a visit was
deep in gloom. He had lost a quarter of his recent cases. The
Anglo-Ethiopian has lost only 6 per cent, so the staff here
feel justifiably proud of themselves.

She cannot shake the awful wounds from her mind, though. She watched Ena's reactions to the wounded at St Leonard's and she has been watching Lady Rosalind this week. She is sure her training is helping her to cope better than they have.

"As doctors, the gentle slow introduction from medical stu-dent days makes it easier. You've done A&E – Emergency Med-icine in Isabella's day – you've seen bad things, not to the same extent, but you're tougher and more resilient as a result," Major Lizzie explains.

Isabella takes a deep breath to bolster her courage, thinking of the rumour that has come through. On a single day this week, apparently, 100 funerals were held in Boulogne. And another 49 on the next. Let alone that there are supposed to have been thirty amputations in just one of the town's hospitals.

"Even now it's a massive shock to see someone with a leg blown off. You never get over the wrongness of it," Major Lizzie admits. And at Frévent, Isabella is on the Western Front. Historians declare that nothing could have prepared any doctors, male or female, for the horror of what they are facing here.

Isabella straightens herself. She cannot give in to the luxury of fearing what may be in store. 'Sufficient unto the day is the evil thereof,' and all that. There must be something hopeful to say to them at home. Ah yes:

The staff are a very mixed bunch – British and French,
civilian and military. To my surprise, everyone seems to be
taking my position as a lady doctor in their stride.

Her mind wanders off again. She has been giving anaesthetics all week. Can she mention that? No. She shakes her head. Definitely not. One patient had reacted so badly to the chloroform that they had had to resort to a local anaesthetic. Not ideal for a ruptured spleen. Not that there had been anything they could do for him – he had been far too badly mutilated.

The week's patients parade through her mind. Will she ever get used to the strange details that every history she takes now includes? The man's regiment, of course, and where and how he was injured. They are obvious, but then there are the extras.

How long since he had a change of clothes? How long did he have to wait for rescue? How long until he was bandaged? How long before those bandages were changed? How many days passed before he arrived at the Anglo-Ethiopian? Does she pull another sheet of paper towards her:

Frévent, 27th March 1915
Dear Jan and Frank,

After the customary greetings, she gets to what she wants to say:

Our patients arrive here after a long journey. Those who cannot walk have to wait for stretcher bearers to carry them from the battlefield. Since it is not safe to transport them in daylight, they sometimes have to endure for many hours. When they do finally arrive at the first aid post, a medical officer examines and dresses each wound, gives a shot of anti-tetanic serum and ties a label to the patient's clothing giving the diagnosis and instructions as to where to take him. The sooner the men receive proper care in a hospital behind the lines, the better their chances of a full recovery.

The moon is full tonight and maybe a shaft of moonlight creeps over her page and makes her look up. Not far from here, wounded men are bumping painfully along on stretchers and carts. Does she let her imagination loose? Does she visualise them yearning for the jolts to stop, in too much pain to consider whether they will live or die, or to fear the perils of moonlight? Perhaps a cry from the ward curtails such fancies. Her job is to give the men the best possible care now that they are safely here. She thinks of something else that will please Mother, Beth and Ena:

One of the nurses told me of a patient who kept declaring that being between our clean white sheets was like being in heaven. He had been several days on the road and thought he'd never forget the contrast between our sheets and the awful mud.

She pulls her mind off another sight: how the white sheets do not remain white, how the red blood soaks greedily into clean white swab after clean white swab as she changes the patients' dressings. And how worse than the clean red blood is the sticky, half-clotted goo, and worst of all – the pus. Nurses write of legs where green slime mingles with bloodied muscles where the bone has been laid bare. They tell of men nauseated by the sight of their own bodies. Every single change of dressing is painful. At the Anglo-Ethiopian, a special supply of champagne is reserved as a reward for the most excruciating cases. She shakes her head. Most of the men are so brave, unlike those despicable malingerers. She continues to Jan and Frank:

There was high drama here on Wednesday. Five men were brought in with sore feet. When he examined them, Dr Jacquin came to the conclusion that they had injured themselves deliberately. By injecting their feet with castor oil they had produced such blisters that they were unfit to march to the Front! If their injuries do indeed prove to be self-inflicted, they will certainly deserve their punishment.

Perhaps she pauses to ponder Major Jacquin, their Doctor-in-Chief, newly appointed by the French Army. Apparently he had heard rumours that the hospital was incompetent, so has been digging his nose into everything, determined to bring the place up to scratch. The rumours have proved false, but his interference has so incensed her friend, Dr Cockett, that he has threatened to leave and join the RAMC. One of her unexpected jobs this week has been coaxing him to stay.

Early morning sounds begin to slip up from the courtyard. She picks up her pen again:

When I arrived here there were some very old ambulance wagons in the yard, dating perhaps from the 1870 war with Germany. They were disgustingly dirty and completely covered in mildew, but in the middle of the week soldiers arrived to repaint them so they can be brought back into use. Can you imagine using ancient horse-drawn ambulances like those nowadays? I'm very glad I won't be a wounded man in one of them!

The maids' chatter reminds Isabella of an easy way to sign off, and she hastily scribbles the same paragraph into each letter:

Working in French is proving no problem. The men come from many different regions of France and beyond, but

although some have thick dialects, most are intelligible.
They are usually very careful to mind their language when
the other women and I are around, but occasionally we
catch them out. Oh how we laugh as their blushes creep up
beneath their beards!
Yours in good spirits,
Isabella

Letting the sound and light of my own 'now' return, I notice a man wheeling himself through the door of the Hospice. I doubt if he knows that other men, younger men, were wheeled and carried through that same door so long ago, but as the door swings, I catch a tantalising glimpse inside. There are stairs, stone stairs, and they are certainly a century old. I fix on them. Perhaps next morning, as Isabella goes up to her first floor ward, the sound of voices bounces down to her. An older woman booms deep, staccato commands. English and Scottish orderlies improvise brief phrases, their utterings harmonising with the percussion of this and that as they move around the ward. A nurse croons soothingly in French. Deep beneath the layers of sound rumbles the rich growl of Frenchmen. Suddenly, louder than all, a solo voice lets fly, "Seester, Seester!"

"They try," thinks Isabella, "they really do. The trouble is they have no idea of rank. From the lowliest orderly upwards, everyone is 'Seester.'" She is used to it. It happened constantly in Edinburgh and Liverpool. The shriek repeats itself. "That will be No. 7," she thinks, hurrying on. As she opens the door, there is a mass fumbling as the men hasten to extinguish their cigarettes. As many as can, stand to acknowledge her arrival. The crooning nurse attending to No. 7 looks up, relieved, as Isabella comes over.

Since arriving here she has been round with the dressing trolley at least once a day, re-bandaging damaged fingers, amputated arms and mangled legs, let alone the stomachs, chests and heads. She has long lost count of the number of filthy swabs she has discarded. She is getting used to the pus and the risk of sudden haemorrhages. Her nose is becoming inured to the iron smell that comes from even healthy tissue, less so to the stench of infected wounds. She still hates how noxious material splatters her as she works.

As she removes No. 7's soiled dressing, she listens to the ward bustle. One man is demanding a drink. It is their blood loss that makes them thirsty, she thinks. Another is too hot. He is begging to be fanned. She shakes her head, laughing quietly as another pleads for a blanket. Oh, and is that No. 5 asking for his cigarette to be lit? He must have forgotten she is here. She works carefully as she nears her patient's flesh, ready for a leak of blood. Or will it be pus, or, oh this would be too, too marvellous – not that it is likely in view of his fever – is there any chance that his wound might actually show some improvement today?

Most of the patients in the Anglo-Ethiopian are 'seriously wounded' and remain in the hospital for a long time, I learn from a Red Cross report: seriously wounded because while the trenches may protect the body, they leave heads vulnerable; seriously wounded because bombarded trenches collapse, crushing and suffocating the soldiers they had sheltered; seriously wounded because the hundreds of rounds of ammunition that fly from the barrels of the new machine guns hit so many men, so many times; seriously wounded because the other new weapons – grenades, mortars and high explosive shells – are even worse, dismembering and mutilating their victims.

However the wounds come about, the end result is that many of the casualties have multiple wounds. Even doctors in the regular army have never seen damage such as this war is producing. Isabella may be new to the military, but she is not alone in her ignorance. Every medical officer along the Front is learning on the job, trying to work out the best way of treating these novel injury combinations.

5

'Madame Curie turned up this afternoon,' records the diary that night. The words may be perfectly legible, but I find them unbelievable. Why should Marie Curie, the world-famous pioneering scientist, the woman who has been awarded Nobel Prizes in both Physics and Chemistry, come here, to the Anglo-Ethiopian Hospital in Frévent?

X-rays, of course. The moment X-rays were discovered in 1895, doctors grasped how useful they would be for pinpointing the precise position of bullets lodged in the body. When Mme Curie learned that the French Army was not installing X-ray machines in its new military hospitals, she moved fast. Teaching herself radiology and anatomy, she arranged for an ordinary touring car to be converted into a mobile X-ray unit. When she drove it out to the hospitals, the doctors were so grateful that she grew that first outfit into a fleet of twenty sky-blue 'Petite Curies' that range the Western Front. They almost match the new uniforms the French Army has just begun to issue.

Disturbed by the clatter of the vehicle's arrival, Isabella and the nurses peer down from the ward windows. The nurses grumble as they see that this is not just any old Petite Curie. The great lady herself is climbing out of the car. She is not entirely popular at the Anglo-Ethiopian. Last time she visited, they tell Isabella, she arrived unexpectedly in the middle of a January night and politeness had forced them to concoct some sort of bed for her despite the lateness of the hour. "To cap it all," they continue indignantly, "the next morning she simply swept off, claiming that her machine was broken."

Today's visit too is a surprise, an impulsive diversion on the way back to Paris, explains Mme. A dark room is quickly rigged up. Hurriedly, the doctors confer to select the cases, standing to one side as Mme Curie's men cart in the bulky X-ray equipment and the generator. Soon, a 'lung' – a man with a chest wound – is lying on the table. Madame sets the machine going. Time passes. No, it is not yet finished. They wait longer. It is a very slow process.

Isabella is the most recently qualified doctor here – the only one to have learned about X-rays at medical school. Ever since she sat through Dr Dawson Turner's physics lectures, mesmerised by his enthusiasm, she has known of their power. Perhaps she has spent this week deeply frustrated by the lack of the facilities she has been used to – if only they could see inside these wounds, if only they could simply take an X-ray, they would be able to provide far better care. The nurses may be ambivalent about Mme Curie, but I suspect Isabella is thrilled.

Over dinner, Mme Curie explains that the Army has banned her from roaming the Front without a doctor, so she is travelling in secret. Nothing and nobody, she declares, can be allowed to get in the way of her mission. But of course, that mission does not allow the Petite Curie to stay at the Anglo-Ethiopian, and in the morning it whisks Mme away over the cobbles, leaving Isabella and her colleagues to return to their work somewhat the wiser as to how to care for a few of their patients, but still struggling on in ignorance with most of their cases.

Looking towards the gates, I ponder the traffic which follows the Petite Curie into this courtyard. A General and his son drop in. Over dinner they give a blow-by-blow explanation of the recent battle at Neuve Chapelle that satisfies the staff's hunger for news – the papers do not reach them here. Day by day more and more patients arrive, some in military ambulances, some staggering up from the station. There are constant surprises – an officer who claims to have been injured by a toy pistol; a man whose ear has been sliced off by his friend; an English parson who wanders into theatre during an operation and invites them to his Easter Day services.

Surgery for one of their gravely injured new cases is scheduled for 5th April, Easter Monday. Newly arrived nurses offer to help but are invited instead to watch, with the medieval-sounding promise that, 'It's to be a great entertainment.' Isabella and Mrs D-W give the anaesthetic. 'The operation went off all right,' reports the diary, 'It took about 1½ hours. His hip bone was broken in about a dozen places. Black spongy and infarcted, which had to come out. Dr Cropper did the plaster assisted by a Matron from London. The smell was awful and the place a pigsty when we'd finished.'

Afterwards, Isabella and the team have to tug off their stinking gowns. Despite the harsh soap, I can see them scrubbing themselves clean and heading for lunch. But as they eat, they are interrupted. An orderly hurries in, "Please Sirs," he urges, "Sister says the hip is in trouble. Please come. Quickly! Come!" Downing cutlery, the doctors all hurry to their morning patient. Desperately, they apply one technique after another – anything to save him. But it is no use. He dies in the early afternoon. They leave his bedside sad and deeply puzzled. He reached the hospital not long after being hit – his prognosis should have been good …

Danielle, the anaesthetist, comes up with a disturbing fact, "Young people, as these war wounded were, hold up well even after big blood losses, but may suddenly fail when an event such as the giving of chloroform takes place."

'An event such as the giving of chloroform'? But it was Isabella and Mrs D-W who gave the chloroform. Did this young man die because of something Isabella did, or failed to do? I try to digest the idea. I want to be accurate and academically dispassionate but somewhere deep inside I want Isabella to have been a good doctor. I want her to have been doing her job well. Now I have to ask myself if she could have done better. Slightly shaken, I remind myself that she was part of a team. In which case, was she part of an under-performing team? Could they all have done better? Or were they, at that time, ignorant of this particular risk? Or perhaps there was nothing they could have done. Perhaps this poor soldier was doomed. Without his operation he would have died; with the chloroform his operation required, he has died.

Not that there is time for reflection or regret. The doctors are again scrubbing up hurriedly. The arm they operated on two days ago needs re-opening. As they work, I read the second grisly description of the day, 'He'd been scouting and met some Germans doing ditto and he got two holes into the same part of his arm. The whole arm was black today. Dr Jacquin said because blood had clotted in his arteries and stopped circulation. Anyway we had the stinking piece off and hope the man will be all right. His fracture was bad on the table.'

Isabella is used to surgery, but the mess and stench of these operations in Frévent is new. And all her life she will bury their memory. At any moment the slightest trigger might kick them into life, but not a whisper, not one blanch of her cheek will reveal their existence. Why? Were they too horrific to revisit? Were they too disturbing to discuss with others? Could her silence be part of the great taboo that stopped so many veterans saying what they saw in this war? Or could it be that even horrific things become normal. Normal is unremarkable. Memory does not bother to file 'normal'.

The mess and blood of that Easter Monday morning are already considered 'normal' for this war. It is the stench that is the worry, the noxious sign of gas gangrene. Later, it too will become 'normal', but in April 1915, it is still new to everyone.

"It has a pseudomonas-like smell – a real fug of dying flesh that hits you and sticks in the back of your throat," explains Danielle. The staff try everything to get rid of the stench: they discard contaminated clothes, scrub themselves for hours, and sprinkle their sheets with perfume, but nothing rids them of its pervasive stink.

Gas gangrene is not only new, it is frightening. It makes even the most innocent wound ominous. A demon that appears as if from nowhere, it races along limbs at terrifying speed. In no time, they become gangrenous, and then, just as quickly, dead. Against every instinct, surgeons lop off toes, fingers, arms and legs, leaving raw stumps. If there was any other treatment which gave their patients a chance of survival, they would grab it. But, so far, amputation has proved the only remedy and even that is often futile. Frequently, the infection has already invaded the rest of the body and kills the patient anyway.

I read how Medical Officers the length of the Front are searching for a better way of beating this scourge. They have discovered that it is brought on when bacteria from the fertile fields where the men are fighting get into any wound. But, with the trenches carved from earth laced with centuries of manure, the whole Front is contaminated. Any bullet or piece of shrapnel carrying something as ordinary as a scrap of torn uniform thrusts millions of lethal bacteria into a wound. And a man instinctively slapping his dirty hand onto an injury will inadvertently inoculate it with those same deadly germs.

Later in the war, they will discover that irrigating a wound with a weak solution of bleach helps, but now, in spring 1915, neither Isabella and the doctors at the Anglo-Ethiopian nor any of the other medics along the Front know that. They are all just trying to do their best. On 8th April the diary reports, 'The man who had his arm amputated developed gas gangrene this morning and in spite of everything which could be done, injections of peroxide, free drainage, he died at 4pm today.'

I drive out to the town cemetery. The war dead are easy to find. Their graves parade in serried ranks beneath a Tricolor. Do any men who died on Isabella's watch lie here? Possibly. Yves Marie Leguellaf, 5th April 1915 announces one tombstone. In my mind, his grave merges with the diary's description of the blackened tissue, the smell, the mess and the blood of that Easter Monday operation. He could well be the one. Metaphorically doffing my hat, I take a moment's silence. And it dawns on me that the bodies beneath these graves are mangled. Hardly any of them hold skeletons laid out straight and true like textbook diagrams. Quickly or slowly, these men died agonising deaths, their bones broken, their bodies shattered. If Yves Marie Leguellaf is Isabella's Easter Monday patient, his pelvis is probably unrecognisable.

In their silence, these war graves cry out to me of the dilemma that Isabella, and all war doctors, face. Even as Isabella is putting Yves Marie to sleep so that Dr Cropper can extract the dead, black spongy parts of his hip bone, the staff all know that he is unlikely to fight again, but if he lives, what will the future hold for such a wounded veteran? Again, I let myself risk imagining what Isabella might write to a medically qualified friend:

Frévent, April 23rd 1915

Today, we bade farewell to 18 men. How wretchedly different it feels from sending patients out at home! As doctors, we work to bring our patients back to health, but here, should we succeed, the men we have worked so hard to save will be sent back to a place where they stand every chance of receiving further injuries, if not being killed.

The faces of the men who knew their departure was imminent betrayed their fears. It is hardly surprising that some of them suddenly developed all sorts of fresh aches and pains; anything that might put off the evil day. Of course, when today came, they acted as bravely as anything and showed not one jot of fear, as we knew they would, but one cannot help but find it a disquieting procedure.

On the other hand, of course, if we fail to bring the men

back to health, they are doomed to a future filled with ill-health and insecurity. The pension received by a man invalided out of the French Army depends on his wound, apparently. We had a fisherman here who begged and pleaded for an amputation. He thought he could make ends meet for his family on an amputee's pension, but he was terrified that the smaller sum due to a wounded war veteran would not cover their survival.

Altogether, the thought of what is going to happen to the men to whom we waved farewell today rather haunts one. What shape will they be in after another spell in the trenches? And what about those who are being sent on for further treatment, for artificial limbs and the like? It does not bear thinking about.

What keeps me going is knowing that we have to stop the Germans. We have been warned to expect a big rush, so we know that more casualties will come to fill our empty beds. However grievous it may be to see yet more battle-torn young men, we really must win this war. Helping its casualties seems to me to be the very best possible thing to be doing just now.

As I look at the tombstones around me, I remember the words of a WWI nurse who firmly pinned all blame for casualties at the Kaiser's feet, and remind myself that, in 1915, most of the population of Britain believed completely in the necessity of this war. If Isabella did not, she would not have volunteered to be here.

But I am not Isabella, and other convictions grip me. Will this site seem as barbaric to an archaeologist of the future as a dark age mass grave does to us? Will he or she begin to understand why these men died? Do I?

6

No war can prevent the April days warming up and the evenings drawing out. Nothing tells the birds to stop nesting or the buds to stop forming, but 1915 is not a normal Spring in Frévent. As farmers wonder whether international affairs will allow them to harvest the seed they are sowing, its streets fill with the sound of marching. French soldiers coming down from the North report that British troops have taken over their positions. By 14th April, 40,000 troops are swarming around this tiny town. Billets in houses have long since been filled. Men are put up in cottages, on floors and in gardens. When the straw mattresses run out, they sleep on the ground.

A brass band arrives in the building next door to the Hospice, and the sound of rehearsing fills the air. Some days are warm enough for Isabella's patients to be carried into the yard for an airing, and they return to the ward cheered and slightly less pallid. Some jolly British aviators lose their way in the skies and take refuge at the Anglo-Ethiopian. But space is limited and they have to sleep in the 'death chamber', the room that has seen six of the hospital's eleven deaths.

With the end of winter and its quiet skirmishing, it is time for the Allies to launch an offensive. Not that Isabella and the other staff know that. That is hindsight. All they have to go on are the rumours they pick up and the evidence of their own eyes. Something is up. Opportunely, the hospital takes delivery of a new Vauxhall ambulance. Beds that have lain empty all winter start to fill, and by 20th, the Hospital has forty-six patients.

An Army officer comes to warn them to make space for more. "Be prepared to requisition one of the Auberges in town," he advises them.

Speedily, they evacuate as many men as they can. The 23rd is St George's day and, St George being the patron saint of Ethiopia as well as England, I read how they celebrate by hanging the Union Jack, the flag of the Red Cross, and the national flag of Ethiopia from the window above the main door.

Immediately, I dig out the photograph from Mrs D-W's box. Yes! It is a perfect match. Someone must have decided to mark the occasion, shuffled the staff this way and that until satisfied, then: Click! Now that I have studied the diary, I want to work this photograph out. These are Isabella's colleagues, people whose stories are intertwining with hers. Which is which? Who is who?

A historian identifies a man wearing a French képi as a Major. That means he must be Dr Jacquin, the only Major on the staff. According to the diary, he was furious about the flags. I can imagine that. With his hands in his pockets, he looks as if he has only just simmered down. He had not been at the hospital when they were put up, and I imagine his puzzled wrath as he comes through the gate …

"Flags? Why flags? *Zut alors* – there is no Tricolor! Why is the flag of my nation missing? Are they celebrating the birthday of their King? Is this an insult? I will raise the flag of France myself! I will raise it now. It must fly exactly with your flag and with the others! The town has seen your flags and she too is *en colère* … "

He calms down a little when Mrs D-W and the other staff

explain that, no, they are not celebrating the King's birthday. The flags simply spell out the name of the hospital. But they offer to fly the Tricolor elsewhere, and soon the flag of France is flying cheerfully from the gate where all the world can see it. Perhaps Major Jacquin can even see his Tricolor flying soothingly just out of shot.

I look back at the two men standing next to Jacquin, hatless but uniformed. Online, I had stumbled across a picture captioned 'Dr John Cropper'. To my surprise, it had matched the older man exactly. Now, I study him. Apparently he is a 51-year-old ophthalmic surgeon who has spent most of his working life as a missionary in Palestine. His expertise is not in war surgery, but in the infectious diseases of the Middle East. I gaze at his large moustache, sticking-out ears and military bearing, sceptical. Of how much use is a deep understanding of malaria in Northern France? I remind myself that he has other talents. If he is not operating, he will be dancing round the roof mending leaks, or down on his knees painting the theatre wainscotting or, as a prize-winning artist, he may be out sketching. He is certainly energetic and hard-working. Beyond all this, he is car-crazy. From the diary it sometimes seems as if his chauffeuring and mechanical skills are almost as vital for the Anglo-Ethiopian as his proficiency as a surgeon.

The other man, by process of elimination, must be Cockett, the doctor described in the diary as Isabella's friend. Can I see sadness in his face, or is it exhaustion, or perhaps an air of detachment? I know he wants to leave. A few days ago he finally handed in his notice. Apart from being utterly exasperated by

Dr Jacquin's continual interference, he has become convinced that he should not be out here treating Frenchmen. It is his patriotic duty to look after English war-wounded. As soon as his notice has run its course, he has told them all, he will be going home to join the RAMC.

Beside these men cluster a bevy of pale-clad nurses, all unidentifiable, many elderly. They come and go so quickly there is no hope of keeping track of them. Isabella is having to adjust to new nurses as often as she is adapting to new patients. Four weeks ago, war wounds were new to her. Now, she is no longer the novice. Already she has been here longer than some of these women. She may even be teaching them. I look at my utterly recognisable grandmother. Nonchalantly un-uniformed, she is relaxing against the wall, her beam as broad as when she was playing with the dog a few years ago. A photogenic pose, or a genuine clue that she is happy here, that the gruelling work is not sapping her spirits?

My eyes track downwards. Apart from Isabella, the only person not in uniform is the black-clad woman sitting on the pavement. She has to be Betty Sandford, who has come over from Addis Ababa to do duty as the housekeeper. I like the idea that this jolly woman, with her intimate knowledge of Ethiopia, is in charge of disbursing the Ethiopian prince's bounty. And in her nurse's uniform, sitting beside Betty, is Mrs D-W. She is smiling nicely for the camera, but tonight she will record how severe neuralgia has made her vile tempered all day. She believes it has been brought on by sick worry about her husband, Dick. There has been no letter from him for more than three weeks.

7

Three days later, on 26th April, a letter, at last, arrives. It is not yet 7am, but the maid takes it upstairs. Hesitantly, she wakes her boss. Mrs D-W is immediately alert. Dick? Her face falls. No, it is only from General Chailley.

General Chailley? The name may fill Mrs D-W with sick disappointment, but it excites me. Surely the purple-printed letter which led me to the Anglo-Ethiopian in the first place was from Chailley? Fumbling, I get it out. Yes! Chailley did write it. But it is not the same letter. My letter is dated is *le 1er Mai*. It must be a second letter. There are four more days to go before this letter and the diary match up.

Reluctantly, Mrs D-W opens General Chailley's letter. The French Army are moving all foreign hospitals away from the Front, she reads. "That is fine," she sighs, "We are not a foreign hospital. We are *Association des Dames Françaises.*" But the end of his letter puzzles her: 'When will you find it convenient to move?' he asks. On enquiry, it becomes clear that the French authorities really do intend the Anglo-Ethiopian to move, and in no time Mrs D-W, standing on her dignity, is off to Paris to pull strings.

It is dark by the time she gets back. I picture many of the staff staying up, unable to rest until they hear the news. The car draws in, and Mrs D-W starts talking almost before she is in the building so it takes them a little while to untangle her triumphant tale. She had caught Lord Granville just before lunch.

He had popped over and had a word with a chap at the Foreign Office, who had dropped into the War Office, which had arranged for Mrs D-W to see the great man himself, de Puzack. "Oh," she crows, "he was putty in my hands! Everything will be fine!"

The next day the relieved staff are on-fire to beat fractures, shrapnel, gas gangrene, wounds of the chest and abdomen, eyes, heads … Bring on the next batch of wounded! But at 10.45 am, a messenger dashes in from the Post Office. "Quick, Dr Jacquin, come! There is a telephone call. *Vite!*"

At 11 o'clock, Jacquin returns. Quietly, he finds Mrs D-W. Intent on their work, the staff do not spot her, too, flying to the Post Office. Nobody observes her coming back, or hears her shout for the chauffeur and jump into the car. Nobody notices how fast it careers out of the gates. It is lunchtime before the news breaks.

I imagine Mrs D-W standing and tapping on the table to make her solemn pronouncement. "This morning Dr Jacquin was called to the telephone to be informed that an ambulance will replace us this afternoon or tomorrow. I immediately telephoned Lord Granville in Paris. He promised to see to things there. Then I went up to HQ to talk to General Chailley, but had to make do with his Chief of Staff, a most disagreeable man! Rules are rules, apparently, and since all foreign hospitals must go, he said, we must go too." She sighs deeply, "The only thing I got out of him was an eight-day stay of execution. After that, he insists that we clear out!"

She pauses, remembering how she mustered every argument for their cause. She is far too furious to consider how her staff are taking the news. Breathing deeply to brace herself, she delivers her next salvo, "I said too that I could not move till the Service de Santé had found us a place to go to. My dream was dispelled by my friend telling me that the military doctors had something better to do than to bother about a *loco* for us. I must run round the country and find for myself."

These volunteers will not take such news quietly. Is there a cacophony of complaints against the French? Loud sympathy? Quiet panic? Noisy objections? Or are they more pragmatic?

"What will happen to the patients?"

"Will they have to be moved?"

"Are they fit to be moved?"

When Isabella returns to the ward perhaps she goes straight to the bed where a cumbersome wooden device holds No. 4's leg firmly in traction. Ears pricked for the sound of the new ambulance coming to take their place, she tries to work out how well the leg will withstand disruption. She moves over to the congested lungs, then on to the irrigation tubes on the smashed shoulder, trying to foresee difficulties and solve problems as she goes. She can tell by their faces that the men have already heard. They have that resigned look, as if gearing themselves up once more for the nightmare of wartime transport: jolting, dirty, uncomfortable, tiring – dangerous. This place has been a haven for them. One of them catches an indiscreet moment of anxiety flit across her face and before she knows it, he has called for a game of cards when the doctor has finished, the moment has passed, and he has given them all strength again.

The next day, the 30th, they work on as if no change is threatened, as if there is no tomorrow to take care of. No. 6 has the shrapnel extracted from his leg. A Petite Curie draws up and they gather for the show.

"What, no shrapnel in No. 26's lungs? Ah, really thought we'd find some there – metal in his leg, though. Have to deal with that."

"Those fractured legs are healing well – but wait a mo, look at that one, still shrapnel in there and he's already had both his feet off poor chap! We'll have to take him to theatre again."

Does Isabella – do any of them – consider whether staying on is their best way of helping in the war effort? With no new location for the hospital, is it worth staying, waiting? After all, Dr Cockett is leaving … But Dr Cockett takes them by surprise. He has, he announces, agreed to stay on for another month or so. His wife has volunteered for night-duty. His wife? Then there was never any chance of his being a romantic thread in Isabella's tale? Dutifully, I scrap my sentimental dream. Patriotically, I recognise that with the wards full and the hospital having only a few days' grace, now would not be the time for romance.

The 1st May dawns. Mrs D-W is bending over her dressings when a telegram is placed beside her. Juggling it between soiled bandages, her face flushes with jubilation as she reads. She wants to leave the wound to run and tell everybody, but she limits herself to a whoop – yes, I am sure she whoops. "Lord Granville has been in touch with Headquarters about the Anglo-Ethiopian," she informs everybody who can hear, her voice shrill with excitement. "He has every confidence that we will not have to move. In the meantime, we are to do nothing." Almost trembling with relief, she carries on working, breathing as deeply as if she had run a race. Ten minutes later, another telegram is thrust hurriedly towards her.

8

'Pray God comfort you. H.M. Doughty-Wylie,' reads the second wire. To begin with, I do not understand. Why should Mrs D-W suddenly need divine comfort? Who is 'H.M. Doughty-Wylie'? Slowly, as I decode a few more sentences, light dawns. Mrs D-W's beloved husband, Dick, is dead. Wire-savvy and terse, Dick's father is sending his condolences to his son's wife.

'The shock was terrible,' writes Mrs D-W, 'I don't quite know what I did for the first 60 seconds, I was nearly mad. Then I pulled myself together and went back to my dressings and then to the Post Office to phone the Embassy and ask them to let me have news of Dick by phone to the War Office if possible. I also wired the War Office.

'I never passed a day in such an agony of misery. It was physical as well as mental pain. Something seemed to clutch at the region of my heart and my inside. Food I could not look at, though I attended meals. I did my work in the theatre where there was an operation, but I could have screamed aloud. Oh the suspense! It was the worst of Hells. I solemnly believe that this day has expatiated many sins. To lose Dick, it seems the end of everything.'

I can feel her crazy autopilot. The flood of adrenaline that takes over when a crisis happens and the mind shuts down and the doing carries on and the awfulness hits later. The collision of calamities when the replacement ambulance really does arrive the very same afternoon. And in the evening, the wire from the War Office that confirms Dick's death.

Her diary sucks me into her grief and I would resist, fearing being dragged away from Isabella's story, but for a letter that lies deep within Mrs D-W's boxes. Written by Dick only days before his death, it is not the letter his wife had been longing for, but a worried letter to her mother, Mrs Jean Coe.

Extract from letter from Dick to Mrs Jean Coe,
Llandysul, Carmarthenshire (Received 5th May 1915)

General headquarters, Mediterranean Expeditionary Force,
20 April, 1915

I want you to do something for me. I am going to embark tomorrow on what is certainly an extremely dangerous job. If the thing went wrong, Lily would feel intolerable lonely and hopeless after her long hours of work, which tell rarely on anybody's spirits and stability. She talks about overdoses of morphia and such things. I think that in reality she is too brave and strong-minded for such things, but the saying weighs on my spirits. If you hear I am killed, go over at once to France with H.H. and seek her out. Telegraph at once that you are coming and want her to send a car to meet you at Boulogne. Don't leave any time, but go and look after her. Don't take her away from the work, for it will be best for her to work, but manage to stay somewhere near and see her through. Tell her what is perfectly true that the work cannot go on without her. I haven't told her yet of this trip because I don't want her to know till it's over.
This is only by way of precaution. She has a great friend

with her, one Dr Isobel Stenhouse, and a Miss Sandford,
sister of my helper in Abyssinia, a very good girl indeed,
and on the whole she is in the best place possible, and I am
unduly worried about her.

Dick's pencilled words rivet me. An upper-class husband is consumed with worry about his wife. A Lieutenant Colonel in the British Army is urgently mustering his allies to protect his spouse from herself. Facing death, he is desperately begging his mother-in-law to rush to her daughter's side. And Isabella is one of the people he is relying on for his wife's safety. Why? What is this great friendship between my grandmother and Mrs D-W?

The trust Dick shows only makes sense if they have known each other for years. But how can a medical student, or a junior doctor, have made friends with a diplomat's wife? Before the war, Mrs D-W had been shifting between Turkey, Addis Ababa, London and South Wales. Where could she and Isabella have met? The more I fiddle with the conundrum, the more I fail to find common ground, and the more I realise the sheer quantity of detail I must be missing, the desperately fragile, filamentous nature of the threads I am pulling together. Then another researcher sends new information: Mrs D-W is ten years older than Isabella and trained as a nurse at Edinburgh Royal Infirmary. Is this, at last, a connection? Many of the nurses at the Anglo-Ethiopian have Scottish names. Many of them are evidently old friends. Has Mrs D-W kept up with her alma mater? Is Edinburgh the place her path crossed Isabella's, the place where their friendship was forged?

Humbled, I return to Dick's letter. Very deliberately, he has pencilled a little omission mark to insert Isabella's title, '*Dr*', above the line – it almost seems to echo the omissions I must be making, but it is more important than that. Dick has taken the trouble to honour Isabella. I have seen this letter quoted in a published book, but now I am looking at the original, I can see that its author has chosen to misquote Dick. She has 'corrected' his insertion to 'Sister' Isobel Stenhouse. But that is not what Dick wrote. He knew that Isabella was a doctor.

Suddenly, the significance of the matter hits me. So great is Dick's fear for his wife, that it is almost a matter of life and death to him that Isabella is a doctor. Stalwart soldier that he is, he may not fear battle, but he is terrified that his wife will commit suicide. And he is convinced that, as a doctor, Isabella will know how to help, she will know how to manage potential suicide. Her presence and her skills bring him comfort, and he is confident that they will be just as reassuring to Mrs Coe.

His words shift my whole perspective on Isabella's status within the Anglo-Ethiopian. I can no longer view her simply as an eager junior doctor on the fringe of the team. She is part of the inner circle. She is one in whom Mrs D-W will confide. Mentally, I add collaborating with Betty Sandford on suicide watch to the list of jobs Isabella is now carrying out under the looming doom of the hospital's move to a new, as yet unknown, location. I can see them helping Mrs D-W to bed this first, grievous night. Perhaps it is even Isabella who suggests that Mrs D-W takes a dose of bromide.

But the letter does something else too. It makes me question my understanding of Mrs D-W's character. The diary has painted me a picture of a pushy, upper-class British woman. Come what may, she *will* get what she wants – nothing will stop her, nothing will get in her way. Dick's husband's-eye view has taken me by surprise. Was I wrong? Is Mrs D-W as strong as she makes out?

As I investigate, I find myself drawn into house parties that include morning canters, pig-sticking and snoozy siestas. Even in the depths of Turkey, dinners are taken in full evening dress. The meals are followed by whisky, soda and 'smokes' around the fire.

Most of the tales gel with the Mrs D-W I know from the diary: a cocktail of English-ness and upper-class-ness laced with huge shots of both humour and hospitality. But they tell too of her overriding passion for nursing. Not only has Mrs D-W nursed victims of bubonic plague in India, she took herself out to South Africa to tend the wounded during the Boer War, and followed that by setting up a hospital in the Balkans during their 1912–13 war.

All the evidence of her career makes her seem like the tough cookie the diary presents, but not everyone sees her that way. Dick was worried about her reaction when he accidentally took her into a bloody siege in Turkey. One of their visitors regarded her as a pale character with a predilection for frilly white garments who rarely risked the open air without a parasol. Where does the truth lie? What sort of woman will Isabella be having to tend?

9

The next morning, a wire gives more details about Dick's death. He had been killed in Gallipoli on 29th April. Mrs D-W still cannot believe it. She tells everybody that she is sure there must have been a mistake …

Throughout the world, countless families are receiving similar news. The number of men who have been killed is vast but the number who are grieving is even larger. Mrs D-W is only one among thousands of women who have been widowed since the war began. The grief she pours into her diary must echo scores of others, "What am I going to do? How will I cope?"

As I had transcribed her words in the academic austerity of the Imperial War Museum, they had appeared self-pitying, but here in Frévent, with a deeper feeling for the war, I have more tolerance for her. I am, after all, peering into her inner world. She never meant her words for general consumption or to generate sympathy. Perhaps only Isabella and Betty are allowed to glimpse her less than stiff-upper-lipped face while she shelters behind a bolder, very British mask to the remainder of her staff. Not that she has the luxury of time to stop and grieve. Far from it. The renewed fighting has already landed them a fresh wave of casualties, while the ambulance that will replace them is lurking in the yard, a predator waiting to pounce.

On 1st May, the diary records, another letter arrives from General Chailley. A little thrill of pride runs through me as Isabella's and Mrs D-W's archives collide. Solemnly, I pull out Isabella's purple-printed letter. Has every member of staff been given a copy, or is having her own copy another clue that Isabella has special status, I wonder, as I translate the General's words.

He begins by confirming that all foreign health units must leave the Front without delay. This is not a personal slight directed at the Anglo-Ethiopian, he assures them, it is a general order. He tells them, as if they did not know, that a French ambulance will be coming to take their place. But his next sentences bring better news. Contrary to what they had heard earlier, he is offering the hospital a new home, the old casino in St Valery:

> ... *a little building work will turn it into a very satisfactory hospital. Orders have already been given for the work to be carried out without delay. Please let me know if you would like to accept this solution ...*

> *I regret that I am unable to keep the unit which you direct in Frévent. Its services have been greatly appreciated by the Tenth Army.*

I imagine their reactions to the General's offer.
"St Valery sur Somme? Where on earth is that?"
"Cropper will know, he'll have driven there."
"Cropper, where is St Valery?"
"On the coast?"
"Miles away!"
Soon, the buzz is going round that their move is the consequence of a spy having been found in a similar voluntary

hospital. They are absolutely certain that not one of them is a spy, but they do admit that no risks can be taken, and Dr Jacquin and Mrs D-W set off to explore St Valery's casino.

It is late in the evening before the Ford pulls back into the yard. Isabella and her colleagues listen keenly to the travellers' verdict. "The General may think the casino will make a good hospital," declares their boss, "but I don't! It's kilometres away! It's a horrid wooden building. And you should see inside – it went bust three years ago and it's filthy! Absolutely filthy! Since the war began they've used it as a billet for Colonial troops and immigrants. Just imagine the state of it! There's been a battle of the plates in the kitchen. It's sordid, quite, quite sordid!"

Isabella and the other staff shuffle. They need to break her flow. Dirt can be cleaned. What will they have in the way of wards and theatres? Jacquin nudges the tirade, "The Army will clean it … "

Mrs D-W interrupts him, "The whole place wants paper or paint. The laundry wants doing. Everything wants doing! And General Chailley thinks I ought to do it. I don't! It's his job not mine! It is dreadfully inconvenient … "

They have their in-point. "In what way is it inconvenient," asks someone, "Surely we can concoct some wards?"

Mrs D-W is off again. "'We can make the bar, restaurant and theatre into wards. That will give us thirty beds, but upstairs is useless. It has endless small rooms that will only take one or two beds. It's quite dreadful! Absolutely awful!"

Inconvenient, awful, filthy: they have no choice but to prepare to move. The spy has seen to that. In the chaos of packing, constantly shifting arrangements and telegrams of condolence, Isabella remains on her ward. The other patients have gone, but hers have not. And on 8th May, the whole hospital sets off.

10

My trek to St Valery may be comfortable, but it too is dogged by war. Cemetery after cemetery lines the road. Signpost after signpost bears the name of a battle. Even Agincourt and Crécy inscribe their names on my route. My unusual reason for coming to St Valery has intrigued the host of my Bed and Breakfast, and almost before I have come through the door, he has leafed through the pages of a book and placed it triumphantly on the table. Together, we pore over old photographs of the Casino. Playbills flaunt themselves from its walls. Smartly dressed hotel guests lounge on its verandah, a glass-roofed verandah. I examine it carefully, certain that I remember the diary featuring a verandah.

"Where is it?" I ask, wanting to go and see the place straight away.

"That Casino has long gone," my host explains, apologetically. But he hands me a map and sends me out, insisting that the new one stands on the same site.

I navigate successfully to the bottom of the hill, but find myself transfixed by a white house set well back from the road. With a vast lawn sweeping down from its façade and towering trees shielding its remaining sides, it is more of a mansion than a house and it mesmerises me. Some sixth sense is telling me that this is where Isabella arrives that late night in May 1915. My irrational conviction is so strong that I begin to imagine the next morning ...

The dawn chorus in the woods percolates through Isabella's

open window. A notorious insomniac, the energy of the birds quickly infects her. She wriggles, then sits up suddenly. This is a pleasant room. The house has been shut up all winter and the Mayor only provided the keys at tea-time yesterday. She is lucky to be in a proper bed – some of the others are sleeping on the floor.

She leans back, wide awake. How soon will they see this casino? The hundreds of battle-stained soldiers they saw yesterday are refusing to leave her mind. The ambulance trains drawn discreetly into sidings were even more dreary. The needs of this war feel more real than ever! Oh, to begin work – but when will that happen? How long will it be before the new hospital is ready? She cannot abide the thought of being idle in the face of such need. Anxiously, she reaches down beside her bed, groping for her medical bag. Relief. It is there. It has not vanished overnight. Many of her belongings have had to wait behind in Frévent but she utterly refused to let this leave her side. Who knows when it might be needed?

Another thought gets her out of bed. Carefully testing each floorboard, she tiptoes to the door and guesses her way to the kitchen. It may be early, but cook will be up and she is hoping Betty Sandford will be too. Low murmurs tell her that her wish is being granted and she eases open the heavy door. Betty looks up. They recognise each other's worry. Mrs D-W has refused to touch solid food since she heard of Dick's death and is getting weaker by the day. Somehow, they urgently need to persuade her to take some food – apart from her own welfare, if she goes under, the hospital will sink.

Leaving them to work out how to encourage their boss to eat, I purchase my own copy of the book of old photographs and walk on to the Casino. It is a standard municipal-style red-brick building flanking a square filled with parked cars. At first sight it looks closed, but when I get to the door, I discover that it is more than closed: it has gone out of business as surely as its ancient predecessor. An open café, La Terrasse, clings to its river side. Tempted, I go in, buy a latte and choose a seat with a view of the water. Laying my new book open at the page of photos of the Casino, I continue reading Mrs D-W's diary.

In Frévent, the staff of the Anglo-Ethiopian had been all set to treat a rush of wounded. Now, it is Sunday, and there is nothing for them to do but exercise patience and hope that their new building will soon be ready. They straggle across the town, exploring its byways and buildings: the ancient church that still nestles inside the medieval town walls, the Jeanne d'Arc heritage that the town still flaunts, and the mud of the Somme that still appears and disappears twice daily as the sea breathes in and out.

It is only when they return to the house that they hear the dreadful news. The Germans have attacked the RMS *Lusitania* and the whole ship has gone down. Imagine! She was a passenger liner! How can they attack a passenger liner? And she was full of Americans! Citizens of a neutral nation! How low can those Germans sink? The atrocity is so unspeakable that it has taken only two days for the horrific news to reach this isolated spot.

Anger against the enemy rekindled, Isabella and her colleagues watch impatiently as the army works on their filthy old Casino. By mid-week, the mess has been cleared and the alterations can begin. 'The big glass verandah is to be coloured to keep out the sun and be made into a ward,' I read. The old photos almost wink at me, as if to say, here we are, remember us. My eyes flip between them and the diary. The match is exact. But wait ... I scrutinise them more closely. There is the river, there is the square, there are the trees. I go round the loop again – square, trees, river, trees, river, square ...

Am I working this out correctly? Can I really be on the site of that verandah ward? Surely that would be too much of a coincidence? But no, however many times I check, I always reach the same conclusion. I am drinking my coffee exactly where Isabella worked.

Except that in May, while battles rage in Festubert, Artois, and Ypres, she cannot work. I imagine her looking at her instruments with exasperation each morning. They should not be lying unused when each day they hear of more and more casualties.

At the moment, Isabella's only task is looking after Mrs D-W. Ordinarily, there would have been a funeral by now, but Dick's remains, assuming he really is dead, lie somewhere on the other side of Europe, and the British Army has already decided that no more bodies will be shipped home. Unable to see and touch his corpse, Isabella's boss has been left, like so many others, desperately hoping that it is all a mistake and that her beloved will walk through the door again.

With no funeral, there has been no moment for friends and relatives to gather and console one another. There has been neither a eulogy, nor a collective remembering of the beloved. There has been no chance to say 'Goodbye'. And as if that was not bad enough, relatives are being asked to control their tears and celebrate. Their deceased was a valiant defender of the nation who has gloriously sacrificed his life for the Cause. They are being urged not to put on mourning – their soldier would not want them to grieve. But with neither body nor funeral, it is very hard to come to terms with reality.

Somehow, think Isabella and Betty, Mrs D-W must be made to face the truth. Hoping the idea will give her the jolt she needs, they point out to her that Dick can no longer inherit her belongings. Reluctantly, she agrees to draft a new will, the grudging acknowledgement of her transition from adored wife to grieving widow. As they assure her that Dick would be proud of her, are they aware of the anxious letter he had written to Mrs D-W's mother? Mrs Coe has marked the letter, 'Received, May 5th', so I scour the diary for her arrival. But there is no sign of her, no hint that this mother-of-the-bereaved will be turning up. Why? If I received a letter like Dick's from my son-in-law, nothing would stop me rushing to my daughter's side. Mystified, I scan through other bits and pieces copied from Mrs D-W's boxes and stumble across a couple of letters she has dated 'May 1915'. Even better, they are addressed to her mother.

Instantly, everything becomes clear. No reinforcements are going to hurry to Isabella and Betty's rescue in the shape of the elderly Mrs Coe. Mrs D-W has banned her from coming. When her mother presses her case, Mrs D-W explains vehemently, 'I particularly do not want any member of my family to come out here … I feel it easier to behave with the dignity

of my position as the head of an English Hospital by myself …
anybody else would only upset me … '

Her words ring true. In her stiff-upper-lipped British way, she
conveys those times when responsibilities are the last bastion
before breakdown, when the least word of kindness might collapse every defence and upset is best battened within. 'I am
perfectly fit, and all my staff is sticking to me like bricks. Leave
me alone to worry things through in my own way,' she continues. In almost the next sentence, comes Isabella's name. 'The
girl next to me is Sandy's sister Betty. Miss Stenhouse is standing up also out of uniform.'

Slowly it dawns on me. Mrs D-W has sent Mrs Coe a copy
of the St George's Day photograph. In the light of Dick's letter,
Mrs Coe has asked her daughter to identify Miss Stenhouse
and Miss Sandford, the people she is thinking about all day and
every day, knowing her daughter's welfare is in their hands.
As I think of her praying that these women will be given the
strength and wisdom to keep her daughter safe, it hits me that,
courtesy of the Imperial War Museum, I have brought Mrs D-
W's letters back to the place where they were written.

Thrilled, I follow the thread of their tale. Whether for sentimental reasons or because she senses their historical importance, Mrs Coe saves the letters and photographs that her
daughter sends to her. When diaries arrive, she saves those too.
At some point the whole collection is donated to the Imperial War Museum. There, I pick up exactly the same photograph that Mrs Coe was holding when she asked her daughter
to identify Miss Stenhouse, the very photograph that led me

to *L'Hospice* in Frévent. The circle is complete. Shivers ripple down my spine.

But if Mrs D-W is placing herself firmly in the hands of Isabella, Betty and the rest of her staff, were Dick's fears of suicide groundless? And, whether or not she is suicidal, how will they take care of her? Surrounded by so much untimely death, how do people keep on, and on, and on, comforting the bereaved?

I leave the café and round the corner. The woods around the white house invite strolling, and in my mind's eye I see the May sunshine dappling onto Isabella and Betty as they walk with Mrs D-W. In her grief, she is developing an unshakeable conviction that she will soon join Dick.

"Dick and I began everything together and finished everything together. I really cannot see why it should be any different this time. He escaped with his life twice: third time, they got him. I've escaped twice too: it should be third time lucky for me too," she confides. "It would be ever so much jollier for me to go on doing things with Dick in the next world, than to drag along here by myself."

What are Isabella and Betty to make of this? With Christianity being the standard foundation for a late-Victorian woman's understanding of death and the afterlife, I walk through the medieval gateway and up towards the church, a Catholic church. Not only is Mrs D-W convinced that she will soon join Dick, she is confident that he is communicating with her, 'He has promised me that he will let me know when I can come, and I am sure he will.' Disrespectfully, her writing makes me feel that Mrs D-W envisages an after-life modelled on the British Empire, with Dick asking permission for her to join him as a man in India might seek authorisation for his wife to come out from England. With my cynical hat, I note that her death will eventually be reported in *The Times* in 1960. But in May 1915, Mrs D-W's confidence that Dick is calling her and that she will soon die is unshakeable.

How worried are Isabella and Betty that she will raid the pharmaceutical cupboard and give herself a lethal dose that will make her dream come true? Perhaps not as much as Dick had feared. As their charge sits and broods, a sense of calling takes root in her life. By the end of the year, the Dardanelles campaign will be recognised as a disastrous failure, but now, in May, hopes are still alive, and nothing can quench Mrs D-W's growing obsession that she must go and work in the Dardanelles, near the place where her beloved Dick lost his life.

It will be several years before Freud's ideas on Mourning and Melancholia are published, so Isabella is not familiar with bereavement theory. At university, her training in mental illness consisted of only six lectures and ten clinics, a drop in the ocean in comparison with the hundreds of lectures and months of placements she sat through in most disciplines. In caring for Mrs D-W, she is working by instinct, common sense, or whatever customs and beliefs she herself has imbibed. Her decision astonishes me. She asks her medium friend, Mrs Gillies, for help.

Why am I so surprised? Because her training as a doctor was firmly based on rational scientific thinking. Because she carried no hint of a belief in spiritualism and its practices into her later life. Because such beliefs are often considered to be at odds with the Christianity she continued to follow until her death. But my shocked incredulity diminishes when I read how the longing to reconnect with the loved ones who have so suddenly and unexpectedly vanished from their lives is driving many of the bereaved to seek out spiritualists. Sir Arthur Conan Doyle, another Edinburgh-trained doctor, has become a prominent believer in spiritualism. Even ministers of religion are not immune to its attractions. Isabella will not be the only person tempted by the idea.

But can this fit with their religion, I wonder. How can faith begin to adapt to the strains of a war like this one? I push open the church door. Brought up a chapel-goer, does Isabella come in here to kneel and pray? Mrs D-W is not the only one who is grieving. On 22nd May, over 400 soldiers from Leith die in a train crash at Gretna on the way to the Front. I picture Isabella's horror as she reads the news in a letter from home. Seven of the men were from Pilrig. Perhaps she remembers them as lively Sunday lads, except that now they are no longer lively, but thoroughly, stone-cold dead. Perhaps she comes up here to take it in. Is she tempted to pray for these dead as well as for the comfort of the hundreds walking the streets of her home town in scandalised sorrow? I imagine her lighting a candle, and light one myself, in solidarity with the grief of this war but none the wiser as to how faith can survive.

I read how the staff of the hospital, apart from Mrs D-W, amuse themselves while they wait for work. Dr Cropper leads sketching expeditions. Local fishermen take them out in boats to catch eels, and they investigate the airplanes they can see over Le Crotoy, the little town on the other side of the Somme. Equally eager to explore, I also make my way to Le Crotoy. The curious sight of an aircraft propellor hanging above a doorway makes me pull up. Even more strangely, I find that it is adorning the entrance to a restaurant, Les Aviateurs. I am obviously meant to go in. Airmen in the garb of long ago smile out at me from the gallery of ancient photos installed on the walls. Model planes and leather flight bags hang from the ceiling. Paper table mats commemorate the Caudron brothers, who ran a flying school here for many years. They often brought their pupils to this restaurant, say the mats.

The past is forcing itself into the present again. The diary records that the staff of the Anglo-Ethiopian had a meal with some English aviators in a small inn in this town. Could it have been in this very restaurant? As I wait for my own meal, it almost feels as if Isabella is sitting at a neighbouring table, choosing from a menu and laughing with the war-weary young fliers.

But on 24th May, at last, the jaunting can stop. The casino is ready. Beds are put up, linen cupboards filled. The little glass-topped tables for the theatre are given a lick of paint. The Scottish staff coo exclamations of thrilled delight when a swarm of bees appears. 'It will bring us luck,' they declare. Perhaps it does, for the next day, after two and a half weeks of preparation and waiting, the Inspectors arrive. They are so delighted with what they see that they decide to get the telephone line working so that the Anglo-Ethiopian can not only fetch its own wounded from Abbeville, but it can fetch and carry for two other hospitals as well. 'Dr Jacquin is to be very much top dog here and we top hospital. Our heads are already beginning to swell,' records the diary.

11

Five days after the inspection, Dr Jacquin hands Mrs D-W a telegram as he hurries in for dinner, late. I imagine Isabella observing her friend as she opens it. What will it be this time? Obituaries and letters of condolence have been rolling in. Why, the Foreign Secretary himself, Sir Edward Grey has even sent a letter. She watches an expression of surprise come over Mrs D-W's face. "General Joffre, the Chief of the French General Staff, is asking to see me," she announces.

"When?" they all ask. She looks at the paper again.

"31st May."

"But that's tomorrow … "

"In Paris?"

An unsettled rustle ripples round the table …

"*Je regrette*," murmurs Jacquin. "I was delayed. I did not know son urgence. *Je regrette* … "

Je regrette does not solve the fact that the last train has gone.

"Quick, we need Cropper."

"Where is that man?"

Eventually, somebody discovers him in deep in the countryside, painting. He promises to drive Mrs D-W to Paris in the morning.

But it is a train that deposits her back in the neighbouring village in the small hours of the following night; her only way home, the road between the salt marshes. It is easy to picture the marshes misty in the early morning. It is less easy to imagine the scene the diary describes: an upper-class British lady trudging past them in her long nurse's uniform, a little dishevelled after twenty-four hours which have included Dr Cropper's car breaking down, a journey on a postman's lap, a visit to a senior Army General and a reprimand for wearing her uniform in the capital. Mrs D-W is carrying a flower and two bags, one of cherries and one of beans. It is her eleventh wedding anniversary and she is miserable. The summer dawn is reminding her of the dawns she and Dick have shared together in Ethiopia, and with each step she is becoming more intensely aware that everything is now over. When she gets to bed, she dreams, and in the morning she shares her dream, dragging Isabella and Betty into a scene way beyond my imaginings.

I seemed to get a message from Dick, in which he said that the last words of his last letter to me saying 'All my love and a kiss till we meet again,' were meant to cancel that part of the marriage service which says, 'Till death us do part,' and he asked me if I also would renew my marriage vow to him on the same terms.

The three of them come up with a scheme. The Cocketts are due to leave, so a feast is being prepared. When all the strawberries and the goodies from Paris have been consumed, Mrs D-W taps on the table and toasts, "Until we meet again!" As glasses are raised with wartime solemnity and joie de vivre, all eyes turn to the Cocketts. Nobody notices Isabella squeezing Mrs D-W's arm. Their eyes connect, but only for a second, then their heads swivel, and their eyes lock with Betty's. The marriage vows have been renewed. Betty and Isabella have been the wedding guests.

Utterly unaware of all this, the Cocketts climb into a car. Equally oblivious, the bystanders wave until they disappear. Mrs D-W is perhaps the only one not suffering from the empty feeling that a farewell brings. Contentedly, she is relaxing into considering herself a widow no longer, a wife once more. Isabella and Betty are perhaps preoccupied. I can see them endlessly pondering their friend's dream and the bizarre ritual in which they have just humoured her.

My preoccupation is entirely different. The white house and the hum of French cars fade as my mind goes to a day when my car radio had emitted the words 'Dick Doughty-Wylie' in the middle of a programme commemorating Gertrude Bell, the British woman famed for helping to found modern Iraq. What took my attention completely off the road was the expert declaring that, at Dick's death, he was in the middle of an unconsummated love-affair with Gertrude. How can he have been, I had shouted at the air, when Mrs D-W loved him so much?

Following this revelation, I discovered that, however concerned he may have been for his wife's welfare, his affair with Gertude was so intense that every book about this intrepid woman included a chapter about Dick. When I learned that she, too, had threatened to commit suicide if her beloved was killed, I found myself shaking my head in amazement. Dick must have been quite some guy to command such passion in both these strong-minded ladies.

In the St Valery of 1915, newspaper descriptions of how strangely Dick had behaved immediately before he fell disturb

Mrs D-W. "He should never have been in the spot where he was killed. What was he doing there? What was he thinking of? It is most uncharacteristic of him!" she puzzles.

One twenty-first-century author even suggests that Dick might have been quite glad to die, stuck as he was between two women who were both so crazy about him. Perhaps there is something in the idea, but I pause. Should I be pursuing this? Is it relevant to Isabella, to her story? Yes, I decide. I need to understand what role she is having to play. There is a world of difference between comforting a widow who believes herself to have been uniquely beloved, and supporting a woman who is fully aware that she has been battling for her man's affections. The key question for Isabella is: does Mrs D-W know about the affair?

During the spring, Gertrude had been working for the Red Cross in Boulogne. Back in January, when the Army were threatening to withdraw their support from the Anglo-Ethiopian, it was she who had saved the day by organising the temporary loan of a surgeon. In March, the two women had lunched together. Some of Gertrude's biographers believe that Mrs D-W knew about the affair and describe a row breaking out between them. But others describe Mrs D-W as simply visiting an old friend, completely innocent of both the affair and the distress she was causing the half-guilty Gertrude.

Determined to root out any trace of suspicion about Dick's faithfulness, I read and re-read Mrs D-W's papers, but I find nothing. All I detect is total trust in his unswerving devotion. Then I discover that the love letters between Gertrude and Dick will be kept private after Gertrude's death in 1926. They will only be made public 34 years later, once Mrs D-W herself has died in 1960. Surely this is another clue that Mrs D-W has no idea of Dick's disloyalty? That Gertrude wants to make sure she never suffers the distress and embarrassment of finding out?

I have to conclude that Isabella's job is to comfort the grief-stricken widow of a happy marriage, not to tend the tattered and wounded widow of a love triangle, but I cannot help a frivolous thought. If Dick is communicating with Mrs D-W, is he also communicating with Gertude? Can a ghost two-time? Could Dick be love-haunting two women at once?

12

With this bonus story weaving through my mind, I return to the café, think 'Hospital', and replace the dinner tables with empty beds, throw off the cloths and lay fresh linen sheets. The smells of starch and British disinfectant replace the aroma of coffee and French tourist cuisine, but I allow none of the characteristic smell of hospital food, pus and sickness. There are no overflowing baskets of dirty linen. There are no filthy enamel basins waiting to be washed. No autoclaves hiss as they sterilise vital supplies. There is no bustle.

Isabella and the staff of the Anglo-Ethiopian are still waiting. Since the euphoria of being allowed to reopen, not a single call has come for their ambulances, not a single patient has come their way. The whole atmosphere is taut with teeth-gritting patience. Every single member of staff is a volunteer and all this waiting is most definitely not why they offered to come. There is no incentive for them to stay. If the French Army does not want them, there are plenty of other places crying out for their assistance. They warn the General vehemently, 'Send us wounded or we leave.'

They watch the Corpus Christi procession from Mme Watel's house in the grounds of the old Abbey. The aviators from Le Crotoy drop in. Captain Yardley from the military police brings them chocolates and other gifts in thanks for the time when they rescued him after his car crashed. A little dog adopts them – but this is not work. This is not helping the war effort. This is not using their skills to help heal the wounded. Knowing that the other hospitals behind the Front are working at full stretch, they engage in endless exasperated discussions, "How long shall we wait?"

With her medical kit lying frustratingly idle, the only person who needs Isabella at the moment is Mrs D-W. Dick's apparent communications from beyond the grave have not stopped. Constantly Mrs D-W is on the alert, calculating the odds that they are genuine. Worse still, a couple of mediums have reported seeing Dick weeping.

"It is not what a widow wants to hear," I imagine Isabella and Betty complaining, "Anyway, what would a stout-hearted hero like Dick have to cry about? Why, he has been recommended for the Victoria Cross, surely he would never weep!"

On the very day I had immersed myself in the story of Isabella introducing Mrs D-W to a medium, a friend had emailed to ask if I believed in ghosts. Hmmm, I had replied, it feels uncanny when I reach a place like this, where I know that I am on Isabella's territory. It is surprising. It is delightful. I could even call it elating, but it is not haunting. I have no sense of her presence. As I loiter where she trod and poke nosily into matters she chose not to divulge, it feels more that I am haunting her, as if I am the intrusive spirit disturbing the peace of her self-imposed silence, not the other way round.

Another idea surfaces. Could Isabella have introduced Mrs D-W to Mrs Gillies not through any personal belief in communication with the dead, but as a kind of prescription, a more hopeful way forward than morphia? Whatever the authenticity of the messages, they might bring comfort – except for this problem of Dick being found in tears.

"It would be better for all concerned," Isabella and Betty agree, "if we had work. It would stop the brooding."

Not that work turns up. On 12th June, the staff of the Anglo-Ethiopian find themselves helping to prepare for a village festival. They decorate the side streets by pinning flowers to great yellow fishing nets, but there are plenty left over, so they set to work on the hospital entrance. Soon, poppies, ox-eye daisies and cornflowers are being pressed into elaborate master-pieces – a white cross to represent faith, a blue anchor for hope, a red heart for charity, amongst other such symbolic shapes. Through the café window, I can see Isabella. Annoyed at being reduced to floristry as her war work, she is positively jabbing her poppies into the arrangement. John McCrae's new poem, *In Flanders' Fields*, has not yet been published. Isabella does not know that this year's poppies are the last innocent poppies, that because of McCrae's poem, next year's poppies will be condemned to remind the world of war and dying men, a role they will have to bear for all eternity.

But of course there are no men here yet, dying or living. The flowers mask the large, empty ward overlooking the verandah, the two empty dressing stations, the empty operating theatre, several smaller wards, also empty, and the waiting staff.

The following day, 14th June, a man strides in unannounced, declaring himself to be their new Chief, sent by the Army to replace its previous representative, Dr Jacquin. Mrs D-W hits the roof, but I take note of his name: Triqueneaux. Why does it seem so familiar? I scour through some scanned documents. Yes! There it is! A letter in French from the Médecin A.-Majeur, Dr Triqueneaux, Médecin-Chef St.-Valery-sur-Somme. It is a short, undated letter, but there is a whole sentence about Isabella.

On behalf of the hospital, the Chief Doctor would like to use this occasion to thank Miss Stenhouse, who has used her surgical skills and knowledge unstintingly through the long months.

It makes me proud, but it tantalises me. So far Isabella has done no work here, she has not had the opportunity to earn the praise of any Army Officer. How can she possibly earn this tribute to her surgical skill and her knowledge, let alone to her hard work through the long months, without patients?

13

It is on 17th June, the day before the end of the Battle of Aubers Ridge, that a telegram addressed to the Médecin-Chef finally arrives, but not one of the senior doctors can be found. Typical! It gets me agitated and anxious. If nobody can open the telegram, are they going to miss their first batch of wounded after all these weeks? Thankfully, the telegraph delivery girl knows the contents of the wire. She refuses to let the staff wait for the senior doctors to come back, "*C'est urgent! C'est le message* for which you have been waiting. My countrymen are wounded. They have need of you. *Les ambulances! Vite!*"

Everything happens fast. Frantic messages find Cropper. Miss Cadell – there is no time to introduce her now – climbs into one ambulance. Dr Cropper fails to start the other. Clambering out, he stomps to his own car. In convoy, the two of them roar across the Place towards Abbeville.

Isabella, Mrs D-W and the other staff wave them off, go back inside, and carry on waiting. But now it is a different sort of waiting. The zing of expectation has replaced the toxic ferment of frustration. The evening is quiet. Alert and tense, they eat their meal in haste, but although it is nearly the longest day, the sun sinks and their wait continues. Perhaps Mrs D-W repeats the story of how Dick's ring arrived today. She is certain that it is the cause of their luck. Without it, that telegram would never have arrived. Perhaps the odd noise rings out from the hunters on the marsh. Maybe there is the occasional lap of a boat coming or going, one or two horses trotting past. But no mobiles keep them posted, no internet informs them of the current status of trains at Abbeville station. There are no updates about the distribution of the wounded. The 10 o'clock ritual of Mrs D-W hammering on a bell to remind them to curfew their candles gets ignored. It is 11 o'clock before a vehicle stops outside the casino door.

They rush forward. It is Dr Cropper's car. He gets out, but he is alone and weary. He has brought no men for them to treat. All the remaining wounded were stretcher cases, unable to sit in his car. Miss Cadell has stayed at the station with the ambulance. Disappointed, they pull themselves back into waiting mode. Are they silent, or do they talk? Do they play cards, risk a small drink or do they smoke? Perhaps they fidget and wind some more bandages or re-boil the water. It is gone midnight before Miss Cadell drives up with two patients.

Orderlies carry them in and lay them down. Everybody is eager to read the labels on their jackets. Nurses cut off damaged uniforms, soothe off mud and caked blood, dodge and destroy lice. Everyone can smell that one of the men is suffering from gas gangrene. Peeling back the dirty dressings, Isabella and her seniors examine the wounds. There is no electricity. It is hard to see clearly. A proper examination will have to wait for the morning. But come morning, paperwork awaits them: four documents for every man admitted and the same when the man leaves, unless he dies, in which case the number goes up to seventeen. Soon they will be filling in the interim reports the Army demands every five days. It has all begun again. By 29th June thirty-six men are lying here, but despite having the patients they have longed for, all is not well.

14

Old photos of Great War hospitals show me swathed heads, arms in slings and legs in heavy plasters. Bulky contraptions for holding broken limbs in traction stand tall at the feet of many beds. In a replica military hospital that I visited, audio-devices embedded in pillows re-created the laboured breathing of men with damaged chests. I try to import that sound here, along with the thump of crutches, the groans of those in pain, and the banter between beds, but a crowd of people coming into the café interrupts my train of thought. Laughing and chatting, they settle themselves at a large table near the far end. I estimate that it is more or less where the verandah ended, so I fade them out, re-install the verandah and replace them with wounded men in pyjamas smoking at a card table. Isabella comes out. Leaning against the railings, she draws in deep breaths of the gloriously clean air.

"The emotion of it all catches up with me sometimes. People have favourite stairwells they take a moment in," admits Junior Doctor Meg. "I'm not a crier, I've got a good friend I can ring," she adds.

Isabella has no phone. She has to find the bulk of her inner strength here in St Valery, from within and from her colleagues. When things get tough, she cannot even walk away to the house any more. Everybody sleeps here in the hospital now. The house, I read in the diary, has reverted to its owner, Mme Vigné.

Her name niggles me. Speedily, I leaf through my book of old photographs. There it is! Incredibly, 'Vigné' is pencilled on the photograph of precisely the big white house that captured my imagination when I first arrived here. My irrational feeling happens to have been correct! That mansion is exactly where Isabella lived, but now, in late June, she has to both live and work here in the hospital. With Mme Vigné's arrival, the beautiful quiet woods of the white house can no longer provide sanctuary when she needs it.

I watch her gazing unseeingly at the Somme. With Dr Cockett's departure, she has not only lost a friend, she has gained seniority with all its responsibilities. Handling the patients would be enough – the gas gangrene who arrived that first night died within a couple of days. Another case died from the effects of poison gas within hours of admission. On the ward behind her lies a strange case with 'shell shock'. None of them have come across such a case before and they are very unsure how to treat him. His fiancée and sisters have visited. It had been quite amusing trying to work out which one was, in fact, his beloved, but will the couple ever have a happily-ever-after? Will his peculiar walk ever calm down? Will his bulging eyeballs ever relax? And of course it has been non-stop in theatre. The dressing stations, too, have been in constant use, and Mrs D-W is so seriously down in the dumps that she is forever wanting to give up.

These would be troubles enough, but they are not what has driven Isabella out here this afternoon. Now, she wants to calm herself down after acting as peacemaker in yet another row. Back in May, they had created two separate dressing stations because Dr Jacquin and Dr Cropper used to fight so badly. When Dr Triqueneaux took over, it had been clear straight away that things would be no better. She remembers how their new Chief had driven them to distraction even over his first dressings. Within five days Dr Cropper had started threatening to resign. For heaven's sake, she thinks, they began by fighting over which of them did a minor operation – for all the world like small boys squabbling over a toy, but since the beginning of the month …

She heaves a huge sigh and flicks a pebble with her foot. Oh, things have been getting worse by the moment. If they are not quarrelling over an operation, they are quarrelling over the car. Quite a few of the nurses have upped sticks and each day brings a more serious row. They are both as bad as each other. This morning, the two men have been quarrelling over the opening of an abscess. Would you believe it, an abscess! She has managed to smooth it down but she is sure the truce will not last.

She braces herself as she turns back to the ward. Pausing on the threshold, she raises a meaningful eyebrow at a young maid who instantly dodges her gaze and hurries off to her duties. Isabella shakes her head; these young French girls find it very hard to resist the charms of the *poilus*. They have a dreadful habit of slipping out for near-trysts on the verandah. She surveys her charges. No. 9 is worrying them. He has so many injuries, a smashed-up shoulder as well as balls through his jaw and his hand. The Petites Curies do not come out this far, and it had been a relief to get him X-rayed in Abbeville, but X-rays in Abbeville are no solution. Sending the men 20km does them no good. Last week they had decided to purchase their own X-ray machine. As she crosses the ward, I imagine her praying hard for the new machine to come and the rows to go.

Reading on, I discover that Isabella's forebodings are well-founded. The truce between Cropper and Triqueneaux does not last long. Only until the next morning to be precise, when, in front of eight nurses, an orderly and a patient, Dr Cropper explodes at the Chief, "Your rudeness to the nurses is abominable, you treat me like a child!" He storms out of the room and thrusts his notice at Mrs D-W. Even more nurses threaten to follow suit, and some do. When Isabella comes into the staffroom after the strain of dealing with further deaths and secondary haemorrhages, it is to hear Mrs D-W confiding that, 'The sooner Dr Cropper goes the better. There is hourly dread of more rows.'

I contrast the young waiters serving in the café with Isabella, working in the same space a hundred years ago. Two years after graduating, a year after winding up the family business following the deaths of her father and her uncle, she is dealing with medical conditions she never studied in medical school, she is comforting a widow who hopes for messages from her dead husband, and, far from trying to fight her way into a male-dominated medical profession as she had expected, she is battling to save the health of foreign male campaign casualties, and to bring peace between warring male surgeons.

The pettiness and dissension that lace the diary seem to me undignified, unprofessional. I begin to fear that the Anglo-

Ethiopian is a shoddy, low-quality establishment. Until I read that the staff in many voluntary hospitals are quarrelling. The stress under which they are working makes squabbles inevitable, explain understanding observers. Displaying a sanguine trust that has utterly vanished with the century, these observers confidently declare that the staff never fail their patients. I cannot help a good dollop of twenty-first-century scepticism creeping in when I read their assurances that the volunteers always forget their differences and rally to give their all for the welfare of the wounded. Can that really be possible? Can men who argue over something as small as who has the car, ever collaborate for the greater good?

Reading on, I discover how two French ladies come to the door. Blissfully unaware of the tensions among the staff, they draw artificial flowers from their baskets. "The colours of France for the heroes of our nation," they explain. Soon they are decking the ward with blue, white and red flowers, telling tales of the bombs in Dunkirk as they stretch and snip. The *poilus* laugh as the ladies mimic the sound of cracking window panes, but when they describe their fear for their lives, the soldiers' private terrors flood back, and I imagine them silently echoing the ladies' very public relief at having ended up here, in the safe tranquility of St Valery.

And then the ladies are gone. The staff of the Anglo-Ethiopian let the news drift onto the grapevine. Chairs are dragged from all corners of the building, and, next day, visitors arrive. The *poilus* can scarcely believe their eyes. Ladies from the village are bustling around offering refreshments. English visitors have strolled down from the hotel. The wife and sister of the Canadian doctor have made the trip all the way up from Abbeville. Patients from other wards have been wheeled in. The ladies bring out their instruments and the Bastille Day concert begins. Nothing like this has been heard in the Casino since it died as a holiday destination. Even the upper-class Brits are delighted.

"The music is very good!"

"One would hardly have expected that out here in the Styx."

"And the patients. Watch their faces when those local lights give them comic songs."

"It is so good for them, they are only boys, after all."

"Three cheers for the refugee ladies of Dunkirk!"

Perhaps Isabella observes her particular charges closely. She has hopes for these concerts. With so many being severely wounded, they often have to lie on the wards, bored and inactive, for weeks. The locals feel sympathy too, and soon the hospital has gained itself a kind of unofficial supporters' club. Somebody makes sure concerts take place every week. Mme Watel invites all the patients who can walk to stroll in the grounds of her Abbaye. But these are the healthy options. There are other treats that would have no place in an NHS hospital and make me laugh – a feast of goose and port wine to commemorate Dick's birthday, vintage wine for the most seriously ill and cigars for all.

But simultaneously, the squabbling is continuing. Soon, Mrs D-W, still raw with grief and torn between her longing to get to the Dardanelles and the depressingly urgent need to find a surgeon to replace Dr Cropper, gets sucked in. And somehow, I cannot stop myself feeling that she actually relishes the tales of Triqueneaux's latest iniquities as she takes tea with Isabella and Betty, 'The manners of a bear with the character of a blancmange that man has!' Perhaps they chuckle and nod in agreement, and remember nostalgically how blissful it had been on the three days when he had been ill. Of course, their tiresome chief is not their only worry. They are extremely anxious about how to manage the X-ray machine.

One of the neighbours has offered to supply electricity for the new machine from his generator. To begin with, the hospital staff had been overjoyed, but gossip has now reached their ears.

"There are three 'ladies' living in his house!"

"Not one of them is his wife!"

"Their behaviour … !"

What are they to do? Will it be possible to power this vital piece of equipment without offending their new friends in the village? Will keeping the 'ladies' away from the hospital on visiting days suffice?

Picturing cables trailing across the road, the generator roaring, the great and the good of the village tutting as they pass, and Isabella longing to locate the shrapnel in No.5's leg, I move on to the next episode of this drama.

15

Perhaps it is her increasing seniority in the team, perhaps it is the comfort she has given to Mrs D-W, but as I read on, it feels as if the diary is mentioning Isabella more often. To my joy, these references shed more light on her character. Here she is on 4th August, a year to the day since this horrific war began, making a move I would never have predicted:

The chief came in about nine and said he was spending the morning operating at the Civil Hospital and Belle hurried through her dressings to get off to join him.

I imagine her briefly greeting the new doctor who has just arrived to replace Dr Cropper as she dashes out of the main door. Trying to push both the unusual magnificence of his uniform and war wounds, out of her mind, she gets the ten-minute walk to the civil hospital down to seven. Scurrying through the huge entrance door, she tries to remember anything she ever knew about surgery for women, children and the elderly, and scrubs up opposite Triqueneaux. Thankfully, none of the people they operate on this morning will be suffering from the war wounds they had feared were coming their way a few nights earlier, when strange noises had woken everybody. Many had believed there were Zeppelins overhead, and they had all braced themselves for bombs. But they had never fallen.

I take myself up to St Valery's solid old hospital. Why has Isabella come up here? As a volunteer, nobody has forced her. It is entirely her own choice to assist Dr Triqueneaux with more surgery. Why is she so willingly taking on extra work for a man with whom her friends and colleagues are quarrelling? Could she simply be grabbing experience wherever it offers, determined to further her career?

"You have to be willing to get involved. The more you push yourself the more they give you to do," explains Junior Doctor Meg.

I think back to the mixture of motives that took women doctors out to war: patriotism, a wish for professional development and a spirit of adventure. If Isabella has come out here particularly intent on furthering her career, I reflect, it would match the drive that sent her all the way to London for her midwifery tuition instead of being content to muddle along in Glasgow. I decide I must keep my eyes open for corroborating evidence.

Which turns up the very next day. That is when the X-ray machine, at last, arrives. From the corners of their eyes, Isabella and Mrs D-W watch the new radiographer running cables from the neighbour's house, setting it up. They are itching to try it out. When he has finished, they descend on him. "*Je suis désolé*," he apologises, with a graphic Gallic gesture of his arms, "*le Médecin Majeur Triqueneaux* has forbidden the use of the machine unless he is present."

That is not going to stop Isabella. The moment the Chief arrives, it is she – perhaps she is the only one on speaking terms with him – who demands that they see the new machine in action. He refuses her request outright. Declaring that there is no electric current, he walks off dismissively. Seething, Isabella and Mrs D-W linger. But as they look longingly at their new gadget, it is the radiographer who explodes. "*C'est pas vrai,*" he exclaims, "the electric is working. The machine is perfectly ready to use!" Isabella's look, Mrs D-W's look, and their sighs of exasperation say it all: Triqueneaux!

The man does not seem to be able to prevent himself from behaving badly. Next day, I read, Dr Cropper is all set to depart. It may be a relief that the threat of rows will no longer haunt the place, but everybody is sad. Dr Cropper has been working with them for months. They gather on the Place to wave him off, remembering the anxious moments they have shared, the intense satisfaction when a case has recovered, the enjoyment of excursions and outings. There is a melancholy to his leaving. His car is loaded, the faithful car which may have broken down many times, but has, nevertheless, carried numerous wounded men and countless loads of essentials to the hospital. He shakes each hand.

Suddenly, an agitated figure catches their attention. It is Triqueneaux, hurrying across the Place from his lodgings. He is gesticulating wildly. Has he come to make peace and bid his enemy farewell? No, he is shouting. In no time Dr Cropper is shouting back at him. Isabella and the others shift and shuffle.

"Do I gather that it is fuel that is the problem?" one mutters to another.

"Is the Chief accusing Dr Cropper of theft?"

"Surely not? Cropper is entitled to fuel. His car has been constantly engaged on hospital business."

The argument is loud and bitter. With the townsfolk gawping, it is also devastatingly embarrassing. There is a collective wince as Dr Cropper dips into his pocket and tosses some change at the Chief. The farewell they had wanted to give their man has been tarnished.

I imagine Isabella waving sadly as Dr Cropper's car crosses the Place. She has learned much of what she knows of war medicine and surgery at his side. Perhaps he has been a mentor. Maybe she has helped him too. Her recent education may have brought the older doctor up to date. Above all, they have struggled together to work out the best way to tend each wounded life. This has been a bad way to end things. But after her departing colleague's fights with first Jacquin and then Triqueneaux, perhaps she prays silently that smart new Dr Hibbert will prove to be a peaceable fellow who gets on well with Triqueneaux.

It does not happen. A few days later, I discover Dr Hibbert outside the X-ray room, reeling from an encounter with the Chief. Isabella and Mrs D-W are beside him, just as shaken. They were there too. They know what happened. "If you had not been in the room I would have struck him, I am sure of it," gasps Hibbert, "I am so glad you ladies were present. And on top of yesterday ... "

Yesterday had been bad. Not content with pulling Dr Hibbert's wrist back just as he was locating a piece of shrapnel, Triqueneaux had later banned the British doctor from the X-ray room. Mrs D-W had stepped in, insisting that the two men had equal rights to the room. But her words have obviously fallen on deaf ears. The Chief has just done exactly the same thing again. And today it is not his word against Hibbert's. They were all there, they watched him do it.

Soon, I find Isabella herself becoming his target. Their clash happens one morning when the Chief announces that he is deferring an operation. It is not the first time. It is becoming a habit, and Isabella and Mrs D-W have had enough. The patient has been starved in readiness for his operation and, today, however rudely Triqueneaux behaves, there is no way these two strong-willed British women are going to allow this boorish Frenchman to prevent the poor man receiving the surgery he is awaiting. Without losing one jot of her steely Scottish politeness, Isabella tells Triqueneaux exactly what he must do. Mrs D-W adds her cut-glass iciness to the argument. Blancmange-like, the Chief caves in, and the patient goes under his knife. The diary records that 'The operation was a success and a very large piece of shrapnel and part of the nickel nose of the shell were taken out.'

But however successful the operation, I need to step back. Isabella is working in an environment as chaotically toxic as a medical soap opera. It is all very well for understanding observers to make excuses and simply accept that quarrelsome behaviour is found in most voluntary hospitals, but these people are allies. They are supposed to be working together to beat the common enemy, Germany. Why do they seem incapable of working in harmony? I begin trawling the diary for clues.

'The chief informed me that he regards his orderly as my equal and when I pointed out that English ideas with regard to orderlies and matrons were somewhat different, also English ideas with regard to a man of the shopkeeper class and mine, he then said English ideas belonged to the middle ages. He is really very funny,' writes Mrs D-W after one squabble.

Is this my clue? Are the rows erupting when the hierarchical principles of the British Empire crash against the egalitarian ethics of the French Revolution? Yet even as I ask the question, I give myself a warning. The class-conscious, imperial values that Mrs D-W communicates would look as medieval in twenty-first-century Britain as they do to Dr Triqueneaux. Indeed, they would have been considered unacceptable in Britain for most of the last half of the twentieth century. But instinctively I find myself wanting Isabella to be a 'goody', a feeling totally at odds with a proper, detached, academic examination of the evidence. I find myself wanting to make her into a paragon who saw things differently. I am tempted to credit her with politically correct, twenty-first-century sensibilities. But just because she broke the mould by becoming a woman doctor does not mean that she was a mould-breaker in any other way. It is far more probable that, like most people, she lived by the norms of her day, the same politically incorrect norms that Mrs D-W expresses. I force myself to picture the two of them chuckling together at the Chief's funny ideas.

But when I return to the diary, I find I can list a plethora of minor complaints, not one of which is related to *entente non-cordiale*. They all hinge on who is 'top dog'. As the Director, matron, financial provider and donor of this voluntary hospital, Mrs D-W expects to run much of the show. As the Army appointed Chief Medical Officer, Dr Triqueneaux expects to be in charge of medical matters and administration. As Senior British surgeons, Drs Cropper and Hibbert expect status at least equal to that of the Army man. Result: nobody has the status or power they feel they deserve, everybody is unhappy, conflict is inevitable.

Then, just as I think I understand the problem, I read the most vivid story yet. Dr Triqueneaux has just left the hospital. As Isabella and Mrs D-W set about their work, a French General in all his grandeur marches onto the ward. It is General Very, the Chief of Chiefs, the Director in charge of the Northern Region Health Service, a man of whom Triqueneaux is terrified. Today, the General announces a spot inspection. Mrs D-W leaves her post and begins to usher him round. He is dignified, she respectful – he has the power to close them down. They pause beside the Greek patient. With nobody able to speak a word of his language, the only conversation he gets is a few words of Turkish from Mrs D-W. Isabella watches the two of them move on to the Algerian, a spunky character who had been so determined to get himself treated at the Anglo-Ethiopian that he had rolled himself off a moving train as it passed St Valery. It had been 10 o'clock at night before he had been discovered huddled in the station.

As they move along the line of beds, the General notices an Arab patient urgently beckoning him to come. He walks over and bends to listen. Mrs D-W retreats. She and Isabella watch from a distance. It is a delicate matter. This Arab has been in real trouble in the last twenty-four hours. Yesterday, the Chief had accused him of insubordination. It had been totally unfair. The poor man had barely understood anything the Chief had said. How can being unable to speak the language be insubordination? Tinpot, Triqueneaux had sentenced him to eight days in solitary confinement. In revenge, the moment the Chief had left the room, the man had jumped up. Announcing in his broken French that if he was to be punished, his punishment might as well be deserved, he had vanished. It had been late at night before they had tracked him down and brought him back in, and this morning it had been all they could do to stop him disappearing again. They had thought it would soothe him to know that the Chief was planning to send him to the big Moslem hospital at Berck, but the Chief's name had proved the reverse of soothing. The moment it was mentioned, he had shouted out for all the ward to hear, 'Call him a Chief? I call him a pig and a drunkard!'

In twenty-first-century Britain, notices plaster public transport, hospitals and government offices: "We do not tolerate physical or verbal abuse towards our staff." Calling the senior doctor 'a pig and a drunkard' is surely verbal abuse? Surely it invites retribution? But, once again, I find myself hardly able to believe what I am reading. The staff of the Anglo-Ethiopian do not punish this man. They do not even reprove him. Instead, they comfort and console him.

It is this man who has now button-holed General Very. Isabella and Mrs D-W are agog. The General is listening intently. Soon, he straightens up. The Arab is grasping his hand. Is it a gesture of gratitude? They busy themselves, masking their curiosity as General Very walks smartly over to them.

"That man is not to be placed in solitary confinement," he declares, overruling his junior's sentence. He fixes them with a penetrating gaze, "Do you get on with Dr Triqueneaux?" The "Yes" that Isabella and Mrs D-W give is laden with such menace that the General continues his scrutiny, silently demanding clarification.

Relieved, Mrs D-W yields, "Every soul in the Hospital detests the man," she blurts out.

And Isabella, not content with being obliged to work alongside him every day at the Anglo-Ethiopian, is perverse enough to choose to help this loathsome creature at the civil hospital. If even Triqueneaux's obnoxious personality cannot spoil her appetite for work, her drive must be phenomenal, her motivation unbelievably strong. Could this be how she earns the glowing testimony he will write?

16

Accounts of WWI medicine tend to show a maelstrom of incoming bodies, mud, blood, lice and never a moment of quiet. But such reports come from front-line units where casualties are being patched up ready to travel to safer places for full healing. Working here on this quiet coast in an evacuation hospital like the Anglo-Ethiopian is completely different. Many of Isabella's patients stay under her care for months. Some of those who arrived in June, fresh from the Front, will still be on the ward in September. These young men, who should be bounding with strength and energy, are virtually trapped by their injuries. Many can see only the ceiling. Anything that whiles away the endless hours is welcome.

During one of the weekly concerts, a fleet of English Red Cross barges is spotted steaming up the river. The British dash excitedly for Union Jacks, then hurry out, leaving a single nurse and a bemused pianist in charge of the *poilus*. As I track the enthusiastic staff up-river, I pass fishermen sorting tackle and cruisers taking tourists north to see the seals at the mouth of the estuary. Isabella and her colleagues pass masted ships as they follow the slowly moving barges across the Place and on towards the station. Their flags encourage the heavily laden vessels as they chug past the yachts moored at the marina and beside the avenue of trees to the lock. It is a very small lock – they must have been very narrow barges.

On my return I people the quay with the French figures Isabella and the others pass as they go back – girls in smocks and boys in baggy trousers, horses towing carts and dogs on the scavenge, dark-costumed women in long skirts, and a different sort of fisherman – the village as Isabella will remember it.

Their long-stay patients do not need operations every day. The doctors and nurses do their best, but after that they can only watch and wait. One day, I read, Isabella finds herself free to go into Abbeville, the town to which the ambulance trains bring casualties from the Front. She climbs into the draughty ambulance beside Miss Ruby Cadell, and I follow them south. Not that the town I drive into bears much resemblance to the one they enter; the destructive power of WWII has seen to that, and I draw up at the station without much hope of spotting anything they will see. It is a strange building, a bit like a gingerbread house. Its arched windows are iced white, its classic wooden planks are toffee-coloured icicles, and the whole confection is topped with cute little turrets and a clock-tower. Then, incredulous, I notice the date on the pediment: 1912. Was this frivolous building the setting for the seriousness of the First World War? I try to picture military supplies streaming beneath its toffee icicles, orders echoing through its iced windows, *poilus* in sky blue and Tommies in khaki, singing and waving as they jolly their way to war and, in the opposite direction, sinister trains filled with wounded soldiers drawing up at its platforms.

Fading out the parked cars, I let Isabella and Ruby pull up amongst a flock of other ancient ambulances. Ruby knows the place well. A fierce and fabulous nurse, she has been keeping watch at the station ever since the hospital re-opened. She has become expert at 'bagging' wounded. The pair hurry into the building, eager for new patients and the latest gossip. But today, the siding reserved for ambulance trains is empty. There are no walking wounded hobbling onto the platform, no seated wounded being carried by their pals, no *grand blessés* being hurried to ambulances by stretcher bearers. I picture Isabella and her companion heading over to the British Red Cross post in the hope of news. Its tiny dressing-station and kitchen have been concocted out of packing cases, and its cupboards are full of bandages, tinned milk, cocoa and other necessaries for passing Tommies.

Since the ending of the spring offensive in June, the whole Front has been quiet. Slowly, the wounded of previous battles have healed, leaving empty beds in every hospital and the staff wondering when the next onslaught will come. Today, however, a rumour is circulating. As the Anglo-Ethiopian's ambulance winds its way back to St Valery, its empty stretcher racks clattering, Isabella and Ruby are buzzing. Two Generals are said to have come through Abbeville promising more wounded 'soon'.

"How soon will 'soon' be?" they speculate, "What's up?"

They may be excited, but I am not. To me, it seems a mercy that the racks are empty. Six men who have not been wounded are not lying in agony at risk of premature death. But for Isabella and Ruby, further battles, despite their inevitable casualties, are vital for victory, and without victory, life as they know it will end. So as I wind my way back to St Valery in their tracks, echoes of their joy at the news resound down the century to me. How splendid it would be if an offensive was in the offing!

But in the meantime, with the hospital quiet, Isabella and her friends grab the moments. One day Dr Hibbert goes over to try out a flying machine at Le Crotoy, and they rather fancy seeing how he is getting on. Taking a ferry for the first part of the crossing, they have to disembark for the final stretch and they walk cautiously across the sands, dodging little rivulets and sinking mud. It is the first time Mrs D-W has been over here, and as they order afternoon tea at the hotel, I wonder if the outing could be a sign of her recovery. Are Isabella and Betty no longer needing to watch her quite so closely?

After their meal, they meander down to the beach to watch the flying machines. 'It is very pretty to see them run along the sands, rise and float away like giant dragonflies,' observes Mrs D-W. As the final plane trundles to its field in the early evening light, they turn, unwillingly, away. And stop. The waters have risen. The path is flooded. There is no way round. Cautiously, they wade in, and become painfully aware of eyes. Le Crotoy Hospital overlooks the sands, and every window is filled. Friends there must have noticed their predicament before they did themselves. A huge crowd has gathered to watch the fun. And it is fun. The flat surface of the water conceals holes. In no time, Betty is wet to her waist, Lady Lamington is displaying her rather fat legs beneath her khaki coat and Mrs D-W's uniform is tucked up almost to her waist, her cloak and veil floating in the wind. Thankfully, they are all laughing uncontrollably. Isabella, the diary records, lifts her skirts to reveal 'legs festooned with unmistakeable frills.'

I could not have dreamed this up if I had tried. Not the frills, those are predictable. Isabella wears frills in every photograph. The utterly improbable, completely unanticipated part is that this quest should have led me to my grandmother's underwear. A strange synchronicity makes it even more unbelievable. Only a day before I transcribed this section, Major Lizzie had explained how, "I always wore uniform, but someone sent me some pretty knickers, which I dried discreetly." Her sentence had resounded through my head as I transcribed the word 'frills'. There in the sterile whiteness of the Imperial War Museum archive, the century had disappeared. Could Isabella's frilly undergarments, like Lizzie's knickers, be a secret survival tactic for her feminine side? Might they be cocking a covert snook at the harsh realities of war?

Every day, I have watched bands of tourists step gingerly out onto the estuary mud to cross the Somme. Invisible paths, known only to locals, thread between the watery channels and the sinking mud. Their fluorescent waterproofs make the tourists easy to spot, but this place is full of concealment. Birds I cannot see are lying low. Huntsmen are lurking in carefully camouflaged hides. Each is fully alert to the other. And I chuckle quietly as I realise that not one of them would detect any trace of the long-skirted British women who preceded them.

17

Ever since Dr Cropper handed in his notice, my suspicions have been growing that the Anglo-Ethiopian's days are numbered. There have been odd phrases, veiled hints and oblique references. Now, in mid-August and towards the end of the final notebook, my suspicions are confirmed. A general comes nosing around, eager to work out what the British will leave when they go. Mrs D-W is pulling strings ever more vigorously in her desire to get to the Dardanelles. Dr Hibbert can stay for only one more month. Ruby Cadell has already gone. Other staff, too, are on their way. I read how Mme Le Gue, a French nurse, decides to take a souvenir photograph of the men in their beds before she goes. It is not as easy as it sounds. No sooner has she succeeded in persuading one man to climb into his bed, than another man is up and out of his sheets. The procedure fills a whole, hilarious Sunday afternoon, but in the end Mme Le Gue does get her photograph, and in the morning she gets a farewell wave from the hospital gates.

The staff is getting smaller but, except for the Chief, those who remain are working hard. Ambulances are sent to Abbeville. Plates for the Greek's bone are ordered from Paris. Two large pieces of shrapnel and several pieces of bone are extracted from No. 21 before his leg is wired, the staff hoping against hope that all will be well – his skin is far too tender for plaster. Day in, day out they strive to get these soldiers battle-ready, but suddenly, without warning, Isabella's focus has to shift.

Leaving the café, I hurry up the road and stare urgently round. In which of these hotels is Isabella's new case? La Colonne de Bronze? Le Lion d'Or? Le Relais Guillaume de Normandy? They are all ancient, they all match the old photos. A young British lieutenant barged in at lunchtime, desperately anxious about his wife. Isabella and Mrs D-W have hurried up here with him, and I picture Isabella upstairs in one of these hotel bedrooms, taking the history. The blood loss began yesterday, but Mrs Stewart had felt quite well this morning. Isabella examines her. The bleeding is profuse; she has probably already lost half a pint of blood. The couple's fear that they will lose their baby is justified. Dr Hibbert joins them. "The case is very grave," he agrees. "You will both have to remain with the patient tonight."

Poor Mrs Stewart – stuck in a foreign town, fearful for her life, desperate to keep her baby; her husband waiting downstairs, his ears alert for any clue as to what is happening. In the early evening, Mrs D-W suddenly hurries in. "The pains are getting worse," she tells him. "Quick! Run to the hospital and get Dr Hibbert's permission for a dose of morphia."

The word 'morphia' pulls me up short – and I dive again for Isabella's instruments. Can her little cylindrical box, the words 'Medicine Glass and Minim Measure' lightly indented in its lid, be up there in Mrs Stewart's bedroom? Inside, ingenious cardboard rings prevent a stout blue medicine glass from crushing a fragile measuring cylinder. The historian had told me how doctors would measure a volume of water into the cylinder and pour it onto a pill in the medicine glass, hydrating it ready for administration. Morphine, for example, he had said. It had felt wrong for Isabella to be giving morphine. I had not wanted her to see pain so severe it needed such powerful relief. Now, I imagine the young officer's anxiety as he runs back up the street. Hurriedly, he gives his message. Isabella gets out her little kit and prepares the dose. Soon, Mrs Stewart's tense body is relaxing as her pain subsides, and I find myself glad that Isabella knows what to do.

Curfew falls. A messy clot comes away. Isabella and Mrs D-W swap between monitoring the patient and dozing in the armchair. At midnight they give another shot of morphia. By morning, they are exhausted, but satisfied. The bleeding has ceased. The patient is still alive. Perhaps young Lieutenant Stewart brings up coffee, croissants or whatever delicacies the war-bound hotel can muster. But when Dr Hibbert returns, he is not so sanguine. As he removes some sort of clot, he admits that he suspects this is not a true pregnancy, it is molar.

Memories stir deep within my mind, memories of a grossly distorted 'something' pickled in formalin in a glass cage: a 'hydatidiform mole' safely locked behind the glass doors of a pathology museum. The words 'haemorrhage', 'cancer', and 'danger' flash before me. This is no normal threatened miscarriage. Mrs Stewart is suffering from something much more complex and far more sinister; something so rare that Isabella has probably never encountered such a case in her short working life.

For a couple of days, the patient does well, but they are all waiting, knowing that the danger has not passed. It is day three, 5th September, when her temperature spikes. Curettage is the only solution. It takes almost all day to turn the little bedroom into an operating theatre. Thankfully, most of the *poilus* are enjoying an afternoon outing, so require no attention, and at 5 o'clock, the operation begins. As he works, Dr Hibbert is gloomy. Knowing the likely prognosis of such pregnancies, he predicts dire post-operative complications, but Isabella and Mrs D-W refuse to agree with him. They have spent more time with the patient. They are convinced she will pull through …

On 6th September she is looking well, and Mrs D-W reports gleefully that, 'It looks as though we were going to be right and Dr Hibbert wrong.'

Then comes 7th September, and probably the longest entry in the whole diary.

For Isabella, it begins in the dim light of the X-ray room. The radiographer is insisting on experimenting and, as the morning drags on, I picture her growing increasingly restless. "Hurry up man!" she longs to say, "It is only a painful arm. We've simply got to get the shrapnel out. Just get a move on and tell us where it is!"

It is almost lunchtime before the calculations are complete. Straightaway, the arm is brought into theatre, and Isabella operates. Gowned up and in charge, she draws out several troublesome splinters of old bone, but no shrapnel. When the Chief deigns to come in, he decides to scrub up and look for himself, but despite 'raking about all over the place', he manages to find only one tiny piece of shrapnel that Isabella has missed.

Oh, I feel as proud as any parent! Metaphorically at least, those surgical instruments that Isabella left behind have been in action. By now, she must have assisted at countless operations, but today, for the very first time, the diary has recorded that it is she who is actually cutting, ligating, retracting and probing. She is the one who is performing the surgery. However many times she may already have done this unrecorded, this entry proves beyond all imaginings, beyond all doubt, that Isabella has gained enough skill, and earned enough trust, to be on her way to becoming a capable surgeon.

Not that the day is yet over. Leaving theatre, Isabella has to pay a visit to Mrs Stewart. She walks alone and I trace her route. She passes the neighbour's pariah house – useful for charging the X-ray machine's accumulators, but awkward. She passes Mme Vigné's white mansion – the summer flowers are fading. She passes the police station with its yellow and blue ceramic sign, *Gendarmerie National*. She passes the small shops. Autumn is coming, and her memories of this place are growing. She walks through the hotel lobby and climbs the stairs to Mrs Stewart's room. She has got to know her well over the week – another case to add to her bank of experience.

When she plods wearily back into the hospital at 6 o'clock, somebody warns her that the water is off, but, "Not to worry. Betty ran for plumbers. They're in the attic now. It'll be sorted out in a jiffy." Before Isabella has even had time to feel the inconvenience of not having running water when she needs to do her dressings, the whole building is echoing to the cry of FIRE!

18

I happen to be in St Valery on the anniversary of that fire. Sitting exactly where the blaze broke out, the diary suddenly makes far more sense than it did in the archive ... I watch pyjama clad soldiers hobbling onto the Place. Some glance fearfully over their shoulders. A few cradle treasures – tins of tobacco, a pack of cards, sheafs of letters. Here comes a huge man racing a wheelchair to safety. Nurses are commanding and pointing. Beds are hurtling out. A couple of soldiers' mothers, here to watch over their critically sick sons, are bringing their boys out themselves. In no time the whole town seems to have rallied. Buckets are appearing from every direction. Water from the Somme is swinging up the bank, across the path, into the hospital. It swooshes on the flames. A human chain lurches the buckets back down. Fill them, raise them, aim them, down again, up again, over and over. Water sloshes, the path muddies, people watch.

Staff and townsfolk are braving the blaze and coming back into the building again and again, salvaging as much as they can. Timbers seem to be falling. I duck; crockery is crashing onto the verandah glass. Shards are raining onto rescuers trying to dodge cascades of water and avoid slipping.

Now, I can see the scale of the drama. I can smell the burning, and the danger. I too, want to risk myself to rescue the wounded. I too, want to jostle back into the blaze to do all in my power to save the hospital, adrenaline quenching my fear.

It takes only twenty minutes for everything and everyone to be out on the Place. Breathless, people listen to the crackle of the flames and the hiss of the water, waiting. The men are fingering their lucky charms. I too am breathless, shaking my head in admiration at the diary.

We only lost one wing of four rooms, and the only ceiling that actually fell was the preparatoire. The whole roof went of course.

It is the 'onlys', and the 'of course', that take my breath away. Oh, and this bit:

We dined at the Hotel and then came back, collected beds from the highways and hedges and slept in the casino, the fire having been got under.

Collecting beds by moonlight, sleeping on wet mattresses, nostrils full of the smell of fire. It is so magnificently 'Keep Calm and Carry On' – the expression could have been designed for today.

By the next day it has become clear that the blaze began as the plumber was soldering a pipe.

"It is hardly surprising," the staff comment, "the whole wall was only made of wood, paper and canvas."

"Could we have got away without clearing the hospital? Things must have been pretty damp after all the recent rain."

"Yes, and there was no breeze to fan the flames."

"Better safe then sorry. Think what might have happened."

And they continue trying to collect their belongings from the different houses of the various enthusiastic townsfolk who have squirrelled them away for safe-keeping. Isabella has lost a ring and a bracelet. They have all lost stockings and nighties. 'We have been dreadfully robbed,' states the diary. They know which house they suspect. Should they go to the police? Perhaps there are other, even more precious treasures they are regretting. "Friends sent stuff out," explains Major Lizzie, "I felt more loved and cared for than ever, and I knew I was in people's thoughts." Lizzie hung her cards and postcards on a string near her bed, and I imagine Isabella having made her sleeping quarters into a similar home from home. Perhaps it too, has vanished in the chaos of the fire.

But there is no time for sentimentality – there are patients to care for. By two o'clock the following afternoon all the men are back in the hospital and Isabella is doing her dressings as usual. Work is already underway to create a new operating theatre and replace the rooms lost to the fire. Curious visitors are arriving. Those who saw the blaze can hardly believe that the hospital is carrying on.

The fire has been a major local event. A hundred years on, it merits a mention in the book of old photos. In 1915, no less than two Generals, General Very and General Alix, the Commandant of the Northern Region, offer their thanks to the staff. It is Triqueneaux who is commanded to copy out their flowery French praise and gratitude, and a copy of the letter lies in Isabella's archive:

In the course of a fire which took place on 7th September this year towards 18.30 at Voluntary hospital 39 in St

Valery, the staff of the hospital, as well as its military nurses, showed praiseworthy devotion. Thanks to their sang froid, their energy and their quick actions, the wounded being treated in the hospital were evacuated and the fire quickly brought under control. Lady Doughty-Wylie and the nurses under her direction showed notably unstinting devotion. The General commanding the Northern Region addresses his congratulations to all the health workers of St Valery for their praiseworthy behaviour.

He offers Lady Doughty-Wylie and the English nurses under her direction respectful thanks for the devoted help that they willingly gave in these circumstances.

In the evening, I take myself over to the sands at Le Crotoy. Gulls swirl around my head as if they were mimicking the ancient flying machines. On the other side of the bay, St Valery lies in shade, the hill concealing it from the westerly light. The fire had been visible from here, the diary says, but I can hardly make out the casino. It lies, miniature, behind the avenue of trees that line the river bank. If the flames could be seen from here, they must have been huge.

But I have not come here for the flames. I let time slip forward a couple of days and imagine Isabella coming out onto the verandah. Turning her head, she looks to the South East, towards Gallipoli, the site of Dick Doughty-Wylie's death. She runs her hand along the railings, wondering about the tale that the diary assures me is circulating. Had Dick really been here?

One of the nurses is utterly convinced she saw him. It had been a couple of minutes before the fire alarm was raised. She was leaning out of the window talking to a friend on the Digue, when she had caught sight of a figure in khaki leaning over this particular section of railing. Isabella strokes the metalwork again. The nurse had assumed it was just an officer from Le Crotoy, but then his medal ribbons had attracted her attention. With a start, she had realised it had to be Dick, but by the time she looked back, he had gone. The six men playing cards on the verandah had seen nobody.

Whatever Isabella may think about ghosts, Dick, I have recently learned, seems to have believed in them. Mrs D-W seems uncertain. 'There does not seem much doubt that Miss Perdue saw Dick the night of the fire,' she writes in one sentence. Yet a few lines down she is commenting 'That is the yarn, for what it is worth.' Her musings pad the diary, but there is not much diary left now, and little seems to be changing.

The hospital is still snatching for its share of wounded from Abbeville. The Chief is still cancelling operations. On the 13th September Dr Hibbert and the Chief take staff photographs in the Place, photographs that I will never see but which were taken, so the diary records, under the scrutiny of binoculars from no less than three different houses. On the 14th, everybody gathers in the Place again, this time to watch a general decorate two soldiers. They feel for the men. One has a paralysed right arm and the other is blind.

There are only three more entries left, and they are brief. Isabella has a couple of days off and goes jaunting with Betty and some local friends. The patients are given a tremendous picnic, their combined weight bursting the tyres of the car on the way home. Mrs Stewart is well enough to come down to the hospital for tea. And with these trivial, fizzling things, that is it. There is no more space in the notebook. There is no more diary. It has not closed with a neat explanation of what will happen next. No arrangements for handing over the hospital have been detailed. No tales have been told of where the staff plan to go. There have been no farewell parties in the village. It has all just stopped.

Could there ever have been another exercise book, lost like the missing February pages? If there was, I do not have it. The Imperial War Museum does not have it. And this time there is no subsequent volume to tell me that it ever existed.

But a couple of emails ping in, laying a Red Cross report before me. Hôpital Benevole No. 39, St Valery sur Somme, the Anglo-Ethiopian Hospital, will close on 29th September 1915. A week later it will re-open, with French staff. And in 1918 the poet Laurence Binyon will record the final chapter of the Anglo-Ethiopian's story:

In October 1915 the hospital was handed over as it stood, together with a sum of money to pay for the heating of the Casino during the winter, and for the maintenance of a French staff, to the Service de Santé. The head of staff had obtained permission to take out a nursing unit to staff a French military hospital in the island of Tenedos, and left St Valery on this new mission. The unit worked at Tenedos till the French left the island, when it was lent for an indefinite period to the Royal Naval Division, and worked partly at Tenedos, partly at Mudros and at Imbros.

So the end of the diary is, very nearly, the end of the Anglo-Ethiopian hospital in France. And, since Tenedos is near the mouth of the Dardanelles straits, Mrs D-W is going to have an almost happy ending. And Isabella?

I re-examine the letter containing Dr Triqueneaux's tribute to Isabella. She gets the most effusive praise but he is, I now notice, thanking all the staff, even Dr Hibbert and Mrs D-W. Towards the end, I translate this sentence:

The Chief Doctor parts from his colleagues, who all deserve recognition by France, with regret.

So it is not just a thank you letter, it is, "I am sad to see you go. Your work has been exemplary." My mind flips to cases where British women working with the French Red Cross were awarded the Legion d'Honneur. The staff of the Anglo-Ethiopian may not have achieved that distinction, and Triqueneaux may have been an unpleasant man, but Isabella did at least keep this parting eulogy for the rest of her life.

"On behalf of the hospital, the Chief Doctor would like to use this occasion to thank Miss Stenhouse, who has used her surgical skills and knowledge unstintingly through the long months."

Closing the diary, I leave the café. This place has told me all it can about Isabella's war work in France. A little more of her mysterious legacy has become a little less mysterious. Soon, she will be journeying home via Boulogne. It is time that I, too, went home.

Suddenly, right in the middle of packing my bags, I freeze. The string of beads. For all my preparedness, I have hardly considered it since I arrived – I have had eyes only for Isabella and her daily doings. What on earth have I missed? Sitting down heavily, I try to work it out. The diary certainly makes no mention of caring for enemy prisoners, and I have read that even in hospital a prisoner has to be kept under guard. Would the army entrust the internment of an enemy to a voluntary hospital? More pertinently, could Mrs D-W have stopped herself writing about such an exciting event? Surely it would have attracted all her administrative energies and given her plenty of scope to spill her irritation in a late-night session with her exercise book. No, it cannot have been here that Isabella received her beads. Recovering my composure, I place the last few items in my suitcase, close it firmly and head for Dunquerque.

SECTION 5

Dated this 24ᵗʰ day of July 19 16

(here sign) Isabella Stenhouse.

Witness to the signature of the said

Isabella Stenhouse

Amy Hodgson . (Witness

1

My journey to Dunquerque is as haunted as if I was the one who believed in ghosts. Little domestic items spotted in museums come chillingly to life – a toothbrush; a box of *Poilu Camembert*; a packet of *Le Vainqueur* writing paper; a small booklet, *To Pass Time in the Trenches*. Signposts morph into the jolly names of dug-outs. The pong of good old French manure mutates into a sweaty blend of fear and fearlessness – soldiers waiting, breathlessly inhaling the fumes of the mass grave growing in no-man's land, so near and yet so deadly.

The dawning light points menacingly at the pallid gravestones of yet another cemetery. Disturbed, I avert my gaze. Those stones are too clean. They are too tidy, too oppressively, obsessively neat. It is as if they think they can disguise the chaos and carnage of their war, as if they could sanitise the whole outrage. I force myself to glance again. Perhaps the bereaved need that contrast, that quietness after the indescribable. The cemeteries are more than memorials, they are tombs – finally rescued places for lost bodies. If a war memorial depicted war as those who lie there remembered it, how deeply would it horrify those who did not fight?

My roller-coaster journey has exhausted me – and I have only been a spectator from a long, long way off. There has been no real assault on my being and my senses. Anaesthetist Danielle once commented, "Isabella must have been one hell of a woman. The smells and noises would have been horrendous: the patient screaming, blood everywhere, putrefying flesh from previously amputated limbs that had not been removed, poorly ventilated rooms, chloroform … " Will I ever grasp my youthful grandmother's experience? My car flinches as a container lorry careers past. From my comfortable middle-aged bubble, is it remotely possible to edge between the myths and clichés of her conflict? Last night I chanced upon a new snippet about dressings which challenged the stereotype that the men were phlegmatic and brave. In reality, the article declared, many soldiers called the dressing trolley the 'Agony Wagon'. Some began to scream even before they were touched, dreading the pain they were about to receive. The thought of pulling dressings off deep, raw flesh, of hot poultices and liniments … What did Granny do in the war? One hell of a woman …

The signpost to the port. I am about to leave France. There must be families in this land whose ancestors were treated, successfully or otherwise, at the Anglo-Ethiopian; ancestors who cannot fail to persist in Isabella's memory as she begins her journey home. As I draw up beside the ferry, it dawns on me that if my Grandmother had really wanted to expunge her war, she would have taken the trouble to destroy her few documents and photographs. And if she had done that, I would not be have been able to come here and sniff out her story.

Aboard the ferry, my tongue finds itself tangling rapidly into German. Some women – descendants of the enemy – are on their way to London and want my advice about shopping. Breathing deeply, I re-arrange my mind for this future. Their ancestors lurked in U-boats beneath this sea, intent on torpedoing my grandmother's ship. It had to zig and zag to dodge them. Their ancestors would have jumped at the chance to get to London. Yet over soothing lattés, we manage to conquer history and compare the merits of Marble Arch and Oxford Street.

As if I am not disorientated enough, my car radio quickly picks up a raging discussion about the musical *Oh What a Lovely War* and all the ramifications of the 1914–18 conflict. I long to fight back, "Be fair! The returning staff of the Anglo-Ethiopian don't have the luxury of hindsight. How can they be expected to assess what they've been doing? It is enough for them simply to manoeuvre themselves between battle-filthy Tommies and squeeze into seats on the London train."

I doubt if they even take a moment to consider how they are feeling. Major Lizzie was exhausted on her return from Afghanistan. Weariness from the endless months of constant alertness made her sleep long hours. "There was a lot to process. One of the officers in Afghanistan had said, 'We won't grieve now, we'll grieve when we get back home.' It's very true." The army gave her a fortnight of 'normalisation' before allowing her to rejoin her family, but that too, is a 'luxury' that Isabella does not have. She simply crosses London and vanishes rapidly northwards, leaving me at a loss. She has left no hint of her plans, and Mrs D-W has no more evidence to offer. I pull out an old, purple document. On 24th July 1916, Isabella will sign it, but that is not good enough. Even if an archive chase can tease out this particular signature's tale, it will be almost ten months before it can be woven into Isabella's story, and if a day in politics is a long time, how much longer is ten months in this particular war? I need something for now.

But where am I to look? Nothing invites enquiry. Nothing is tempting me into believing that it might be the key to the forthcoming weeks. Dejected, I decide to check on the rest of Isabella's family. At least that will fill time until serendipity strikes, and their stories will set some sort of backdrop for Isabella's own. But as I explore, my grandmother's return starts to come to life …

Somebody meets Isabella at the station. In no time, they are approaching the front door. Scottish voices surround her. Her coat is eased off. There are hugs. Someone enquires about the journey, and she tells them about the signal failure at York or the delay at Durham or whatever other trials the system has thrown up. She looks at their beloved, familiar faces. The smell of home is good. She hesitates. It would be even better if she could still detect her father's pipe smoke. Her mother gets a special squeeze. In no time, she is being ushered into the large room, the one with the piano. Ena indicates that she should take the place of honour. Mother starts to pour the tea. Absentmindedly, she accepts the cup and saucer Beth is proffering. The formulae of polite society must be followed.

"How is dear Mrs McStuart?"

"Did you hear about … "

She knows most of it already. Her sisters' letters have conveyed the hectic vigour of their friends – the signing up and heading off, the fund-raising and philanthropy. She has savoured the froth of feverish patriotism, the gay picnics, parties, concerts and romances. She has tasted their bitter undercurrent of uneasiness, tension, heartbreak. Her mother's letters have been flavoured with the fear and anguish that every parent must repress.

Over the rim of her cup she sizes up her family. To them it must feel as if she has never been away. The other world in which she has been dwelling is so far from theirs that they will not recognise its mark on her. They will see her exactly as she was. This is the way it has had to be. Ever since the day she went through the door of Surgeons' Hall, she has been living a life her family can never share. By going to war she has amassed a whole new clutch of divisive memories, multiplied the difference. But … they want to know. She will have to give them something …

She faces the same dilemma as when she picked up her pen in France, a dilemma shared by every other man and woman who has ever returned home from any war. Is it possible to 'tell' anyone who has not been there? Can they even begin to understand? Dare she even try? She searches rapidly for a set of anecdotes that will satisfy without causing distress, for reflections that will inspire rather than depress. Reaching for an extra cube of sugar, she catches sight of the old photograph on the side. Good heavens, how innocent they had all been, dressed up in their party frocks! Would that life was that simple now! Laying down her spoon, she begins her tale.

Perhaps she is aware that today will set the pattern. Out of habit she will repeat the same stories to whoever asks, and many will. As she finishes her tales, I envisage her eyes drifting restlessly towards the pile of newspapers on the other side of the room, her fingers itching to get at them. She had picked one up in London and devoured it on the train. Such a relief! But there is so much to catch up on, so many details to grasp before she will once more be confident that she understands what is happening. It all seems so very gloomy. The Battle of Loos is not going well. Nor is the fighting in Serbia. And there have been how many zeppelin attacks? How many people have been killed and injured? She drags her attention back. What is her mother saying? Jan is expecting a baby? All being well, it will be born in March! It will be Janet's first grand-child. Enthusiastically resolving to visit Jan as soon as she can, Isabella watches her mother.

She is not going to tease them, is she? "If it goes on this way I will only have Power grandchildren." Isabella hopes she will stay quiet. She, Ena and Beth may be spinsters, but they all know only too well that this war is claiming so many young men that it has already turned countless brides into widows before they have had time to become mothers. It has already left many babies fatherless.

Isabella's eyes linger on Ena. Last Spring, at the exact moment when Jan got married and Isabella left for the Anglo-Ethiopian, Ena's papers show that she gave up working as a VAD. It puzzles me. With VADs proving themselves invaluable in this war of countless casualties, why should Ena have chosen to stop 'doing her bit'? Not that stopping work seems to have damaged her prospects.

"The rules have just changed," she is explaining to Isabella, "Not many VADs used to be sent overseas, but now any girl aged twenty-three or over with three or more months of experience in a military hospital in Britain can apply for service overseas." Ena's words tumble over each other as she explains how she had seen that she fitted the bill, had filled in the lengthy forms, the letter inviting her for an interview had arrived. She pauses for dramatic effect, "They have accepted me. Isn't it grand?"

"But you may be near the front line," shudders Janet.

"Don't let yourself worry, Mother. The Army will keep us well back from the fighting."

"She might not even be in a hospital. She might be running a canteen like the one in Abbeville."

"Or in the Mediterranean."

"With those poor men from Gallipoli?"

However much Janet may tremble at the thought of Ena risking her life near the front line, or crossing the U-boat infested sea and facing whatever horrors and dangers may materialise once she lands, in her heart of hearts Janet knows she cannot complain. She has long-since forgotten the concerns she harboured about the propriety of Isabella training as a doctor. Now, she is just grateful that she has no sons to wave off into the certainty of enemy gunfire. She will never have to live with the ever-present threat of their mutilation or death. She has observed the different disguises her friends adopt to conceal the shadows of their fear. She has watched their struggles to remain composed after receiving one of those dreadful telegrams. At least Isabella has returned safely. At least she and Beth will remain here. She looks at Beth, her third-born.

I too look at Beth. She has no news to share at the table, simply because I have not been able to unearth a shred of information about her. She has not married. She has not joined the Red Cross. She is not listed in any archive that I have checked. My sole clue is still her autograph book. Since Isabella signed it in 1906, Beth has gradually been filling its pages. I flip past black verses scribbled by scratchy Scottish pens, past rough portraits, stilted ships, static windmills, and a finely cross-hatched castle. I linger longer over the entries that intrigue me most, the ones dated Cassel, 1910. Beautiful and illegible italic scripts by Lisbet and Grete, Louise and Anna-Sophie appear to greet 'Dear Miss Stenhouse' in numerous foreign languages. I identify German and French, perhaps Italian, and maybe Dutch, but by far the most exotic is four vertical lines of delicate Chinese script. Every greeting hides a story, invites enquiry and offers no answers.

One autograph book! It is *so* frustrating. Beth is Isabella's sister, she is part of Isabella's story, but it is almost as if she did not exist. Why was she in Cassel? Why did she go back there in December 1911, and again in December 1912. And why, at that point, did she stop collecting autographs? There are plenty of blank pages, but since December 1912 she has added not a single signature – not a soldier leaving for war, nor a friend or relation passing through. Maybe, quite reasonably, she has just grown out of the whole idea, but the consequence is that I have no idea at all how she has spent her days since the war began.

Not that Isabella's trail is exactly proving easy to follow. Indeed, knowing Jan and Ena's activities merely adds to the frustration of the ten-month void that is still gaping between Isabella's return from France and the document that she will sign next July. The iniquity of the execution of Edith Cavell drops into the chasm, then air-raids that kill and injure hundreds of people, but nothing personal to Isabella is even hinting at how she crosses this gap.

Should I have been less eager to say goodbye to Mrs D-W? The French Red Cross was begging her to take her St Valery staff to the new hospital in the Dardanelles. Could Isabella be about to squeeze in a visit to Tenedos? I check the hospital diary, just in case, but discover no hint that Isabella heads East with her old boss. What is she up to?

2

At some point, a letter arrives warning Ena that she should prepare to embark for Malta on 12th December. But is Isabella, the one who took herself off to medical school, the one who took herself out to France, the one who has so recently been praised by the French Army, now going to limit herself to waving goodbye to her sister? Surely keeping an eye on Jan's healthily swelling abdomen, and aiding and abetting Mother and Beth in whatever mysterious things occupy Mother and Beth is not going to satisfy her drive?

I read how many returnees find it hard to slide back into life at home. Shopping for fripperies, driving comfortably in broughams, and exchanging respectable niceties at plays and parties jars on minds conditioned to battling the suffering of wounded and dying warriors.

This Autumn, disabled veterans, unfit to fight another day, are appearing on the streets of Edinburgh. Convalescents have become national heroes who travel for free on trams. Theatre managers give them the best seats in the house. Middle-class ladies parade them at tea parties and bazaars in a valiant attempt to maintain sympathy levels and boost revenue. The poorhouse not far from the Links has been converted into a military hospital. From the John's Place windows, Isabella may even be able to see the recovering patients strolling in the autumn sunshine, their bright blue suits becoming daily more evident as the trees lose their leaves. The war is not so far away, after all.

Bemused, I pull out the Flower Press box again. The beads slither cold and glassy past my hand. I ignore them – Isabella is not going to be given beads by a prisoner now she is back in Scotland, is she? Further into the box, my fingers find themselves lingering on her anatomy dissection kit, so I pull it out, unhook its little clasp and flip it open. It is a higgledy-piggledy mess, the scalpels lying anywhere except in their allocated wooden slots. Impelled by an urge for order, I twist them this way and that, but however hard I try, they refuse to fit. A long-dormant myth-memory starts to slice itself free. Did Isabella say that she taught the first mixed anatomy class in Edinburgh? It seems unlikely. After all, it was only in 1908 that the university had categorically refused to allow mixed classes in the Faculty of Medicine, but I steel myself for a long and tedious wild goose chase through the volumes of the Medical Directory, just in case. Today, however, I am in luck. As early as 1919, Isabella has recorded herself as being: 'Late Demonst. Anat. Edin.'

I examine one of the scalpels with fresh fascination. I had never noticed before, but now I can see that the blade is faintly blackened and flawed. The tiny screws which hold its wooden handle to the metal blade have corroded to a coppery green, but inside the wooden box, the brass fittings are still shiny and gold. This scalpel has seen life – or rather, death. Not long after her student days, Isabella uses it again. With this very blade, she helps medical students grasp the structure of the human body, but – typical Isabella – she has given no dates, and I need dates. I need to know whether demonstrating anatomy is the task that fills her days until she signs the purple document.

Eagerly now, hoping that more details will slip out in subsequent volumes, I return to the hunt. Twenty odd years later, in 1941, she refers to her time in the dissecting room again: 'Carnegie Demonstrator in Anatomy at Edinburgh'. Carnegie? A couple of clicks and I discover that Isabella's post was funded by a trust set up for the benefit of Scottish universities by Andrew Carnegie, a Scotsman who had made a fortune in the American steel industry. Very interesting, but not the answer to the question of dates. With the purple document next July due to tie Isabella down for who knows how long, this 1915–16 academic year may be her only chance. Not that the date is the only problem with Isabella's claim. If she is to teach men as well as women, she will have to find a way past the University of Edinburgh's unshakable opposition to mixed medical classes.

As I explore, I gradually discover how very much times have changed. With the thousands of casualties needing vast numbers of doctors, medical schools have increased their intake of women as well as men. In Edinburgh, the 106 women who started the course in 1914 made up only 11 per cent of the total, but by 1918, 28 per cent of the nearly 1700 medical students will be women. The figures are staggeringly large, especially set against the fact that, when Isabella qualified just over two years ago in the summer of 1913, only 4 per cent of the total of 98 medical graduates were women. But with thousands of qualified doctors now in the army, who is to teach all these students? Sometimes, I discover, terrified undergraduates find themselves forced to act as fully-fledged doctors. In about 1916 I read, perhaps more out of desperation than from any commitment to equality, the University of Edinburgh …

I slow right down – can this be true? 'The University of

Edinburgh agrees to train male and female medical students on equal terms.' The next sentence gives me my answer: 'The University gives its official blessing to mixed classes.'

The gap is filled. Now I know what Isabella does when she returns from France. She is one of the doctors who steps into the breach, teaching both men and women their anatomy, preparing them for action. The peculiar tribulations of the times have placed the responsibility for teaching the first mixed anatomy class firmly in her hands: the myth-memory has proved strangely true.

I start picturing Isabella back in the dissecting room, then wonder why. Why should a woman who has spent the last few months fighting for the lives of wounded French soldiers decide to return to the dissecting room, when fresh casualties who would benefit from her experience are arriving every day? Why, for that matter, would any fully qualified doctor choose to teach anatomy rather than treat patients?

It does not take long to discover that Isabella is following a well-trodden path – the path to becoming a surgeon. Not that many women doctors actually succeed in becoming surgeons. Miss Pringle, the doctor who demonstrated anatomy when Isabella was a student, tried but she has ended up as a GP in Dundee. By 1919–20 there will still be only four female Fellows of the Royal College of Surgeons of England and possibly two in Scotland. Even by 1990 there will be only 320 female Fellows of the Royal College of Surgeons of England, and in 2013, "Surgery is still very male dominated," says Junior Doctor Kate.

Mentally, I revisit the operations that Isabella helped with in France. Had she been digging out her Cunningham to revise the relevant anatomy before each procedure? I have read of other women doctors doing that. With such badly maimed bodies, it cannot always have been easy to recognise what was what. No wonder she wants to improve her knowledge of anatomy.

Over in the dissecting room, I picture her opening her textbook and studying the pages. Lifting a scalpel from her box, she begins to incise the skin of the awkwardly draped cadaver's back, preparing to expose the fascia beneath, and I begin to follow her actions in another ancient Cunningham, purchased to replace Isabella's own. Her next job is to expose the nerves, blood vessels and muscles. It takes time, but at last she steps away, a satisfied look on her face. This prosection is now ready to show the students. When they find it tricky to locate their *rhomboideus minor, serratus posticus inferior* or *trigonum petiti*, she is confident she can guide them.

The young men and women who later trickle into the room are perhaps even more embarrassed than Isabella and her all-female group were when they first faced a male body, but France has cured Isabella of any such sensitivities. She begins to greet her students. The first mixed anatomy class has begun.

Respectfully, I lay Isabella's not-quite-fitting scalpel back in its box. It was perhaps a replacement for an original that got lost in the hurly-burly of daily use.

3

In case the global enthusiasm for the digitisation of archives throws up anything new and relevant, I periodically re-google 'Isabella Stenhouse'. One day, a whole page devoted to her loads before my eyes. To add to the thrill, it has been signed by Isabella herself. I scour for a date. Oh, it could hardly be better – 31st December, 1915! Has another gem, polished and ready for weaving into the tale, simply landed out of the cyber-blue? I dip further into the website and discover that Isabella's page is part of the *Index of Doctors in Scotland During the First World War*. What is this Index? What is Isabella signing up for, or agreeing to, or declaring? What is this all about?

The *Index* proves to be the work of the Scottish Medical Service Emergency Committee, a work that fits into the bigger picture of waning enthusiasm for the war. As the spring of 1915 had warmed into summer, the number of men signing up to join the Army had gone down, causing the government grave concern. Without volunteers, how were they to maintain the army, let alone run the nation's key industries? An Act of Parliament had enabled them to register every man and his skills, so they now know what resources lie at their disposal. Parallel concerns have motivated the Emergency Committee's Scottish Index. How is the military's need for doctors to be squared with the health needs of the civilian population?

I scan through the pages. Amongst all the male names, the women lie few and far between. One of the women who graduated with Isabella in 1913, Celia MacNeil, is working in the military hospital across the Links. Another, Laura Davies, is working in Edinburgh War Hospital, but I count only 14 women among the 527 doctors listed in Edinburgh and Leith. If all these doctors gathered in one place, the women would be a mere sprinkling of long skirts nudging at the outer fringes of the sombre mass of suited masculinity.

The Emergency Committee has sent a letter to every qualified medical practitioner in Scotland requesting details of their present work and a signed pledge that:

At the call of the local War Committee for my area, as instructed by the Scottish Medical Service Emergency Committee, I am prepared to render the service or services marked above. This offer is subject to the condition that, in the event of such service requiring me to leave my present work, I am enabled to make arrangements for having it carried on during my absence.

The 'service or services' that the doctors can offer are limited and age-dependent: part-time civil work, part-time military work, locum work, or serving as a Lieutenant in the RAMC at home or abroad, but that makes it exciting. Most official records deal merely in facts and figures – what, where, when. These forms are different. They offer a window into the thoughts of these medical men and women. "If you were called upon, what … " They explore willingness and desire. There are promises and apologies. Gradually they morph into weft for Isabella's tale, and a meeting of the Edinburgh branch of the Association of Registered Medical Women concocts itself in my mind …

It is just before Christmas 1915 and, a little late, Isabella and Celia arrive together. Nodding silent and enthusiastic smiles at Laura, they sidle quietly into seats. Apologies for absence are being offered on behalf of Dr Georgina Davidson. Her family has sent word that she cannot join them because she is in France, serving with the French Red Cross.

"Let us remember Dr Ada Macmillan," the Chairwoman is continuing, deeply solemn. "We have received news of her imprisonment by the enemy in Serbia. Let us pray for her speedy release."

The atmosphere is sombre, very different from the bold confidence of the meeting in Liverpool last year. Since then, most of these women have suffered bereavement of one kind or another. Some, like Isabella and her friends, have diverted their careers to tend the wounded. There is much they would like to air, and the moment the Chairwoman calls, "Any other business," a young woman jumps up.

"Would the distinguished ladies please give their advice as to how to respond to the call of the Scottish Medical Emergency Committee's letters, which I believe everybody has received?"

"Your name, doctor?" enquires the Chairwoman.

"Dr Gertrude Herzfeld," replies the questioner. A ripple goes round the small gathering. Herzfeld, clearly a Germanic name. Whatever the young lady's credentials, she will have a hard time persuading anyone in authority that she is no spy and has the welfare of the nation at heart.

"Your age and present employment?" continues the Chair. Gertrude is working at the Hospital for Sick Children. She wants to offer the only service that befits her age – working as a

Lieutenant with the RAMC – but is aware that the RAMC have, hitherto, refused to accept any ladies.

A woman in her thirties stands up, identifying herself as a bacteriologist, "I sincerely hope that this opportunity signals the turning of the tide and that we will be released to go where our services are most needed. I, for one, long to get out to the Mediterranean and help fight the peculiar infections of that region that threaten our troops."

Perhaps Dr Grace Cadell herself takes up the debate. Ever optimistic, she urges the younger doctors to go. Elderly now, she declares herself fit only to continue the work in which she has become expert during her long career. "But," she continues, "civilians still need treatment. The fulfilment of the needs of the various Fronts must not be allowed to cause suffering at home. Old fogeys like me will just have to retrieve our stethoscopes and forget our aching bones."

A quiet young woman stands up. "I am only 25, and hate to appear cowardly," she begins, "but I feel far better qualified to take on the job of releasing a man for the Front than to go over there myself. It seems absurd for a man to stay here dealing with complaints I understand while I dash into working with soldiers when I have no idea of how to treat them."

In reply, an older woman eases herself stiffly up. Her skin has the weathered texture of one who has spent a lifetime in the sun. "I am as eager to help as the next woman," she declares, "but the plain fact is that I am not qualified for military medicine. I have spent my life working for the church in India. The Hindu ladies refuse the attendance of a male physician, so their welfare has been my chief concern. I agree with you, Dr

Cadell," she nods towards her contemporary, "I do need to dig out my stethoscope." Her eyes move over to the nervous young doctor, "I also echo this young lady's feelings about the absurdity of some of us attempting military medicine, but there is something else I worry about too. I have not practised in this country for many years, and I can only consider myself competent to undertake the most minor of tasks. It would be a dreadful mistake to go about the place doing more harm than good."

"Oh surely that is an unnecessary fear," interrupts another voice, "I haven't practised for 12 years, but I'm sure I could pick it all up in a jiffy. I'm with you," she looks at Gertrude and the bacteriologist, "I'll be in the military hospitals before you can say knife."

Half the meeting flinches. It's all very well and good to be sure of yourself, but this is a bit rich, isn't it? When even old hands are finding the new wounds of this war a challenge? The woman is carrying on, "Isn't it funk to cry off doing the hard stuff? We've always said we can do everything just as well as the men."

How many times have they heard that before? At the moment, this war's reality is making the truths that seemed blindingly self-evident last year seem more like bravado to some. One woman apologises for her inability to offer to work more than part-time with civilians – there is nobody else to care for her three children. Two GPs explain that they are already at full stretch covering for men who have gone to the Front. They regret that they can offer no more.

Once Christmas is over, Isabella sits down and pulls the letter from the Emergency Committee out of its envelope. Unfolding it, she begins to read.

Present work? She quickly jots down that she has been 'Recently serving in a French Army Hospital and is at present living at home'. The next bit is harder. What kind of medical service is she is prepared to offer, should the need arise? She studies the list of options carefully. The only one truly applicable to her age is 'Group A (under 45) Lieut. RAMC', but she hesitates.

Could she be thinking, "What would be the point of choosing that one? However much I want to go, I am a woman. The RAMC would never have me." Or could it be, "I have a post in which I am gaining the knowledge I need to be of real service. Once my tenure is complete, I will have far more to offer. That will be the time for something new."

She checks the remaining choices. 'Group B (45 to 55) Part-time home military work'. She could select that one. Friends have described having to resort to options outside their age bracket. The alternative, 'Group B (45 to 55) Part-time home civil work', is a definite 'No'. Far from scaring her off, France has provided her with experience in war surgery that many doctors of both genders lack. She is certainly not going to rule out the military. What about the last choice, being a locum and releasing another doctor for the Front? No thank you! Reaching for her pen, she marks a cross in the red circle beside 'Group B (45 to 55) Part-time home military work'. She signs and dates her form, then lays it ready for the post.

4

Cunningham's manual guides me through Isabella's year. After the back, she tackles the upper limb and shoulder: cutting, retracting and exposing, determined to embed the twists and turns of each muscle, ligament, nerve and blood vessel in her memory. The preservative smells terrible, but at least it does not send her to sleep as chloroform does.

As the manual guides them down to the lower limb, I imagine Isabella looking at the disabled veterans lining the streets with professional eyes. What injuries necessitated such extensive procedures? What operations might have been performed to produce those effects? What were the alternatives? Where did the surgery take place? Under what conditions? Could she herself have carried it out?

My own *Cunningham* falls open at a diagram of the foot – adductor *obliquus hallucis, adductor transversus hallucis*, the external plantar nerve and artery. There is a story about them that Isabella can her students ...

"It began with a young *poilu* who reached the Anglo-Ethiopian late one night in June. He was one of our first patients," she recalls, looking up from the cadaver's foot. "His leg was in such a sorry state that we knew we would have to amputate. It was just a question of when and where." She gestures along the leg to indicate the various positions they had considered. The students pay unusually close attention, profoundly mindful that this war means it may not be long before they themselves face the same awful choice.

"But we had to wait until the infection died down before we could decide how much needed to come off," Isabella continues. Moving the soft tissues carefully, she explains how, with meticulous dressings and plenty of irrigation, the infection had retreated, the damage repaired. "We waited and waited, but the moment to operate never seemed quite right and, by September, all we had to amputate was one toe!" she crows. "It was a long wait for the poor man, but oh, it was so satisfying to let him go knowing he could use his whole foot. It wasn't pretty, but it worked. He will be able to earn his living."

The months pass, and Isabella and her pupils dissect their way through the male perineum, the rectal and urogenital triangles, up through the abdominal wall and into the abdominal cavity. March arrives. The female pelvis and reproductive system are the very last dissections of Volume One. The newspapers are full of bloodshed – Verdun, Isonzo, East Africa, Persia, Egypt and Salonika. Occasionally, the classifieds carry job opportunities for women doctors. In January Mrs St Clair Stobart wanted ladies to help with maternity work in Petrograd. Now she is seeking surgical women for Serbia, while the Scottish Women's Hospitals need help in both France and Serbia.

As yet another veteran catches her eye on the way home from work, Isabella's mind perhaps drifts back to the form she filled in for the Emergency Committee. Will her offer of assistance be taken up? This month, she would prefer not to be needed. She has become an aunt – Jan has been safely delivered of a baby boy.

Suddenly, I understand the quaint old expression, 'Safely delivered'. For all the efforts of Dr Annie McCall and her kind, many women do not survive childbirth. I can sense the relief that flavours the Stenhouses' kissing and cuddling and passing of the baby parcel – Jan has survived. And yet I feel for her. Maternal nervousness seems to blend with the pride pulsating from the photograph of her and baby Bill as she presses Bill's small, warm cheek tightly against her own. Conscription has been introduced. "Please God," I imagine her murmuring, "make this war end. Keep this precious new living, breathing bundle safe." Perhaps she dares not contemplate the moment when Frank may actually join up, when she and Bill will join all the other mothers and children dreading the telegraph boy's knock. Doctors are not immune to death.

5

The very fact that Isabella will sign her purple document on July 24th means that some time before that day, she will receive a mysterious letter that glides, phantom-like, through the archives, a letter that is sent to every woman on the medical register. Well, on that much the sources are agreed. But exactly what it says, and who sends it, is so vague that I set out to find the original – an easy job, I assume. But after trawling numerous archives both on and off-line, I am just as ignorant as when I began. And a whole lot more puzzled. There has been nothing. No trace of an original. Not a sign of a copy in any of the various formats in which archives keep copies. It is unbelievable. If every woman doctor on the Medical Register is to receive a copy of this letter, several hundred copies are required. Yet not a single one appears to have survived, not, at least, in any of the most obvious archives.

Reluctantly, admitting that I am not an expert at tracing missing documents, I concede defeat and return to the literature. That is when I notice that none of the genuine academics actually quote this letter, they merely refer to it. Have they too failed to find a copy? Are they, like me, relying on hints, inferences and each other? It piques my curiosity. How come every single one of those hundreds of letters has vanished? Surely a copy must lie somewhere, in some attic or obscure vault, unloved and unrecognised.

But until it turns up, all I and other researchers can do is quote one another. The letter is thought to have been sent sometime during the Spring, so it may not have arrived by the time a Zeppelin attacks Leith at the very start of April. Strangely, there is more information about that bombing than there is about the missing letter. I can easily picture the scene in John's Place. Janet is, perhaps, in Lancashire with Jan, and Isabella and Beth are enjoying a quiet evening at home when a roar fills the room. The pictures on the wall begin to swing. Rescuing them, the girls dash to the window – but see nothing. It is as quiet as usual. Until they get upstairs. Then they see it. Out of the back window. The ghostly cigar shape of a zeppelin, gleaming in the moonlight. Behind it, towards the docks, the sky glows with the reds and oranges of a huge blaze. Isabella and Beth stare as the Zep turns silently south. Slowly, it glides out of sight. Rushing downstairs, they tumble out onto the Links, where a crowd is silently watching bomb after bomb dropping on Edinburgh. Come daylight, the damage caused by eighteen bombs is clear for all to see. A warehouse full of spirits has been burnt right down. People – including a baby – have been killed. The Castle rock has been hit. Spectators tour the damaged buildings, angry at the unpreparedness of the authorities.

Eight weeks later, on May 25th, the Stenhouses are perhaps among the crowds who gather in Rosebank Cemetery for the unveiling of the memorial to the men who died in the Gretna train crash. As with any disaster, Isabella's thoughts fly right back to when she first heard of the tragedy … She is in the church in St Valery, lighting her candle again, praying for these men and for Dick Doughty-Wylie … so much pain, such a need for everybody to pull together. And her mind jumps to the letter – she has definitely received it by now. How should she reply?

219

She is not the only one wondering what to do. In mid-June, beset by worries as to how to recruit the many doctors the Army requires without risking the health of the civilian population, the Director General of Army Services, Sir Alfred Keogh, makes a public appeal to the medical profession to rally itself. Over the next few days, the papers develop this into a kind of 'Your Country Needs You' directed specifically at the medical profession. As she reads the articles, I imagine Isabella allowing herself the kind of superior chuckle that comes from having secret, inside information. She knows something that the papers do not.

Her letter had been signed by – well, whom? Was it Dr Louisa Aldrich Blake, or was it several such eminent medical women? Perhaps it does not matter. Perhaps what matters is that it had come from a source that women doctors such as Isabella could trust.

What does it say? Isabella reads it for the umpteenth time. Perhaps it begins formally, recognising the contributions of women doctors, something like: 'The Army has taken note of the excellent work being done by medical ladies in France, Serbia and at the military hospital run by Dr Louisa Garrett Anderson and Dr Flora Murray at Endell Street in London … ' But all too quickly, blasting its way from beneath the flannel and the flowery language, the Army's plea explodes, something like:

DEAR LADY DOCTOR,
PLEASE, PLEASE COME AND HELP THE RAMC.
WE NEED YOU.

By all accounts it is not a gently phrased enquiry like the form from the Emergency Committee, it is urgent. If the Army could go down on bended knee, begging for women doctors to come and assist in this grave national emergency, it would. A tantalising hint suggests that the women will be sent to the Mediterranean to provide medical support for top-secret new campaigns. But the source does not make clear whether Isabella and her fellows know this detail. Perhaps all they know is that, at last, their country needs them, and its need is urgent.

On 24th July, as men wounded in the long-awaited battle in the Somme begin to flood home, and hospitals across the British Isles fill, Isabella picks up her pen. With a simple signature on the purple document, she offers her skills to her nation.

To, His Majesty's Principal Secretary of State for the War Department.
I, Isabella Stenhouse, of 9 John's Place, Leith, Edinburgh being qualified to practice medicine and surgery and being registered under the Medical Act now in force in the United Kingdom hereby offer and agree if accepted by you to serve at home or abroad with His Majesty's Forces on the following conditions:-

…

Signed: Isabella Stenhouse, 24th July, 1916

How much selection has taken place? Have there been interviews? Medicals? If I was an Army recruiting officer, I would reject the woman doctor who has not practised for 12 years, however mustard-keen she may be. "Go and prove yourself on the civilian front and come back to me," I would say. But Isabella is a different kettle of fish. She has experience in military medicine and is well on the way to being a fully fledged surgeon. "Yes please, Dr Stenhouse, we will take you."

6

A tiny article about the women doctors concealed between the news reports from the Somme and the casualty lists gets me letting out a victorious, "Yes!"

The War Office has asked for the services of lady doctors to work in regular army hospitals, and forty qualified ladies have been chosen for service, some of whom will go to Malta, where there are important hospitals. This is the first occasion on which medical women have been requisitioned for army service, for the lady doctors serving with the Red Cross units are volunteers. At the moment it is in doubt whether the War Office will give these latest recruits a uniform, but, if not, so strong is the feeling of the ladies on the subject that they will supply themselves with one.

The ladies may be all set and ready to go, but their trail goes almost cold. These particular women doctors seem to figure very little, anywhere. The all-female medical units of WWI – the Scottish Women's Hospitals, Mrs St Clair Stobart's outfits, and the Women's Hospital Corps – have left their trace through books, diaries, letters and articles. But despite the fact that the RAMC experiment is a landmark both for the Army and for the position of women within the medical profession, it has hardly dented the archives – a few lines in an article about women's war service here, a short paragraph there. Soon I work out that one brief mention simply refers back to another brief mention, until I begin to see that they all stem from the same very, very few pieces. The old newspaper may have been told that forty lady doctors signed up, but it is not just Isabella who keeps silent.

Is there a revealing diary that will tell me what these professional women do, how they think and react? It seems not. The Army has banned them from keeping diaries. But my hopes rise when I come across a reference to a letter-writing doctor, Eithne Haigh. I hurry to the Imperial War Museum, only to find that Eithne is annoyingly far from prolific – only three of her letters remain, and one of the first things she writes is:

We have quite settled down here now and I am quite enjoying things so far. Unfortunately there are so many things that I mayn't mention in writing that I'm afraid my letters will feel scrappy and unsatisfactory. I mayn't tell you anything about the hospital, the staff or the work so you must take it for granted that I put in a little work occasionally.

Phoenix-like, my hopes of insight into Isabella's life in Malta rise again when I learn that the women held a meeting after the war to discuss their experiences. I dash back across London to the Wellcome library, and read with increasing puzzlement. One woman reports on the difficulty of basing a diagnosis of paratyphoid on agglutination tests alone in inoculated patients, another on a case of fulminating malaria in which the symptoms began four hours before death, and a third on the differential diagnosis of malaria and dysentery. I suppose that to somebody studying the history of medicine, they would be fascinating, but they are hardly what I was looking for.

Then, gradually, it dawns on me. These reports are, in fact, the very evidence that I have been seeking. They tell me exactly what matters to these female doctors. They tell me precisely what these women feel is worth recording. They almost certainly reflect Isabella's own interests and concerns, but I have been blind to their significance, deaf to the voices they reveal, because they are not what I was hoping for. They are nothing like Isabel Hutton's book of medical school treasures. They are nothing like Mrs D-W's Anglo-Ethiopian diary. They warn me very sternly not to expect VAD-style, introspective accounts from these professional, scientifically trained women.

But that leaves me with a problem. These sparse accounts give me no idea how to slip myself into Isabella's sensible lace-up shoes, so, hoping these earnest medical professionals are not looking, I carry on searching.

A letter written in 1921 by a lady doctor who served in Malta considers their experiences worth only a few sentences, but by 1937, with a new war looming and a desperate wish to learn from experience, letters are flying back and forth all saying something like:

"It is a long time ago, I don't remember."

"Surely somebody must have written an account."

"I understand that Dr Martindale entirely ignored them. One wonders why, seeing that the employment of women as army doctors for the first time was an event of some professional importance."

"Try Dr Lepper."

"Try Dr Hare."

"Figures were not kept."

"There must be something in the War Museum, unless it was burnt in the Crystal Palace fire."

"I never came across any book dealing with the matter, though there must necessarily be, I imagine, some record in the official papers of the RAMC."

"I thought Dr Thorne wrote an article for an old edition of Encyclopedia Britannica but I could not find it."

Clutching at straws, I contact the twenty-first-century team at Encyclopaedia Britannica, but they, too, can find no trace of this legendary article. The discussions go on, but sixteen years later, in 1953, the War Office writes to say that the Army has no record of the number of women serving with them in WWI, and in 1978, an Australian academic pre-empts me by saying, 'It is a pity that so few left any record of their reactions to the war.'

In a change of tack, I try 'the official papers of the RAMC'. 'Surgeon with the French Red Cross' states Isabella's official war record at the National Archives. Ordinarily the simple description would excite me; after all, it does confirm Isabella's ambition to be a surgeon. But just now it merely irritates – I can see it only as yet another layer of silence about her service with the RAMC.

Then my luck turns. A new website, www.maltaramc.com, pops up, leading me to another source of official papers. Soon, I am in the Army Medical Services Museum. The curator lays a file on the table and opens it at yet another trace of Isabella. On thick blue paper, *Record of Special Reserve Officers' Services* emblazoned in bold capital letters across the top, Isabella's first appointment with the Army is written up in black ink: 'Embarked for Malta 12.8.16.'

There! 12th August. Less than three weeks after signing up, Dr Isabella Stenhouse is on her way, and I am restraining another victory whoop.

7

From beneath a round brimmed hat, Isabella is looking at me again. She is seated casually on some steps in the shade of a tree, but this time, I turn away. It is the back of this photograph that I want. Already I suspect it may weave me into the Maltese phase of Isabella's story, for there, on card yellowed by the century, Isabella herself has written:

St. Ignatius Hospital, Malta, September 1917.
'The garden was my great joy. It was old Italian terraces
sloping to the sea. These steps were leading down from a
courtyard to the Jesuit's Garden. The scent of that magnolia
tree!!

Courtesy of such delights as Major-General W. G. Macpherson's *History of Medicine in the Great War,* and Captain G. R. Bruce's *Military Hospitals in Malta during the War: A Short Account of their Inception and Development,* I learn that St. Ignatius Hospital is one of many temporary military hospitals that were set up in Malta during the Gallipoli campaign of 1915. Prior to this, I read, the building had been used as a college by ... I should have guessed! The Jesuits – the very people who created the garden that Isabella loved!

She, too, must know the history of the place: how the Jesuits had taken over the building in the 1870s and turned it into a well-regarded school but had been forced to leave in 1907. By 1915, eight empty years had left the building in 'a very bad condition'. The Royal Engineers had had to clean it, fit gas cookers and electric light, and replace the drains before setting it up as a properly equipped, modern surgical hospital with sanitary annexes, operating theatres and X-ray facilities.

I turn over the photograph and study my grandmother. After making no comment about her six months of war service in France, mentioning next to nothing about 1915–16 in Edinburgh, and captioning none of her other photographs, why does this particular garden tempt her into breaking her silence? And since she has, this once, taken the trouble to write something down, will it prove significant, provide a key to something, sometime? My eyes start searching the background, the balustrade behind her, its sentry-like stone urns ...

It is the classic light-bulb moment. I delve for a huge photograph in which Isabella stands conspicuously pale-garbed amongst countless khaki-clad British soldiers and a phalanx of seated nurses, a balustrade behind them. My eyes track back and forth, forth and back in my customary 'I can't believe this' checking procedure. This time, the soldiers are filling the frame far too effectively. I want to ask them to move over and get out of the way, but the more I look, the more the combination of the balustrade, the iron-work and the trees gives the game away. Isabella on her own may be fuzzy and informal and the military group sharp and formal, but these two photographs are definitely from the same place. Courtesy of Isabella's own comment, I know it is St Ignatius Hospital, Malta.

At this point, my luck strikes yet again. A neighbour's friend, Joe, is a Maltese architect who knows the island's buildings well. He volunteers to act the sleuth and locate this 'St. Ignatius Hospital'.

"There are other photos that might come from Malta too," I warn, "People taking tea, Isabella's sister, and a woman in black."

"Send them over," comes the reply, "I'll see what I can do."

8

I follow Isabella to Malta, but there is something momentous I need to absorb before I can begin to investigate Isabella's life here, before I can start wondering whether it will be here that she receives her string of beads – something vast connected with the woman in black. Joe believes the photographs of her were taken beside the sea in Sliema, so I scramble down onto the foreshore, settle on a suitably seat-like rock, and open the pictures in question. There she is, sheltering beneath a rough structure of wood and straw. And again, sitting on a rock like mine. Finally, she stands beside a road overlooking the sea, enigmatic, mysterious.

"Who is this woman in black?" I had asked Isabella's daughter.

"Oh, that is Granny," she had answered airily.

Granny? Isabella's mother Janet? She went to Malta too?

"She must have gone out to chaperone my mother and Ena."

I had believed her, until I started thinking. Chaperoning may have been all the rage during Isabella's Edwardian adolescence, when young girls were delicately innocent, but in 1916? To chaperone two women in their late twenties who are performing the far-from-genteel task of treating the casualties of war? Let alone that one of the pair has been studying and working independently for eight years?

With the lapping of the sea in my ears, I let the photos take me back. I was on the phone to Irene, a woman who had once worked in 9 John's Place, when I heard the news. Warning me that her washing machine was flooding and she might have to hang up at any moment, she insisted on logging on to a subscriber-only website on my behalf. As I hung on at the end of the line, she clicked hither and thither until she came out with her bombshell, "Bethia Stenhouse died on 31st July 1916."

"I beg your pardon? Please could you repeat that?"

Irene amplified, "Your Bethia Stenhouse died between 9 and 10 o'clock in the morning on 31st July 1916, aged 24."

The fact had not changed. A fuzzy line had not been playing tricks on me. I had not misheard. I had misbelieved. I had always known, dimly, vaguely, that Beth had died. It was one of those facts of family that was just there, that was all there was to it. A fatal fall from a rotten window at the age of 18, so the story went, the story which I had told Irene only a few minutes earlier, as I had wondered aloud precisely when during her medical training Isabella had had to deal with this disaster. The reason why Irene had insisted on logging on.

But now I was hearing that Beth did not die until she was 24. Six whole years after tradition had her tragically dead and buried. It was early during my research and an ominous idea began to creep out of some deep recess in my mind.

"I think that might have been round about the time when Isabella signed up with the Army," I blurted out. "But she can't have died then? Can she?"

A fresh gush from Irene's washing machine suddenly demanded her full attention. As shocked by the news as I was, she rang off, promising to call back as soon as possible. While she mopped, I snatched. Old papers fell out of cupboards and files flew open on the computer as I gathered every relevant scrap of evidence. By the time the phone rang, I was shaking in my chair, but before I had a chance to speak, "I reckon she topped herself," announced Irene, "she topped herself when she found out your Granny was going to the war."

My thoughts exactly ... but ... suicide? Really?

"I agree," I had had to reply, "31st July 1916 was exactly one week after Isabella had signed up with the army. It was the morning after Isabella's twenty-ninth birthday."

I had made sure I read Beth's death certificate for myself. It informed me that she had died 'of a fractured skull, the result of a fall'. Reluctant to accept the obvious inference of suicide, I had returned to John's Place, trudged up and down its gorgeous staircase and taken photographs, lots of photographs. The window from which Beth had fallen is unusually high up. Standing beside the sill I had instinctively wanted to retreat, no matter that the present window looked solid enough. Down in the yard where Beth had landed, I had shuddered. This had not been some gruesome scene in a horror movie, it had been reality. As real as the war, as real as the death having been certified by a 'Dr William Elder', listed in the Emergency Committee's Index as a GP living at 4 John's Place. When I read that, the scene had sprung to life.

Somebody – Janet, Isabella, a maid? – discovers Beth lying in the yard. Have they gone out by chance? Had Beth screamed? 'Whoever' hurls herself up the basement stairs, shrieking for help. She dashes through the hall, slips between the paired porch doors, jerks open the heavy front door, careers down the short flight of steps at the front, races across the front garden … Good heavens this is taking eternity. Why in the name of all that is sacred had they not installed a telephone? … She flies past numbers 8, 7, 6, and 5, before she hurtles up to the door of no 4, hammering and shouting. Dr Elder's maid comes ponderously to the door. A garbled explanation and, at last, the doctor himself is grabbing his medical bag. He heaves himself towards No 9 faster than he ever imagined his 51-year-old body could manage … And there my imaginary journey had faded. I needed hard evidence. What exactly did Dr Elder see as he emerged from the back door of No. 9?

I had consulted the newspapers. Beth's death was announced in *The Scotsman* the very next morning, 1st August – fast work by somebody.

At John's Place, Leith, on 31st July, the result of an accident, Bethia Drummond (Beth). Dearly beloved daughter of Mrs Stenhouse and of the late William Stenhouse, grain mer-chant, Leith.

What about grief? And shock? How was Janet coping? Isabella? The questions began to rush in … I had looked at the announcement again. Unlike almost all the other death announcements in the paper that day, unlike the announce-ments the Stenhouses had inserted when Isabella's father and uncle had died, it gave no details about the arrangements for Beth's funeral. A hint that it was suicide? Or just the chaos of the times? Tucked inside the paper I had found a further brief report:

Fatal accident at Leith: Miss Bethia Stenhouse, 20 years
of age, daughter of Mrs William Stenhouse, 9 John's Place,
Leith, was fatally injured yesterday by falling from a win-
dow on (sic) the top flat of her mother's house to the ground
at the rear of the building.

Disappointing. I had expected at least a big headline and some journalistic snooping but, perhaps, set beside the catastrophic news from the Somme, a single girl dying in an accident no longer mattered all that much. So what if they had her age wrong? So what if a family was grieving? So were so many.

Might a local paper offer more detail, I had wondered, and, winding my way through microfilm copies of the *Leith Observer*, I had my reward. When Dr Elder thundered down the stairs and out into the yard, Beth had not been dead, the newspaper stated, but she had been unconscious, suffering from what today might be described as 'multiple injuries'. Had she ever had any chance? Had Dr Elder, perhaps with Isabella's help, battled to save her life? If so, his efforts had been in vain. Soon, he had no choice but to sign the death certificate. There had been no opportunity to ask Beth what had happened.

Later, her death had to be registered. And for the third time, it was Isabella, her call-up to Malta looming, who took on the task. This time she did not hurry to get to the Registry Office on the same day, and – too shocked, too busy, or just way past pride – she did not include 'M.B. Сн.B.' with her signature.

Whether the papers printed the details or not, Beth's poor, broken body still needed to be buried. Her stunned family still needed the ritual of a funeral. I had taken myself back to the churchyard in Corstorphine, and traced Beth's name on the Stenhouse's polished granite memorial stone. My eyes had tracked upwards to the first name, her grandfather's, 'Erected to the memory of William Stenhouse, Grain merchant, Leith, 1902'. Beneath came his wife, then his two sons, Beth's father and uncle. By 1916, space remained for only one more name – Janet's. In the fulness of time, she should have joined her husband. Yet that summer, a stone engraver was chiselling not her name, but Beth's, into that little empty patch.

A glare of Maltese sun fades the woman in black from my screen. Now I understand. Perhaps it was as early as lunchtime on 31st July that Janet's anguish drove her to her wardrobe. From it, she dragged her old black mourning dress. Defying the conventions of war, my great-grandmother allowed the depths of her grief to show. No daughter should ever precede her mother to the grave. Janet came to Malta not as a chaperone, but to grieve and, perhaps, to escape.

9

Even the Maltese sunshine cannot expunge the image of Beth tumbling past the windows at the back of John's Place from my mind. Had she seemed happy before she went upstairs? Had she told them of her plans for later in the day? Her mother would know. If it haunts me, how much worse must it be for Janet? Every time anybody looks at her, convention will dictate that they offer their condolences. Will they probe? Or will they assume she is suffering from that deadly common grief, the loss of a son? I am certain that not one of them will dare to come out with the question that has gripped me ever since I heard the news. Was Beth's death the accident it purported to be, or was it suicide? Just what sort of death are Isabella and her family mourning?

I had wanted to find an inquest, or a post-mortem – anything which would tell me why Bethia Stenhouse should simply have fallen out of a window and died. But the Lothian Health Archive had assured me that at the time there was no requirement for inquests to be carried out on accidents in the home. The only thing I had found was a 'Record of Corrected Entry' to Beth's death certificate, and the only information it had added was the distance of her fall – approximately forty-five feet – which sounded as nasty as the walls of John's Place had looked. But I had made a mental note that in September, a month or so after Beth's death, someone, somewhere, had decided to do a little more investigating. Someone, somewhere, had been wondering how it had happened.

What was it the *Leith Observer* had printed? 'Miss Stenhouse had always been of a very cheery disposition, and the sympathy of the public will go to Mrs Stenhouse in her great loss.' The words had dogged me, dragging with them an answering phrase from somewhere deep within my head, "Methinks they do protest too much." Slimily, the sentences had seethed and snaked through my mind, together insinuating that, however cheery Beth's purported disposition, the Leith locals would wisely discern that, 'She topped herself.'

In reality, I had had far too little evidence to succumb entirely to those weasel words. One day I would find myself convinced that Beth had committed suicide, but the next I would be telling myself not to be so ridiculous, accidents happen. Utterly trapped in a loop of indecision, I had enlisted a jury of friends. They were allowed to ask whatever questions they considered relevant, and I was to try and answer them, as well as playing devil's advocate and posing counter-arguments.

We started with the full cutting from the paper:

5TH AUGUST 1916
LEITH WOMAN'S FATAL FALL

A distressing accident, which terminated fatally, happened on Monday to Miss Bethia Stenhouse (24), daughter of Mrs Stenhouse, 9 Johns Place, and the late Mr William Stenhouse, corn manufacturer. It appears that Miss Stenhouse mounted a table in order to open the window on the top flat of her mother's house, and that in doing so she lost her balance, and fell over the window sill to the ground, a distance of 45 feet. Medical assistance was at once brought and Dr Elder found her unconscious and suffering from a large wound in the right side, while her skull and right forearm were also fractured. Death took place shortly after the doctor arrived. Miss Stenhouse had always been of a very cheery disposition, and the sympathy of the public will go to Mrs Stenhouse in her great loss.

"Top flat? Why should Beth have been up there?" my jury began. "Wasn't the top floor for servants?" I agreed that I, too, had been taught that the top flat was for servants, so had wondered why Beth had been up there – but it was wartime, anything might have been happening.

We moved on to the window itself, examining the distance of the sill from the floor and how the frame was recessed into the wall. We researched the way the sashes worked. The National Trust for Scotland informed us that 'unless there was very rotten timber it would be unlikely to fall through such a window.'

"But with Beth's window facing north-west it must have caught every winter storm that came Edinburgh's way."

"Yes, we need to give the rotten window story a chance."

But then the table got us. None of us could see where the table fitted in. I began to feel squeamish when one of my friends spelt out all our thoughts, "The only reason I would drag a table over to that window would be to give myself the best possible platform for climbing onto the sill, and the only reason I can think of for wanting to get onto the sill of a top floor window is to let myself fall."

To defuse the tension, I pulled out Beth's little book. Perhaps they would spot something I had missed. Carefully, they leafed through. Nothing. Then, unexpectedly, somebody prised opened the stiff flyleaf to reveal a piece of thin, typewritten paper. Unfolding it cautiously, she read out:

> *Love is life's end (an end but never ending)*
> *All joys, all sweets, all happiness awarding;*
> *Love is life's wealth (ne'er spent but ever spending)*
> *More rich by giving, taking by discarding:*
> *Love's life's reward, rewarded in rewarding;*
> *Then from thy wretched heart fond care remove:*
> *Ah, should thou live but once love's sweets to prove,*
> *Thou wilt not love to live unless thou live to love.*

> *Anon: (from Brittain's Ida 1628)*

'Thou wilt not love to live unless thou live to love ... ' Could this be the equivalent of a suicide note? Tucked in here by the grieving relatives after finding it, perhaps, on the offending table? Quickly we checked out where the verse came from – an epic of innumerable stanzas that had once been attributed to Spencer.

My friends came up with all sorts of suggestions. "Perhaps her fiancé had been killed." It seemed obvious.

"But stiff upper lip was the order of the day. Dead fiancés must have been two-a-penny. Equivalent numbers of girls didn't kill themselves. It just didn't happen."

No, not in general, but maybe here or there, I wondered silently.

"Perhaps she was in love with a German," suggested someone. That sounded plausible, a good reason to keep returning to Cassel.

"Perhaps he died in the Somme? It wasn't just our side that got killed."

But could Beth really have been using the typewritten sheet as a suicide note? Suddenly we realised that it was just as likely to be the crib copy of the greeting she inscribed in other people's autograph books. Timidly, we laughed, pretending the ghoulish moment had been dispelled – we needed it to go. I tried to imagine Beth looking down at us from heaven, laughing at our silly ignorance.

But then somebody remembered the strange coincidence of timing, of how Beth's death matched so peculiarly with Isabella's signing up with the Army and our laughter stopped.

It was time to reach a verdict, and one by one the decisions came. Suicide, suicide, suicide … Every single one of them voted that it was suicide – except me. I still could not decide. I could not get away from the fact that accidents are more likely when somebody is stressed, and the combination of the battle in France and Isabella leaving for Malta would have been very stressful. Surely it could have been an accident – couldn't it?

Would some background information about the suicide of women during the First World War help? I found almost none. Although some laws had been relaxed – for example burial on church property was now allowed – suicide was still both illegal and taboo. Most families chose to conceal 'self-murder', which makes the few available statistics so unreliable as to be almost worthless.

People of the day, like my friends, believed it was the lovelorn who were likely to kill themselves – the lovelorn, or the mad, or the financially ruined. But the academics dispute whether the facts support this belief. They suspect that a high proportion of recorded suicides were suffering from either physical or mental ill-health, exactly as is found to be the case among twenty-first-century suicides.

My imagination went wild. Could Beth have been suffering from some form of mental illness – something unmentionable, misunderstood and utterly taboo? I began to pull together shreds of 'evidence': Ena stopping working at St Leonard's exactly as Isabella left for France, yet going overseas the moment her older sister returned; the strange timing of Beth's death. Could something about Isabella doing her patriotic duty have made Beth crack?

I reined myself in. There was not enough evidence to support that conclusion. If Beth was not laughing at my ridiculous fantasies from her cloud in heaven, she should be angry, "The injustice of it! Your fantasies bear no relationship to the truth. That window was rotten and I fell to my death. I only wish I had not."

The literature explains how, after any unexpected death, adrenaline keeps survivors going for the first few days. They do not think or react, they just do what needs to be done – the numbness helps them cope. But afterwards, the whole, horrendous affair kicks back, details of the dreadful event looping incessantly through their minds in tandem with the endless struggle to grasp the reality of what has happened.

Often, I discover, the families of suicides have known there was a risk. They have been aware that it might happen. It is only a year since Isabella kept suicide watch for Mrs D-W. If Beth had been ill, maybe the Stenhouses had been watching her. Alternatively, maybe they had known that the window was unsafe, had known that a carpenter should be called, had known that their mother was finding it hard to care for the house with Father gone. Could negligence have led to Beth's death?

Whatever the reason, gossip was inevitable. From the moment Beth began to fall, even while Dr Elder was signing the death certificate, the Stenhouses must have realised they would have to provide answers. The little details about the table and the assurance of Miss Bethia's cheerful disposition may have served to fend off the newspaperman and his prying questions, but a mere assertion that Beth had been cheerful was far too blatant. Something much more subtle would be needed to scotch the rumours.

Sure enough, the version of Beth's death which has emerged as family tradition is different from the account in the *Leith Observer*. It leaves out the table. It brings in the rotten window. How did that happen? Perhaps it was the carpenter employed to repair the damage who commented that the frame was rotten. Perhaps his news confirmed that Beth's death was the tragic accident Isabella and her mother had feared it was not. But perhaps they were fully aware that no rotten wood had caused Beth's death and grabbed the carpenter's tale. It gave them exactly the red herring they needed, the socially accept-able story that allowed them to disguise Beth's scandalous deed and maintain respectability.

Nobody will ever know. Yet a scholarly book on modern-day suicide and its aftermath contains a whole section on the widespread phenomenon of the development of family secrets amongst the relatives of suicide survivors. There is no doubt that Beth's death was awkward. It stood in hideous contrast to the daily loss of thousands of heroic and valiant young men on the various Fronts. Whatever its 'truth', the tale of the rotten window meant that the Stenhouses no longer had to fight the whispers that Beth had been deranged, or lovelorn, or – speak softly – suicidal. It gave them an honourable small corner in which to grieve, a corner beneath the shadow of the war heroes in which they could come to terms with their loss.

And of course maybe, just maybe, even Isabella and her family did not know the truth. Perhaps as Janet donned her black dress and Isabella made arrangements for the funeral, they too were puzzling as to whether Beth had fallen by acci-dent or thrown herself out. And uncertainty breeds questions which preoccupy the mind. With the Maltese sun warming me and the Maltese breeze cooling me, I imagine those questions following Isabella and her mother to this very beach, teasing them and taunting them hundreds of miles from home.

10

Crashing into this chaos comes the order for Isabella to 'embark for active service'. She must board the hospital ship HMHS *Gloucester Castle* at Southampton on 12th August.

"What about Mother?"

"We can't let her stay here."

"Everything reminds her of Beth."

"The gossip will never stop."

"But where can she go?"

Somehow, Janet will end up here in Malta, her witch-black garb so potent it has coaxed Isabella's innocuously anonymous photographs back to life, exposing the grief that now stains the warp of my grandmother's tale.

Stiff with story, I stand to ease my aches. I must get to Valletta – Isabella is about to arrive. Yet once stationed on the heights of Upper Barracca, mammoth cruise ships control my view, dwarfing history with their white height and blaring horns. Determinedly, I replace them with a mass of much smaller, older vessels and notch the temperature up a considerable number of degrees. I am here in October, but courtesy of the diary of an RAMC orderly, Private Arthur Lumley Morgan, I know that at 9 a.m. on 20th August 1916, only a day short of three weeks after Beth's death, Isabella is waiting on board the HMHS *Gloucester Castle* just outside Grand Harbour. The dreadnought HMS *Agamemnon* travels rapidly past the ship, then a destroyer. Gunboats and cruisers buzz all around, and Isabella and her colleagues are fanning themselves as the temperature rises still further.

Before the war, the liner S.S. *Gloucester Castle* ran between Cape Town and Britain, but when she was requisitioned for hospital duties, she was re-painted and her cargo and her route were changed. I think back to Southampton, eight days ago …

The casualties have been discharged from the iron cots on the stuffy wards below deck, and the *Gloucester Castle's* staff of RAMC officers are preparing to meet their new travelling companions. Well-practised, they direct smartly marching Private Morgan and his fellow RAMC orderlies to their quarters and their tasks. Then they turn to watch the lady doctors straggle up the gang-plank, a motley collection of bags and suitcases in their hands. The officers have become used to VADs and nurses, but these women are different. To start with, they are not uniformed. True, some appear to have cobbled together something that they must believe looks like uniform, but it is most assuredly not RAMC uniform. It lacks badges. It lacks rank. It is unofficial and it will deceive nobody. Other women have made no attempt. They wear full-blown mufti. As the doctors near the top of the gang-plank, the men's military eyes narrow a tiny fraction. Polite greetings will have to be offered – but what form of polite greeting? These women hold no rank. Where do they fit? Have there been orders? These gals are a puzzle.

Graciously accepting whatever welcome their male colleagues decide to offer, Isabella and her companions navigate the ship's narrow passageways to their cabins. They are not 'gals'. They are not timid and inexperienced VADs. They are not battle-hardened nurses used to obeying orders. They are strong-willed professionals accustomed to standing their ground, and today their mood is especially triumphant. They are marching, invited, right into the Army's yielding, but hitherto sacrosanct, male bastions.

On journeys to the Mediterranean, I read that VADs suffer inoculations, lectures, bandage rolling and extreme measures designed to keep them away from male company. Orderlies such as Private Morgan are tasked with light duties and offered singsongs. But what about the medical women? Lifeboat drill, mealtime discussions, complaints about the dearth of news? Unlike VADs, they are not barred from male company. They may mix as freely as they like with whoever they like, but I suspect their focus is elsewhere. They owe it to themselves and to womankind, let alone to the soldiers of their country, to make sure this experiment the Army is conducting works well.

Have the RAMC officers been detailed to lecture them about the situation in Malta? About the army? About military medicine? After all, these women have had no training. Or do the women themselves demand information? Either way, I can see a blackboard set up in some lounge or dining room, the officer beside it peering uneasily at the phalanx of medical ladies before him from the security of his khaki and badges.

"At the outset of the campaign in the Dardanelles, there was no thought that Malta would be required to play any role in the fight," he begins, "however at a very early stage in the offensive an appeal for help was received from Egypt, where the hospitals were finding themselves unable to keep pace with the flow of casualties. The new Governor of Malta, Lord Methuen, showed his customary foresight in promptly implementing a far greater expansion of medical provision than necessitated by the initial request. The excellent work of the Royal Engineers and the Maltese resulted in a rapid expansion of the Army's existing facilities. Their task was greatly assisted by the presence of useful materials in the cargo of prize ships captured by the Royal Navy. As the campaign continued and the flow of casualties grew ever larger, other suitable buildings were also transformed into well-equipped, modern military hospitals, some tented.

"By the end of the year, the original 500 hospital beds had grown to more than 20,000 and hundreds of staff had been shipped in – VADs, orderlies, nurses, medical officers and consultants. More than 2,500 officers and over 55,000 rank and file had received treatment. However on the withdrawal from the Dardenelles in December, many of these beds became redundant, so the whole expansion was partially reversed. The number of medical officers was reduced from 334 to 140, but 12,000 beds were retained in readiness for future emergencies."

The lecturer interrupts his speech to indicate the map on the blackboard. "Valletta Hospital receives the most serious cases because of its proximity to the harbour," he begins. Gradually he makes his way round every hospital and convalescent camp on the island in minute detail, itemising bed numbers, facilities and the types of cases which they receive. "Imtarfa, being inland and on raised ground, serves as an isolation hospital … Floriana is low-lying … Tigne' is … St George's … St Patrick's … Hamrun … Spinola … " Do Isabella's ears prick up when he reaches St Ignatius? Does she yet know where she will be working, or is she having to absorb and digest a mass of impersonal information?

The officer continues, "An outbreak of malaria in Salonika is proving the wisdom of having retained such a large number of beds. In the first week of last month, 718 men arrived in Malta; in the second, almost 2,000, and over 2,500 were sent over in each of the last two weeks of the month ... "

Quickly the women calculate. Over 7,000 patients arriving in July means that already at least 7,000 of the 12,000 beds are full. The lecturer corrects them.

"On 3rd August 13,000 beds were occupied. Many of the patients with infectious diseases require prolonged hospitalisation. Last year's expansion in bed numbers is therefore being repeated."

Assuring them that inoculation and preventive measures are keeping many of the diseases of the enteric group at bay, he warns them to expect the trench fever and rheumatism that result from all campaigning. "However the wounds in general are not overly severe," he informs them, "nothing like those we saw during last year's campaign. The base hospitals behind the front line in Salonika are well-equipped and treat the men before they come to Malta. Some are sent over only to free up beds on the mainland."

Courtesy of Colonel Walter Bonnici, L/RAMC, the webmaster of www.maltaramc.com, I know exactly which women are travelling with Isabella, bracing themselves for the hectic pace, for patients who are more likely to be sick than wounded. At 29, Isabella is the second youngest, the fourth most recently qualified, and one of five who have already served at one Front or another. The eleven 'war-virgins', their ages ranging from 27 to 53, have been working mainly with women and children, or in asylums, or with the mentally ill, or in sanatoria … in other words they have years of experience in fields that bear no relation to the skills they will need in Malta.

"But the five who have already been out all had to adapt and learn – now it is our turn."

"And we'll do just as well as they have!"

In their determination to be ready for absolutely anything and everything, and in line with Anaesthetist Danielle's information that many of the advances in medical treatment that took place during WWI were passed on by word of mouth, I can see them gathering over tea in some floating lounge …

Elizabeth Moffett is 50 years old, has been a member of the Association of Registered Medical Women for many years and has worked with some of the most eminent women doctors. An active suffragist, like Grace Cadell she once refused to pay her house tax in the full knowledge that bailiffs would commandeer her property. This morning she is perhaps musing as she watches young Katherine Waring offering her opinions on the other side of the room, "Thirty one, but only recently qualified – one certainly needs grit to enter this profession!" Turning her attention to a quiet young woman who has stationed herself near the exit, she hesitates, "That Louise Fraser's a different kettle of fish. Been qualified six years and still far and away the youngest of us. It's really most peculiar that she's never been out to the war before – most of the younger lot seem to have taken themselves out one way or another. They've nothing to hold them back – no practices, no families." Her eyes seek yet another young face, "Look at Martha Stewart – getting herself off to Serbia the moment she passed her finals and running a whole surgery out there! How old must she be? Early thirties?" She thinks back twenty years, to when she herself was newly qualified, "I'd have done it myself at her age, but thank the Lord I've got my chance now."

Beside her, Edith Martin may be looking at the group through different eyes. A member of the Medico-Psychological Association of Great Britain and Ireland, she is hoping to improve the mental welfare of the casualties, but this lot make an interesting study en route. There are plenty of Scots, several Irish, a few English, one who hails from India and a New Zealander, Ada McClaren. Ada has told them a good many hair-raising tales – how she turned to surgery in response to the needs of the Serbs after working in bacteriology since she graduated; how she was taken prisoner and held for two long, cold, winter months in Serbia. "If she can adapt from one discipline to another then come back for more after that spell in a foreign gaol, good for her! She's testimony to the hidden strengths we'll all discover."

On the other side of the room, the oldest woman amongst them, 53-year-old Elizabeth Gilchrist, is perhaps somewhat bemused. At Christmas time she had firmly told the compilers of the Scottish Index that she was available only for part-time civil work at home – she had had no thought of any military service, let alone of going overseas. Yet here she is, apparently as willing and able as all these younger folk. Shaking her head at herself, she pays close attention to the discussion.

It is lively. Like Ada, Florence Bignold and Georgina David-son talk of their experiences in Serbia. Cases are cited, sug-gestions made. Georgina speaks with the additional authority of having worked in France as well as the Balkans. From Elsie Layman, Constance Astley Meer, Nora Williams, Eleanor Gor-rie, Mary Murray and Mabel Hector – indeed, from every sin-gle woman amongst them – the questions come fast, fierce and penetrating.

But what about Dr Stenhouse? Is she chipping in vigorously with tales from the Anglo-Ethiopian? Are her answers spot on, just the ticket? Her mother is not travelling with her, and without that mourning dress to trumpet the family's grief, her travelling companions know only as much about Beth's death as Isabella has chosen to tell them. Perhaps here amongst her colleagues, her unique grief is making her even more intent on proving that she is as bang up to the mark as the next woman. But afterwards, gazing out at sea from this temporary, *Glouces-ter Castle* world, does she wonder whether she imagined the dreadful events of the past few weeks, or if it is this all-engulf-ing present that is imaginary, with these single-minded women and the total dearth of news from the Front? In her cabin at night, does she wake with a start, utterly confused as to where reality lies? Does she join the other women, the officers and nurses for the concert that Private Morgan reports as taking place on 17th August, five days into the journey? Music is so potent, and with adrenaline still pumping from the sadness and stress of all that has just happened, tears would be quite reasonable, if Isabella would allow them.

Since they passed Gibraltar, each day has been hotter than the last. From precious pools of shade, the women have observed the coast of first Algeria and then Tunisia. To the north, Sardinia has slipped past. This morning when they awoke, Malta was in sight. Now they can see Valletta itself.

Their pilot climbs aboard and guides HMHS *Gloucester Castle* through the harbour mouth and past the golden walls of Ricasoli, St Angelo, St Barbara, Barrakka, St Michael's – new names that mean nothing to the women doctors, yet. A troop ship en route from Egypt to Marseilles follows them into harbour, its decks thronged with cheerful Tommies doomed for the fateful assault in the Somme. Beneath them, the sea is teeming with a mass of small, brightly-painted wooden boats, dghaisas, their Maltese helmsmen shouting and gesticulating wildly to one another as they steer their various cargoes from place to place. As soon as the *Gloucester Castle* has docked and officialdom has done its work, the women have to clamber down into one of these cockles. Sheltered from the sun by its canopy, they are carried across the swell to the wharf, where a wartime hum of organised compassion greets them.

Barges are landing sick and wounded soldiers from another hospital ship. RAMC staff are shepherding the men efficiently into waiting ambulances. Red Cross ladies are stepping into dghaisas, bearing gifts for the Blighty-bound men who lie sweltering in the cots on board the ship. From across the harbour comes the clang and boom of the dockyards, where wrecks salvaged from enemy attack are being prepared to fight again.

The officers detailed to meet Isabella and her fellow doctors usher them to their various transports and they bid one another farewell. They have discussed their contracts, the vexed question of what to wear and every medical matter they can dream up until they are blue in the face. It is now that their test will really begin.

SECTION 6

1

At the top of a side street on the far side of Sliema, Joe meets me. Wasting no time, he opens a rusty gate labelled 'St Ignatius Villa' and gestures for me to go through. I hesitate. Surely this is trespassing? But he urges me in and soon I go quiet. Without his gall, I would have missed this. Thanks to him, I am standing in the very spot where Isabella's photographs were taken – the courtyard at St Ignatius.

I struggle to take it in. It is still. It is peaceful. The whole way this quest is working out is almost awe-inspiring. Here I am, standing in yet another of the places where Isabella worked during the First World War. When I began this search, I never dreamt I would get this far. My luck has been incredible – an enthusiastic archivist, an unexpected book, another woman's diary, a useful website, the friend of a neighbour.

After a few stunned minutes, I wade into the knee-high grass to try and reproduce the old photograph. Peering through the viewfinder, I move a little sideways, step a little backwards, stumble into concealed holes. I zoom in and out, but a new wall is cutting off the space and my lens is clearly not the same focal length as the one the other photographer used so many years ago. There is no way I can get an exact match. Perhaps that is a metaphor for the tale I am threading – I can get so far, but absolute accuracy is always one step further – a different lens, a wall knocked down, another document …

Joe is pointing up at the balcony, "The balustrade in the photograph is the same as that one there, but the stone is soft.

Carved objects, like those urn shapes, weather quickly, which is why many of them have been replaced."

True, the whole building is gently crumbling, but the colours are astonishing. Doors blaze blue, yellow and brown. Magenta flowers bloom on evergreen shrubs. Golden stones blush with a long-gone red wash. Fleetingly, I wonder what colour the place was when Isabella worked here. In theory, I can compensate for the fact that the world she inhabits is as colourful as mine, but only in theory. Usually I think of her embalmed in sepia. Today though, the colour is electrifyingly alive.

I lay my hand on the tall grey-brown stump of the very tree under which she sheltered. I climb the flight of honey-coloured steps where she sat, and lean on the green railings that stood above her.

"What about the Italian terraces stretching down to the sea that Isabella so loved?" I ask, gesturing at the concrete apartment blocks in front of me.

Joe turns to look, "Everything between here and the sea has been built since the First World War. When Isabella was here, the gardens really would have stretched right down to the bay at Balluta."

From here, then, Isabella can pause to let the blue sky and azure sea wash away the dirty white and coagulated red of the wards. Then she can descend into the green shade of the Jesuits' terraces. I scowl at the pernicious constructions before me. Isabella's favourite spot must be somewhere beneath them, her magnolia tree perhaps itching to burst through its twentieth-century concrete tomb.

Far too soon, Joe calls me to leave. He shepherds me round to the front of the building, "When Isabella came here," he gestures, "St Ignatius was on its own, surrounded by fields." Suddenly, I can see it. To me, St Ignatius is a small oasis of antiquity dwarfed by taller, newer buildings, but for Isabella, it is the other way round. St Ignatius is the local landmark at the top of the hill. Around it lie small fields bordered by dry stone walls where lizards dart. With grass-hoppers humming and prickly pears tumbling, she has arrived in a place geographic worlds away from Edinburgh and the Western Front.

A call on Joe's mobile catapults him back to work, so I am alone as I cross the neatly paved front garden and approach St Ignatius' green front door. *Brigitte Gauci Borda School of Ballet* announces its ultra-modern fanlight graphic. Brigitte herself welcomes me inside, and disappointment grips me. The outside was magnificent, but this? This is not the hall that Isabella entered. It has false ceilings, uplighters and glass doors. Does anything old remain? Grudgingly, I concede that one door is an original. But that is almost the only trace.

Brigitte leads me round. There are dance studios with sprung floors, mirrored walls, spot lights and barres. Everything is flawless and new, and from my war-engrossed perspective it feels almost sacrilegious that youngsters should be dancing here, on the very spot where the ambitions of other young people came to a halt – young men who had assumed, just as Brigitte's students do, that their ability to run, and stretch, and jump and bend would last forever – but were brought up short. Sensing my disappointment, Brigitte picks up the phone. She arranges for me to visit her friend, Mrs Formosa, in an apartment at the back of the building. I cross the courtyard again, but this time I pause to dip back to the time when Isabella first sees this place …

St Ignatius is busier than it has ever been, busier, they say, even than last year when the casualties from Gallipoli were flooding in. There is no question about whether the staff want women doctors. They are so fully stretched that they welcome them with open arms. Urgently, Isabella buries the memory of Beth's death as thoroughly as Beth's poor body is buried somewhere in the Scottish earth. Wholeheartedly, she plunges into her duties. It is the only thing to do. It is part of doing one's bit, part of carrying on the weary, dreadful task of beating the Germans. But I can see her glimpsing the garden as she passes from one vital task to the next, promising herself that one day she will make time to explore, sometime this chaos will calm, a moment will come …

Fast-forwarding, I imagine the preparations for the staff photograph, a huge camera standing exactly where I snapped my replica – this is evidently going to be a high quality picture. The Regimental Sergeant Major is in complete command. Eight chairs are set out for Matron and the senior staff. The NCOs and orderlies are commanded to their places. The drivers, clerks, cooks, soldiers who tend horses and men from ordnance units follow on. Forty-eight of them, jostling one another in their efforts to squeeze into the positions that protocol demands – this space is nothing like as large as the photograph will make it look. Six VADs find themselves arranged on the ground at the front, their legs tucked modestly and symmetrically beneath their skirts.

Now it is Isabella's turn. She is being instructed to stand behind Matron's chair, so I walk towards the same spot. Feeling more than a little awed, I plant my feet exactly where Isabella planted hers. A slight, Maltese man slides in to my left. Beyond him, a second woman doctor takes her place. A shy staff nurse creeps in to my right, her head bowed. Matron, two more doctors and a quartet of nurses take their seats on the chairs in front of us.

By the standards of Maltese military hospitals, St Ignatius is small, but it is still three times larger than the Anglo-Ethiopian at its height, and it has far greater resources at its disposal. For a start, it has a reliable supply of electricity for its X-ray machine, and blood, sputum, faeces and other material can be sent for analysis in Valletta. On top of that, eminent medical men have been brought over from Britain – surgeons, physicians, bacteriologists, public health officers, anaesthetists, ophthalmologists, dermatologists, otologists, specialists in mental diseases and radiologists. Twice a week, they visit every hospital on the island. Isabella and her five colleagues have a duty to inform them by telephone about every serious case, and to consult them before any major operation. Regular case conferences are held at the university at which all the doctors working with the RAMC are able to learn from one another's experience. The army is genuinely trying to provide the best for its sick and wounded.

In front of me, the breeze is lifting the white headgear of the nurses. Men in khaki are shifting restlessly behind me, but they still obey every order they receive. There should be no Triqueneaux-style bickering and squabbling here. Everybody knows his or her own place, and each cap, jacket, cape, badge, button, stripe and belt declares to the world exactly where its owner fits within the great army machine – which group its wearer belongs to, his or her role, his or her seniority. I glance at the Maltese man beside me. Just by looking at the photograph, Colonel Walter has identified that he is a civil surgeon temporarily commissioned into the RAMC. The black tabs on his collar and the fact that he is not wearing a Sam Browne belt indicate that he is working under the auspices of the joint committee of the British Red Cross and the Order of St John.

The Regimental Sergeant Major is strutting around making final arrangements, his badges glinting in the sun. These men and women are proud of their uniforms. Casualties, I read, hate being forced out of khaki into hospital blue. "You are no longer a soldier," their new clothes seem to shout, "You belong to an inferior breed." Some patients go to great lengths to borrow khaki from orderlies before going out, despite the fact that their blues would buy them free tickets in the local concert halls and cinemas. Even borrowed khaki makes them feel they belong again, that they are still part of the team. Yet amidst all this identification, hierarchy and order, one thing sticks out a mile. Isabella and the other woman doctor are the only ones here who are not wearing uniform.

Isabella is light and airy in a pale suit and a V-necked blouse. She has even pinned some 'badges' to her lapels, but whatever they represent, they are not RAMC badges. The other woman has enveloped herself in a huge coat with acres of lapel over a loose necked shirt and tie. In a world where uniform tells all and countless ladies in a pot pourri of different garments visit the wards on all sorts of errands, what happens when Isabella and her colleague walk onto the wards?

The contracts the women doctors have signed with the Army are not the same as those signed by volunteering male doctors. In 1898, when the RAMC was inaugurated, the experience of previous wars was taken into account. The Army recognised that volunteering doctors could not function properly unless they received temporary commissions and were granted all the privileges of being full members of the Corps. It had no idea that the assistance of lady doctors might ever be required, and now that this brutal war has forced its hand, the Army has been cautious. "No point in making the risk any greater, eh what?" Different contracts have been drawn up. Unlike the men, the women have not been permitted to become members of the RAMC – they are only being allowed to serve 'with' his Majesty's forces.

When Colonel Walter had examined Isabella's contract, he had commented, "Its terms and conditions are rather harsh – look at Clause 5."

In case I shall in any manner misconduct myself, or shall be (otherwise than through illness or unavoidable accident) unfit in any respect for service hereunder, of which misconduct or unfitness you or your authorised representative shall

be the sole judge, you shall be at liberty from and imme-
diately after such misconduct or unfitness to discharge me
from further service hereunder, and thereupon all pay and
allowances hereunder shall cease, and I shall not be entitled
to any free passage home or gratuity.

I had wondered whether this could be a discrete and 'profes-sional' way of treating the women with the same distrust that the VADs are treated, a covert way of saying, "Don't, under any circumstances, get pregnant. If you do, you're on your own."

But Walter had warned me that it was much worse than that, "The contract is very one sided with no right of an appeal. Just imagine being on duty in Iraq or Mesopotamia and ending up stranded because of an adverse report by some colonel or other."

That is not the only problem. What the contract leaves out is just as serious. Isabella and her fellows have not only been given no right to the ration allowances and quarters provided for all volunteering male doctors, they have also had to agree to work 'without rank and without the right to wear uniform or RAMC badges' – the very constraints which the army had long ago accepted were impossible for the men. It is, I read, only the nation's dire need that has led the women to accept such unreasonable terms.

My thoughts are interrupted from beside the camera. The Reg-imental Sergeant Major is signalling his satisfaction. There is a shuffling and a straightening as the officer commanding takes his seat. I try to catch echoes of restrained humour, of barked orders and the deep silence as the army photographer does his work, but as quickly as the assembling and arranging was slow, the group is dismissed and disperses, leaving another piece of Isabella's archive woven satisfactorily to her timeline.

2

Walking to the corner of the courtyard, I ring the bell, and for the second time, a door into St Ignatius opens before me. Mrs Formosa leads me up the wide, stone staircase and into her kitchen – or rather, into the stone-walled, high-ceilinged room in which her cooker, sink and cupboards have been deposited – and relief fills me. This is Isabella's world. The room's ancient walls and stone floor demand something much more imposing than this hospitable Maltese lady pouring lemonade from a plastic bottle.

"The building was converted into apartments after the Second World War," she tells me. "That is when my neighbour moved in. She always said how puzzled she was to find bed numbers painted on the wall."

Bed numbers painted on the wall? This is too good to be true!

"Excuse me, did you say bed numbers?"

"Yes, in my neighbour's apartment."

My sense that this home is perching in history soars. Why, this is a genuine living memory, on site, of the time when Isabella worked here! It is not six degrees of separation – it is touching distance!

I look round the room. Were bed numbers painted on these walls? Could this have been a ward? I hesitate. With its only windows high up on one side and no verandah, I am not convinced. Where would the patients get the supply of healthy fresh air that the British so love? The hospital needs plenty of other, specialist rooms. Could this have been an operating theatre, perhaps even the place where Isabella makes her first foray into surgery since her training days in the dissecting room? I let the room transform. The plastic table cloth becomes a linen sheet draped over an operating table. The chair beside me becomes a glass topped table laden with surgical instruments. Opposite me another chair turns into a stand for enamel bowls. Pristine and empty, they stand ready to receive whatever noxious materials the operation will produce.

My eyes begin to water with the hospital-clean smell. The decontamination never stops. Every morning the orderlies damp-dust the whole theatre with disinfectant. After every operation they scrub it down. The fear of infection drives them all. The dreadful, infected wounds they have seen in the last couple of years have made everybody very, very cautious – not a microbe can be allowed to escape. But sterility is not easily achieved. I banish the kitchen cupboards and set up an autoclave for sterilising the dressings and gauzes. I fill vats with antiseptic solutions for the sharp instruments, and set water to boil for the blunt tools. It gets noisier. It gets hotter. In fact, it is soon very hot.

Isabella is gowning up. First she envelopes her hair in a cap. Then she swaddles herself from shoulders to toes in a thick, linen, surgical gown and slips on cuff-covering armlets. Placing a mask ready to raise over her mouth and nose, she scrubs up. A nurse ties her rubber apron at the back and helps her slide on two sterile rubber gloves. It is far too much for comfort in this heat, but it must be done.

The door opens, and orderlies bring in the patient. These men who have been fighting in Salonika are suffering not only from war-wounds, but from ruptured appendices, hernias, haemorrhoids, cancers – all the general wear and tear of living. Not only that, the infectious diseases of the area sometimes produce complications that require surgery – amoebic liver abscesses, for example, or perforations of the intestine.

Last night the orderlies shaved and sterilised the relevant patch of this patient's skin. Even such a simple procedure requires greater care in this climate. Each surgeon has his own preferred method of sterilising the hot, moist skin and dealing with the almost inevitable infected insect bites that dot the site where the operation will take place. It is part of the medical profession's restless eagerness to do everything better than last year, last month. Constantly, the doctors compare notes with one another. They publish articles in journals, pass on tips by word of mouth and try out ideas picked up at the conferences in the university.

Today, as they arrange the man on the table, he is awake, and clearly terrified. It is time for the mask. The surgeon has requested not the Schimmelbusch with which Isabella trained, but the new Shipway apparatus. One thing the war has revealed is that these hotter climates change the way the patients react to anaesthetics. Many of the surgeons out here in the Mediterranean are choosing to use ether rather than chloroform. The Shipway is a clever new device that allows a warmed mixture of the two anaesthetics to be given simultaneously. Not only does it help to get the men to sleep more easily, but there seem to be fewer complications with their recovery.

Now, however, the patient is flailing wildly, fighting the mask as the ether releases the suppressed horrors of the battlefield from his sub-conscious. Several of the staff pin him down. It often takes a large volume of anaesthetic to help these fit young men slip into sleep. I install some extra shelves and load them with a generous supply of brown glass bottles, brimful of anaesthetic – anything to make life easier for these traumatised men.

Standing opposite the senior surgeon, Isabella reaches for the instrument she needs. I look carefully. Is it one that has been lying in the Flower Press box all these years? A few months ago Lieutenant Colonel David Jones, L/RAMC, looked through Isabella's equipment. Unlike the historian in Edinburgh, he was confident about the silvery kit engraved with Isabella's name, "This is standard Army issue," he had declared. St Ignatius being Isabella's first appointment, perhaps today is its first outing. Her eyes are the only visible part of her face, so I watch them carefully as she co-operates with her senior, moving the implement towards the incision. Slowly, the muscles round her eyes relax, her frown creases into tiny smile lines – her fingers are remembering exactly what to do.

But this heat is new. Apart from anything else, it encourages flies. It is not long before an insect is buzzing around them, a little bundle of lethal infection. She cannot brush it away – that would contaminate her gloves. She raises an eyebrow to the orderly assigned to swatting duties. Flies are a problem beyond discipline, and everybody is trying their hardest to come up with solutions. She has been told that grilles and fly-screens are ineffective and ingenuity is required. In some hospitals, they swear by dishes of formalin which supposedly tempt the flies to drink themselves to a well-deserved and hopefully agonising death. Well-practised, the orderly wafts the fly away and the operation proceeds.

Letting the operating theatre morph back into a kitchen, I recover with a sip of lemonade. Beside me, one of Mrs Formosa's teenage sons is staring at the photograph of his courtyard full of soldiers. He is conjuring uniformed men and women back into his flat – orders fly about, ambulances arrive, salutes are exchanged, leather boots clatter, the smell of ailing men and disinfectant fills the place. Looking over his shoulder, it is as if I suddenly see the image for the first time. I have never noticed how weary these people look. Their eyes are gritted in a sort of grim determination, as if they are forcing themselves to carry on regardless of the nightmare visions they have already faced, regardless of the helplessness of so many of the cases they receive. Now I see the whole picture differently. These are sixty-seven exhausted minds busily censoring what they will dare to remember. They have been at it for two years – nothing will break them now. On the contrary, I have read how the more they see of suffering, the more it troubles them, and the more determined and skilful they become at relieving it.

I drain my lemonade. Mrs Formosa is keen to show me the rest of the flat. First comes a massive display of Lego boxes. Upright against the wall of her son's room, hi-tech images of battle and military advance parade across the stones. The irony of it almost hurts – the previous inhabitants of this room were victims of 'progress' in those very fields! But I cannot stop, Mrs Formosa is leading me along a short corridor. In no time I am standing on the very balcony that features in Isabella's photograph. Magic!

Of course, I cannot see the sea as Isabella can, but I can conjure patients in hospital blue strolling across the courtyard below to the recreation room for a game of billiards, or carrying a book back from the library, or seeking a shady seat where they can write, or joking over a game of cards. I can see nurses supporting men on crutches, orderlies wheeling the fever-weakened out to take the air. The courtyard is a flurry of boy scouts, Red Cross ladies, and well-meaning visitors – all sorts of people eager that these young men return to energetic health without falling into temptation.

I focus on a chaplain talking earnestly to a patient. "Every afternoon … tea … " It is hard to catch all he says, but I get the gist. He wants the young man to go to the Church Army tent on the shore. By the look on the patient's face, I am not sure that he is tempted. The Church Army is not his only option. There are cinemas and theatres and a whole host of other treats designed for the recovering soldier. In Sliema, Mrs Bonavia runs a tea room. The Red Cross have a club. The YMCA organise something similar. The young man is beckoning to some pals. Perhaps he will reject all the offers of tea and instead they will try to persuade Isabella or whoever is in charge of their care to let them go into Valletta.

I have to leave them; Mrs Formosa is leading me inside through the very french door that I have looked at so many times in the photograph. Slowly, my eyes adapt from the sunshine and I decode the television, the well-used sofas, the box of tissues. Then the television fades to reveal the bed numbers on the wall behind. Slowly, beds appear, beds that I know from my reading have scratchy blankets and sheets worn muslin-thin.

Men are lying in them on mattresses squashed hard and lumpy with overuse, but however hard I peer, I cannot see any of the contraptions old photographs show in surgical wards – cumbersome wooden splints busily straightening fractured limbs, glass vessels dangling red rubber tubes that carry cleansing fluids to infected wounds. The smell starts to hit me. It is not anaesthetic this time. Nor is it disinfectant. It is more like – what? Coarse cigarettes mixed with something noxious? It is making me wince. It is so thick, so dirty. This is not a healing atmosphere at all. No wonder they like to open the windows and draw in as much fresh air as possible. I look again at the men. Could this be the stench of fever? Could these be sick men, huddled in their beds?

Isabella may be a surgeon, and the literature may describe St Ignatius as a surgical hospital, but only about a quarter of the patients arriving here this summer are surgical cases. Malaria is endemic in the areas the troops have been endeavouring to secure, and other sicknesses are rife. At the moment such large numbers of men are falling sick, and they are taking so long to recover, that disease is proving a bigger threat to the efficiency of the army than wounds. This month an extra 41 beds will be squeezed between the 155 that already pack these wards. It is not just here – all round the island, beds are being added to existing hospitals and hospitals which were shut down only a few months ago are being re-opened. Isabella's lecturer may have informed the lady doctors that there were 13,000 patients in Malta on 3rd August but, by the beginning of September, there will be 14,000, and the numbers are set to rise all through the autumn.

They are so busy that no hospital can be staffed as fully as the Army requires. And since no wound or ruptured appendix will stop malarial parasites or other nasties from infecting a man, Isabella, too, is having to cooperate in fighting the infections that keep the men in their beds week after week, grey and feeble. Many a time operations have to be postponed until a feverish episode subsides. Almost routinely, a course of quinine is prescribed to reduce the chances of malaria preventing an operation from being carried out. Not only that, malarious patients need particularly careful post-operative care – the doctors are observing frequent flare-ups of the condition in the first few days after their operations. Can I see Isabella standing at the foot of the bed of one of these fevered men? Examining him? Discussing the complex differential diagnoses of his condition?

Music is crackling up above the hubbub of the ward. Ah, there is the gramophone with its huge horn, but I do not recognise the tune – then I see. Mrs Formosa's son is wielding the television remote. The space-age theme tune of his programme is filling the room. Wrenching myself towards the future, I find my hostess insisting that I come downstairs to meet her neighbour.

Auntie Rosa's lounge is much larger than Mrs Formosa's. The shuttered French doors make it dark – keeping out the summer heat, they tell me, is a higher priority for the Maltese than letting in the light. She threads me past huge chairs, small tables, knick-knacks, lamps and mementoes to some photographs in a corner. Peering, I make out St Ignatius, taken from far below.

Even in this light, I can see that the building is much darker than its present honey-pale – perhaps it is the red that I noticed when I was with Joe. When was the photograph taken? Auntie Rosa does not know – she picked it up from a magazine.

As we came downstairs, I made up my mind to rein in my imagination while I visited this apartment and to stick rigidly to the facts, but being 'accurate' is proving hard. What are the facts? I have been picturing Isabella working in a honey-coloured place, but did she? A trivial question, but as I stare at Auntie Rosa's photograph, it crystallises the truth that the amount I can never know is far greater than the amount I will ever find out. There will be other 'facts' that, if known, would completely change the thread of Isabella's story – the whole business of being accurate is proving much trickier than I thought. I could simply say, "St Ignatius was converted into a hospital last year, 1915," but those words are barren. They give no sense of how British officers must have paced this room, their boots kicking up the dust of years as they decided whether it should be a forty-bed ward filled with fresh air from the courtyard or a recreation room with a billiard table, a piano and newspapers. What is historical accuracy? How is the truest tale told?

Auntie Rosa is sitting herself wearily down. Can she tell me anything about the hospital? No. She is interested in Isabella's story, she cannot help. Until today she never even knew that the building had been a hospital. Which tallies with my next fact. It has been remarkably difficult to find out anything about Isabella's life here. The most significant book about the period

Malta, Nurse of the Mediterranean was written in 1915, and the 1915 evacuees from Gallipoli who people its pages had very different battlefield experiences and medical needs from the casualties Isabella is meeting on their arrival from Salonika in 1916. Not only that, the author, Rev. Albert Mackinnon, the pastor of the Scottish Church in Valletta, writes from the perspective of a chaplain, a very different viewpoint from that of a lady doctor. His book gives a strong sense of the Malta he lived in last year, but how similar is that to the St Ignatius Isabella is living in this year? Is any of it close enough to Isabella's truth to weave onto the warp of her story?

In France, Mrs D-W's diary led me day by day through Isabella's life, but here communication by every individual working for the army is subject to the censorship regulations – no Mrs D-W is going to risk gossiping the daily goings-on at St Ignatius. Not only that, most of the official records of the First World War military hospitals have long gone, so I have been scouring Malta, determined to dig out even the tiniest nuggets of information about this place, but in the National Archive, there were so few relevant documents that I found myself back outside in the sunshine of Rabat in no time. In the University Library my task took scarcely any longer. Very little has been published about Malta during the First World War, and the amount of research tucked away in unpublished dissertations and theses is almost as tiny. Valletta was more fruitful, and I managed to spend a useful day under the ornate ceiling of the National Library of Malta, rolling through microfilm of the *Daily Malta Chronicle*.

But there is another fact that makes accuracy hard. In the

crises of this war, rules are being bent. I read of VADs being given responsibility for whole wards. I read of chaplains administering anaesthetics. Necessity is breaking down the conventional boundaries of every role. However long I devote to the task, I doubt if it is any more possible to be absolutely certain what Isabella does each day than it is to know how she feels about it all.

As I bid my hostesses farewell, I focus on one amazing and indisputable fact: after all these years, I have visited the very building where the instruments that have been tucked in my Flower Press box saw service – the artery clamps, the suture needle, the scalpels, the engraved kit. Months ago, Anaesthetist Danielle told me that military surgeons used to send home for the extra instruments they felt they needed. Here, with a sense of the challenges they face, that makes sense. Perhaps it also explains why Isabella has left so many stray tools. Will she, too, be sending home for supplies?

And will there ever be German blood on them? So far, I do not know. My grandmother has only just started using them, but I can be sure that, somewhere in this building, she uses them to operate on British soldiers. I can be certain that she used the stethoscope to listen to the chests of British Tommies. And with so many of the medical instruments seeing service here, could there be a chance that her beads too, will prove to have some sort of connection with St Ignatius?

3

As I cross the courtyard, I dig out a map. It is time for Isabella to meet her sister. Ever since December, Ena has been working at Tigne' Hospital, just down the road. The spring months were slack, but since summer has brought this rush of patients, she has been working harder every day. She never saw Beth's poor, broken body lying in the yard. She never went upstairs with the rest of the family to examine the treacherous window. Nor did she see Beth in her coffin. She did not even have the chance to say goodbye at her funeral. Everything has been second-hand.

Stationing myself on some rocks at the far end of the Tigne' peninsula, a battered, meditative spot, I picture the pair of them. Frenzied bursts of conversation are broken by long, unseeing surveys of the sea. The twenty-first-century literature tells me that for the families of the victims of fatal accidents, grief can be mingled with the most surprising feelings of guilt and anger – why did the accident happen, who is to blame? For the relatives of suicides, these unwelcome emotions are magnified many times over. But 1916 is not the twenty-first century. How much of this complexity are Isabella and Ena allowing themselves to feel? From what I understand, their whole upbringing has trained them to button up, keep occupied and refuse to dwell. Even if they had all the time in the world, they would not linger, self-indulgently, on their own emotions, but at the moment they certainly do not have time. Their patients need them.

Tigne' Hospital is far larger than St Ignatius. I jot down the figures: these barracks alone hold 612 beds, and in July tents were erected to accommodate another 800. But just up the coast, Forrest has 186 beds, St George's has over 1,400, St Patrick's over 1,100, St Paul's almost 900 and St Andrew's coming up for 1,800. Across the bay towards Valletta, Manoel Island has 600 beds, while inland, the Blue Sisters can care for 120 officers, and St John's has 400 beds. With St Ignatius' 155, it makes a total of – I delve for my calculator …

In the space of a couple of square miles, there are ten hospitals with beds for nearly 8,000 casualties of war. Add to that a whole host more hospitals towards Valletta and further inland, convalescent camps to the north-west, an army of staff to take care of the casualties, more beds being added and further hospitals reopening every day … It is impossible to imagine the magnitude of the sadness here, the stress, the strain and the British upper lips exercising hard to stay stiff.

As they leave their rocky refuge, perhaps Isabella and Ena bolster each other with the sufferings of their patients – every day they are seeing people who are far worse off. Even apart from the soldiers, there is Mother. My reading about the twenty-first century suggests that, as Beth's mother, Janet cannot avoid suffering from an overwhelming, all-encompassing, sense of guilt. If Beth was the victim of an accident, she is the householder who failed to make the window safe and let her own daughter die. And if it was suicide? She gets no relief from guilt there. One way or another, the mothers of suicides are said to feel that they should have been able to prevent their child's death. Is it any different in 1916? Janet's actions speak as loudly as any words. She puts on her mourning dress. She makes the drastic decision to move away from Leith. She refuses the logical refuge, Jan's home in Lancashire. Despite the war and the risk of death at sea, she lets her grief drive her all the way to Malta.

The passenger lists show that she did not travel out with Isabella on the *Gloucester Castle,* but is she fit to travel alone? I flip open the pictures again. There is one woman I have overlooked. A constant companion, she stands with Janet in every photograph. Nobody can tell me who she is, but she bears a striking resemblance to Ena – an Ena perhaps in her 40s or 50s. In the absence of any other evidence, I decide she is a relative – 'Auntie' – who accompanies Janet out here on her daunting journey through grief.

It is my turn to clamber up from the rocks, but no barracks and hospital tents greet me. Instead I pass a building site, a high-end shopping mall and blocks of luxury apartments. All that remains of the Tigne' where Ena works is a small stone building with 'Serjeant's Mess' engraved on its portico. Soon, I reach the coastal, tourist crust of Sliema. Somewhere on this island, Mother and Auntie need a home. Ena cannot help them. She is obliged to stay in the VAD quarters provided by the hospital, but what about Isabella? Quarters are not guaranteed to doctors on temporary contract with the RAMC, and I read that only three of the Maltese hospitals provide the women doctors with accommodation and allow them to join the men's Mess. Most of the women doctors are having to rent rooms at their own expense. Maybe she can help Janet and Auntie.

Isabella's daughter has always believed that her mother

lodged with a 'Mrs Gegen who played the harp'. For a long time, I hit a dead end – googling 'Gegen' yielded nothing. But recently I was presented with an old watercolour. On the back of the gilt frame was a note, 'Sliema, Malta. Painted by Ena's friend, Mrs Geoghagan, who she met while nursing in World War I.'

Geoghagan – I would never have guessed that spelling! But it has worked. Typing it in, Google reveals two Mrs Geoghagans living in Malta during WWI, an older woman and her daughter-in-law. Walter has even discovered their addresses – one lives in Strada Torri, the coast road, and the other in Triq Leone, deep within the town. Both are convenient for St Ignatius, so could one of them be the place where Isabella and her relations lodge?

Since I have already passed the few old buildings that remain on Tower Road, I dip in towards Triq Leone along one of the small streets that fight to maintain their existence against the power of commerce and concrete. The buzz of traffic fades. It is quieter here, more Maltese, and redolent with history, but Joe's warning that even many of these apparently 'old' buildings have been built since WWI rings through my head as I wonder how similar these roads are to the ones that Isabella walks. There are magnificent old mansions with ornate iron gates, lush gardens, paths lined with bougainvilleas, and palm trees that peer over their high stone walls. There is the Alhambra, a magnificent late Victorian edifice, but before I reach Triq Leone, the fading light forces me to lay aside hopes of the past and find my way back to my accommodation.

My hostess greets me. She has photos, she says. Her friends have photos. In no time, emails are pinging in. There is the Alhambra again. Uncluttered by the surrounding buildings, the little fields beside it really do look like Sunday School pictures – just as the VADs' diaries say they do. This is indeed Sliema 'as it used to be'. Another image drops in. It is interesting. In fact, it is so interesting that I pause. These cottages seem familiar. I check them against one of my own photos. Yes! It is a complete match. Both pictures show the little houses on the coast road below St Ignatius. Both are taken from the other side of the bay, but while my photograph is cluttered with the 'new' buildings which stretch between St Ignatius and the sea, in the old photograph …

It is so clear that there is hardly any need to zoom in. Despite its burial under concrete, I am looking at the walls of Isabella's Italian terraces and the leafy trees that line them. For some reason, I can smell citrus – lemons, oranges. Soon I find myself beneath the canopy of a mature garden. The leaves are blocking the burning heat of the midday sun. The breeze is cooler here. Is this where Isabella takes refuge from the turmoil of life? If I turn the corner, will I find her sitting beneath her magnolia, recovering from a stressful operation? Or reflecting on the death of a patient? Or summoning the strength to keep burying thoughts of Beth? I find my mind wondering what she will muse on in the garden she will make in old age, when the gentler, English sun will dapple onto her elderly, gardening hands.

Satisfied, I close the blinds on Valletta's skyline and the small boats creeping across the sea. I try to close out the bustle of the street beneath and sleep, but the headlights streaming across the ceiling strobe the fan that whirs to control the October heat. Some sort of siren becomes a military bugle. Clunky, the fan drowns out the bleep of the pedestrian crossing beneath me, but deepens into the rumble of ancient ambulances. Then it becomes the agonised mutterings of the wounded, the fevered cries of the sick. Then Beth. This time I see her lying, bleeding in the backyard, unconscious and doomed to die. I imagine it being one of my own siblings and break out in a sweat before it changes into one of my children and I wake up stifling my screaming. As the headlights flash across my ceiling, I wonder how well my ancestors are sleeping nearby, and whether thoughts of Beth, and their patients, and this war, haunt them too, or whether they are so well-disciplined that their fears and feelings do not break down even under the influence of Morpheus.

4

October arrives, and as I read about the events that surround Isabella, a sense of doom envelopes me. The dreadful slaughter in the Somme, Beth's death, and the 27,000 beds that now lie waiting for whoever the war sends would be enough, but the Germans are managing to sink more and more ships. Again, the figures are incredible: during September, two or three German U-boats succeeded in sinking about 30 ships in an area of the Mediterranean patrolled by 97 destroyers and 68 auxiliary craft.

I read how every conversation is turning to the battle on the water. The news of a ship being lost sends as powerful a shock through the island as bad news from the Western Front does at home. Tension is increasing by the day. Yet when I dig out another photograph from her archive, Isabella is smiling. Dressed in a long-sleeved button-through dress made, perhaps, of linen, she is accompanied by another woman and two gentlemen in mufti.

The group are not seated in some elegant dining room or garden. Instead, they are picnicking on some huge, flat rocks. The unusual geological formation has convinced Joe that the tea-party is taking place beside the sea in Sliema. It is no simple picnic with a rug and a few sandwiches. A large teapot and a tray of china cups and saucers sit on a very sturdy wooden table. Suddenly, I see that this table answers the question of where Isabella lives. It would have been hard to carry that table all the way from Triq Leone, but as easy as pie to pop it across Strada Torri, Tower Road, where in 1916 new Edwardian houses command a glorious view of the sea. Isabella, probably with Janet and Auntie, is lodging with Mrs Geoghagan at 52 Strada Torri.

The anxious expression of one of Isabella's companions draws me back to the photograph. He is completely failing to smile for the photographer. Instead, he is gazing moodily out to sea. Everything that they need for their tea-party has come by sea – the tea, the sugar, the condensed milk and the biscuits. But almost everything else they need is also shipped in. Meat, fish and jam come in tins from Britain. Eggs and chickens come from Egypt, Tunisia or Italy, and every drop of water has to be dosed with chlorine or boiled before consumption.

It is not only food that is imported. Isabella and her friends have all seen the dockworkers disembarking cargo and counting it into storehouses. They have all dodged the carts and lorries carrying urgent supplies of bandages, pyjamas, shirts, invalid foods and toiletries. They have watched the Red Cross cars filled with heavy crates of new books for the hospital libraries and boxes of fresh records for the gramophones that cheer up every ward. They have seen the Red Cross women giving out imported chocolate, cigarettes, writing paper, pencils and sheet music by the ream, but more serious and more basic than all these are the medical supplies. Every treatment the hospitals offer relies on imports – surgical instruments, splints, chloroform, ether, disinfectants, the supplies for the X-ray equipment, morphine and other pharmaceuticals … the list is endless. But while everything depends on safe transport across the sea, the sea is far from safe.

Steam ships pass these rocks on their way into harbour. No less than thirteen ships have gone down in the waters quite close to Malta. To the southeast, to the west – the place is surrounded. Not a single route is safe. It is not that the Germans are targeting the island. They want the much bigger prize of controlling the Mediterranean, closing the Suez route and preventing access to the East, but Malta has a lot to lose. If the Germans can gain control of the seas, no patients will be able to get here. No soldiers will be able to return to battle. None of the long-term sick will be able to go home. The staff will be marooned and life will become increasingly difficult. Supplies of food and even water will run low. There will be insufficient medical equipment and pharmaceuticals. News will be limited to the brief Reuters telegrams that are printed in the local newspaper, and there will be no mail. Yet despite the terror of the times, Isabella and her friends are taking tea. Even though they live with the daily threat that there may be no tea tomorrow, the table has been carried down to the beach, and the china teacups still have saucers.

Not that their picnic is the only one. From my position in the twenty-first century where a single terrorist action provokes a global response, it is easy to imagine fear, but it is not fear that dominates the accounts I read of this period – it is tea-parties, gatherings and outings. The British seem to be playing as if there was no tomorrow, war or no war, U-boats or no U-boats. Perhaps the very fact that for so many poor chaps there has already been no tomorrow makes their play even heartier – let us eat, drink and be merry, for tomorrow we already know that

285

we really do die. Perhaps too, they are pre-empting the spirit that refuses to be terrorised by terrorists, that declares, "If we give in to fear, we have let them win."

Grabbing every opportunity to get away from the foetid wards and forget the fear, there is plenty for Isabella and her friends to see here even if, with the wards so busy, they have to fit most of their outings into half-days. I can see them heading out to the new excavations at Tarxien. Only a year ago Professor Zammit began uncovering a beautifully preserved temple from the Stone Age. He himself guides them round the excavations, gesticulating wildly as he explains the lay-out. He directs their attention to the delicate drawings on the stones he has unearthed, then leads them over to the gruesome bony remnants of animal sacrifices and some tiny shards of painted pottery. When the tour is over, he points out a pleasant spot where they can picnic among the ruins before walking the mile or so back to the tram for the short ride back to Valletta.

They will go to the garden parties thrown by the governor and his wife. Isabella knows Lord Methuen, the governor and commander-in-chief of the island, from his tours of the wards. Dressed in the full black and gold of his Field Marshal's regalia, he regularly limps round every hospital, greeting each patient. When party day arrives, Isabella and her friends catch the little train in Valletta. By British standards it is a ridiculously short journey – a deep dive through a tiny tunnel then a quick steam across the dry Maltese countryside. The poor engine snorts and grunts as it strains to tug the extra first-class carriages that have been added for the party-goers. At Attard, Isabella's group follows the crowd into the fleet of *carrozin* and jolt out to the palace at San Anton. As they take tea and saunter through the orange grove, they survey their fellow guests. The island is small and densely packed. Unexpected acquaintances pop up all the time.

But however hard they play, they cannot escape the war. There are now 21,000 patients on the island – almost as many as there have ever been. Every member of staff is working at full stretch, whoever they may be mourning, whatever they may have seen. Diarists and letter writers are soon pointing out that the glorious red sunsets are being followed by nights of crashing thunder, flashing lightning and the clattering thumps of shutters and doors blowing open. As they write of fierce winds forcing cascading rain through every crack and crevice, news arrives of yet another sinking.

"The P&O steamship *Arabia*? A passenger liner! Eleven dead? Why, she wasn't even a military target!"

In the twenty-first century, news footage of a boat filled with refugees from Africa sinking not far off-shore makes it easy to picture the plight of the survivors of the *Arabia* in 1916. To begin with, they need medical treatment. The military doctors and nurses know the ropes well by now – over the past couple of months hundreds of shipwrecked sailors from merchant ships have landed in Malta, bedraggled and with nothing but the sea-soaked clothes on their backs. All autumn, the shops in Valletta have been doing a roaring trade in the replacement of belongings, but now supplies are beginning to run out, and I imagine Isabella doing as the other staff do – digging through her own wardrobe for garments that will keep these poor souls warm. And of course it is not only the clothes – sometimes there is not even tea and sugar with which to console the ship-wrecked because the tea and sugar too have gone to the bottom of the sea. The whole thing is relentless and hardly have they got used to the idea of the enemy sinking a liner, than another whisper is going round, "The *Britannic!*"

Most of them know HMHS *Britannic*, the sister ship of the *Titanic*, now requisitioned and serving as a hospital ship. Many of the staff have travelled on her. I can hear the facts and figures flying round the island – and the sheer horror that a hospital ship, protected by international law, should have been violated.

"When did it happen?"

"21st November."

"How did she go down?"

"Nobody seems sure of anything except that there was an explosion at the foot of the main staircase just after breakfast. Mercifully, the wards were empty."

"Thank God! What about the staff?"

They care about the staff – many of them are acquaintances, even friends. On the wards, the nurses relay the good news that all the sisters and VADs have survived. The RAMC rank and file perhaps concentrate on the eight orderlies who have been killed. The first one was blown up right at the start of the disaster, in the explosion at the foot of the main staircase. The others were thrown into the sea when their lifeboats were smashed to pieces by the lurching propellor of the sinking ship. Over in the club, the figures are bandied about – most of the 1,100 people on board made it to the lifeboats, but thirty have lost their lives.

In the officers' messes the buzz is about how the medical officers remained on board until the end, then clambered towards the sea down wire ropes that ripped open their hands. Again and again they repeat the minutiae of how the doctors fought their way through waves that swirled and sucked them back towards the sinking ship. And the name on everybody's lips is 'Cropper'. Captain Cropper is the only officer to have been killed in the disaster.

Curious, I google his name. The photo that comes up is familiar, horribly familiar. The dead Captain Cropper is the very surgeon with whom Isabella worked at the Anglo-Ethiopian. Staff who travelled with him on the *Britannic* sing his praises – he was such a marvellous lecturer, his teaching about malaria and the other infectious diseases of the Mediterranean was magnificent.

How will Isabella react? The last time she saw him was that embarrassing argument with Triqueneaux as he departed, but before that? There had been outings, mealtimes, operations, cases … hundreds of memories. A colleague – a friend, perhaps – has died. But I know so little. How many friends has Isabella already lost in this war? How has she been reacting? How hardened has she become? Not that she has much time for reflection. Within days, another hospital ship, the *Braemar Castle,* has struck a mine in the Aegean. She does not sink, instead she limps to Malta, where she will sit in the naval dockyards for three months before she is repaired. She is followed by two more passenger liners: the *City of Birmingham* is torpedoed on 27th November and the *Caledonia* on 4th December.

Does twenty-first century Malta remember this? Has the

island forgotten her role in this war? I cross the city to the War Museum at St Elmo. As I go, I cannot help picturing the streets speckled with dazed shipwreck survivors in cobbled garments.

Inside the museum, a monstrous black tube dominates the display in the first, tiny room. About 60 cm in diameter, it has a red ball like a nose at one end, a propellor with tilt devices at the other and fills a whole wall. Puzzled, I look for the caption. 'This is a G6 AV torpedo that failed to detonate after being fired at a Royal Naval Squadron patrolling the Sicilian channel. It was picked up by HMS *Laburnum* on Christmas Day, 1916.' Instantly, I am transported.

5

St Ignatius is all but unrecognisable. Paper chains and streamers adorn the ceilings. Palm trees lurk in corners. Every spare surface is festooned with decorations. I have read that the hidden talents that emerge from their patients startle the medical staff but this is phenomenal. It must have taken days. It is most certainly Christmas, but is it anything like the happy, fireside, Christmas in the 'dear old homeland', that the *Daily Malta Chronicle* has been urging its readers to create? To my jaundiced twenty-first-century eyes, it is Christmas taken hostage by more than two years of death and maiming.

I tiptoe along the corridor. Each ward has its own personality. It is still early, but in one I spot a couple of men already up, perfecting their elaborate creation. I guess they do deserve the very best Christmas, whatever the rights and wrongs of the conflict – they are so far from home and they have been through who-knows-what physical and mental pain.

Of course, it is not only the patients who will find today difficult. Janet will too. She may have escaped the sadness of John's Place and the gossips of Leith, but she is not going to escape the nostalgia that is 25th December. Every month, the *Daily Malta Chronicle* has advertised countless concerts and bazaars in aid of one good cause or another – blind soldiers and sailors, Belgian orphans, Turkish wives, the Archbishop's Bread Fund, Lady Methuen's Distressed Families Fund, the Wounded Entertainment Fund, the Ladies Guild Fund for the Wounded, the Lord Kitchener Memorial Fund, the British Red Cross and more – but this month, on top of the charitable appeals, there have been the exhortations to buy, buy, buy – mince pies here, costumes for amateur dramatics there – and don't forget, the mail boat is leaving soon, presents need to be sent home.

Valletta is the place to go. Perhaps Auntie reports how she and Janet had a lovely cup of tea before braving the throngs, and enthuses over the marvels they had considered – silk shawls and cotton tablecloths from India, Egyptian cigarettes, fine lace, necklaces, Maltese nougat and Gozo buttons. She goes into minute detail about the delicate collar they had agreed on for Jan, the little bonnet they had chosen for Bill and the inlaid match-box case that had seemed just right for Frank. "Fingers crossed that they get through," she ends.

But what about Janet? Is she just as enthusiastic? Or does she complain how dreadfully noisy it had been – what with the street vendors, the chattering Maltese, the dirty goats and the crowds of shoppers. Or worse still, is she depressed and silent? How has she been reacting to Beth's death? How have Isabella, Ena and Auntie been helping her? Even if Janet is managing to put on a brave, wartime face, she will not find today an easy day.

A nurse emerging from a festive ward disturbs my thoughts. A few of the patients are already disappearing towards the church – there will be a service at quarter-past six – so I follow them out of the hospital. Among the classifieds in the *Daily Malta Chronicle* is a column entitled 'The Wounded in Malta'. Usually it is full of desperate enquiries about pals last seen on the battlefield, but for the last month, gratitude has replaced anxiety. Little groups of recovering soldiers in hospitals around the island have been banding together to publish 'Thank you' messages to their RAMC staff. One lady doctor is described as being, 'like a mother to us', and another is honoured for her kindness.

As the men ahead of me turn into the church that abuts St Ignatius, I wonder whether they are Isabella's patients and, if they are, how they have reacted to being tended by a woman. Many soldiers have never encountered a lady doctor before, but across the war-zone, the women doctors are confident that their patients love them. Yes, I have unearthed a trio of complaints – one grumpy soldier in England determined to have nothing more to do with his lady doctor because she had altered his treatment, a VAD moaning about a female medic whose over-prescribing made the medicine basket back-breakingly heavy, and another VAD furious that a woman doctor had refused to give a man with a freshly broken arm so much as an aspirin, but on the whole, the lady doctors seem to have been accepted everywhere, and in Malta the classifieds have been overflowing with thanks.

Another group of patients drifts past me. These are the men who have been left behind. From June to November, ambulances delivered more and more new patients to the doors of the hospitals, but this month has been different. Empty ambulances have drawn up. Men ready for the next stage of recovery have clambered aboard, their pals and the staff cheering from the hospital doorstep. There are 7,000 fewer cases in Malta than four weeks ago.

Is happiness or sadness more appropriate? It depends where Isabella and the other medical officers have ordered their departing patients to go. Everyone wants full recovery but full recovery means going to the dreaded convalescent camps to the north of the island, then back to the fighting at the front; and while nobody wants ill-health to continue, continued ill-health comes with a ticket home.

Meditative, I join what is now a throng going into the church. Squeezing in at the back, I examine the congregation, resting my eyes on the blue pyjamas of the patients, the khaki of the orderlies, the Red Crosses of VADs, the frilled hats of the fully-trained nurses, the Sam Browne belts of the male medical officers – and Isabella and her colleague in mufti. Everybody appears to be joining in a carol they must have sung many times, yet each of them, whatever their rank, must be on her or his own journey to assimilate or avoid the indigestible conundrums this conflict has hurled at their faith. And as the utterly recognisable ritual rolls on, I ache at how they can bear to celebrate the birthday of the Prince of Peace when man's horrific inhumanity to warlike man has never been clearer.

By the time the service is over, the bright light of Christmas has dawned – hours earlier than in the 'dear old homeland'.

"Happy Christmas, Sister," echoes across the stillness.

"And a Merry Christmas to you, Sergeant," comes the brisk return.

"Seasons Greetings, Miss Stenhouse," they address Isabella.

"It is so mild," they all say, "does anyone know if there is snow at home?"

I follow the crowd inside. Soon the men will be opening their little packets from the King and Queen. What will they make of the accompanying card with its royal crest and its gold-lettered message?

Grateful thanks for hardships endured and unfailing cheeriness. The Queen and I are thinking more than ever of the sick and wounded among my sailors and soldiers. From our hearts we wish them strength to bear their sufferings and a speedy restoration to health.

A cluster of VADs bustle past me, chattering secretively. Bathing, dressing and feeding their charges brings these women close to their patients. Somewhere on each ward they have hidden piles of presents purchased from their own earnings.

From the kitchens seeps the smell of Christmas and at midday I watch Isabella and the other doctors serving their patients a full roast dinner. It is so warm that tables have been laid in the courtyard. The men tease and laugh – who would have imagined this when they were injured or became sick in Salonika? Courtesy of the *Daily News* and the *Daily Telegraph*, there are even proper Christmas puddings.

All day long visitors come and go – and it is not only Lord Methuen and other dignitaries. Former patients wander in from convalescent camps, friends from other hospitals drop in and, in mid-afternoon, the concert party arrives.

The Red Cross has managed to assemble enough performers for every single hospital to have its own Christmas Day recital. The musicians and entertainers wear wonderful costumes and applause rings loud – the programme is the perfect balance of songs from the music hall, operatic arias, piano solos and comic turns.

Come dusk, fairy-lights twinkle from the balcony as tea is served. And if thoughts of Beth come over Isabella, Janet, Auntie and Ena, why there are thousands of families who have lost members this year. Look at all these men. Everyone here has lost somebody. Let's toast our precious, absent Beth and keep busy …

Later, amusing tales will be told of how the baritone interrupts tonight's performance of *Madame Butterfly* to arrange a duel with a member of the audience, but I doubt if the Stenhouses attend. With the young heroine committing suicide, it would hardly be the most relaxing evening's entertainment.

And as night descends, Christmas, so brief, shiny and brittle, passes. Somewhere off the coast, the sailors on HMS *Laburnum* have picked up an unexploded torpedo and are bringing it, cautiously, in.

6

On a burning hot day, I turn away from the vehicles hurtling along the dual-carriageway outside Valletta into a peaceful Pieta side street, where I go through an iron gateway. The thick Maltese walls instantly dull the roar of the traffic. I can hear insects, and even in the midday glare I can see that this cemetery is unlike any I saw in France. Cypresses stand sentinel over a field of flat tombstones that lie between hard baked paths: their dates 1915, 1916, 1917, 1918. This is where the soldiers who the hospitals fail to mend lie buried. Many of the stones bear three names. The Maltese ground is so hard that the army has had no choice but to let the flood of dead share one another's graves. They have had no choice but to lay many of the tombstones flat, as if to greet the sun. If I took the time to count, I would find 1,303 victims from Isabella's war. That is almost one every day from the start of the campaign in Gallipoli in 1915 until the signing of the Armistice in 1918. But I do not count them. Instead, I turn back towards the gate, letting time and the weather slip to the winter cloudiness of Tuesday 30th January 1917. An article in the *Daily Malta Chronicle* makes me think that Isabella will come here this afternoon.

As I wait, I thread together the information I have gleaned about the last month. Many of the churches started this third New Year of the war with a week of special prayers, but the German U-boats did not stop. Instead, they sank four merchant ships passing near Malta before the month was even nine days old. Not that there were many casualties, but tons of sugar, barley and other grains were lost. From home, tales of women and children queueing for hours in the winter cold and wet for basic supplies of bread and meat have been coming in from every quarter. The letter-writers try to put on a brave face, but the envelopes spill stories of supplies running out and shopkeepers having to come to the door to dismiss the queue. They tell of the weary families, frozen to the marrow, trudging home empty-handed, wondering how they will survive. Rumours abound too of discontented murmurings among the soldiers on leave, furious that while they have been risking everything for the sake of their nation, their nation has not looked after the women and children they have entrusted to its care. And the British in Malta have agreed that although they may be bored of canned meat, canned fish and the everlasting condensed milk, for now they are having the best of things.

My thoughts are interrupted by music. It is a quarter to four. Other people have joined me – a few nurses, some orderlies and a little crowd of men in hospital blue. Quiet, we crane to see. In front of the band marches a cluster of uniformed men who I know from the *Chronicle* are members of the Royal Garrison Artillery. They pass so slowly that I can count them, forty in all, pacing solemnly to music so sad that it alone makes my eyes moisten. As the last row of the artillery passes, the band itself comes into view. Eyes front, the Band of the Royal Malta Artillery is setting the rhythm for the whole procession, the dignified tones of the *Dead March* from Handel's *Saul* resounding from their instruments; swinging from their drums, black crepe. Solemn minutes tick by before the coffin comes into view, and every hat around me is doffed, every head bowed. Lying on a gun-carriage pulled by six mules, the coffin is escorted by privates, lieutenants, captains and colonels, each bearing an elaborate wreath. Just beside me at the gate, the cortège halts, and the band falls silent. The Union Flag draped over the coffin moves eerily in the January breeze.

Hundreds of funeral processions may have come along this road in the last two years, but this one is different. It is no soldier who lies inside that coffin. It is one of the lady doctors, Dr Isobel Addy Tate. Respectfully, her coffin is lifted gently from its carriage and placed on the pall-bearers' shoulders. Even their names make the *Chronicle*, so detailed is its account. The priest is leading them into the cemetery, but I wait, watching the crowds who have followed Dr Tate. There are numerous Medical Officers with their RAMC badges. A cluster of civil surgeons, and a throng of Matrons, Sisters and Staff nurses pass before, at last, the group I have been waiting for comes into sight. Instantly recognisable by their motley garb, I slide in with the lady doctors. The paper does not mention Isabella by name as one of the attendees, but at the end of the list of names it adds, "and many others". Surely only very urgent duties in the hospital would keep any of them away from paying their last respects – I am certain that Isabella is here. Slowly, we process towards the grave. The place is packed. Every path is full, and the grave is awkwardly near a wall, but the men are moving back to allow these women, Isobel Tate's closest friends and colleagues, to be the nearest to her burial.

As the priest conducts the service, the two neighbouring tombstones catch my eye. These are not shared tombs, each grave holds the remains of a nurse. Only one space remains in the row, and I shudder. At the rate this war is going, it too will probably soon be filled. Somebody who is now living and working, maybe even one of these women standing near me now, will be lying in a coffin for an interment as ceremonial and certain as Dr Tate's today.

The priest finishes the ritual and the artillery men raise their guns. Three sharp volleys snap the silence and the tear-jerking strains of the Last Post echo from a single trumpet. Deciding not to peep and pry into who is dabbing a handkerchief, I bow my head and wait while the lady doctors file past the still open grave. Then solemnly and quietly, they leave the cemetery. Does their conversation slowly come back as they walk towards Porte des Bombes?

"So sad."

"So far away from home."

"How did she die?"

"Congestion of the brain associated with typhoid, they suspect."

"She had taken over the bacteriology in Valletta Hospital, hadn't she?"

"Yes, and she was ill in Belgrade when she was out there last year, I believe."

"She deserves recognition from the authorities."

"Yes, she has given her life for her country just as surely as any wounded soldier or victim of malaria."

I keep an eye out for Isabella. Did she know Dr Tate well? There are over 70 women doctors here now. They have arrived in dribs and drabs all through the autumn, but a few have already been invalided home. Dr Tate is the first to die. She was considerably older than Isabella but she was a highly-qualified radiologist. If they have not met in the general mêlée of life in Malta, they may have come across one another over some complex case in an X-ray room.

I imagine the lady doctors clinging together after this shock. Perhaps they make their way to their usual haunt, the Union Club in Auberge de Provence on Strada Reale. And perhaps the conversation gradually moves away from dear Isobel and towards their daily preoccupations, diagnosis for example. Will Dr Dorothy Hare raise the problem of how inoculation is obscuring the results of diagnostic agglutination tests for para-typhoid, the case she will discuss after the war at the Medical Women's Federation? Will Dr Elizabeth Hurdon expound on the differential diagnosis of malaria and dysentery, and will Isabella's shipboard companion, Dr Elizabeth Moffett, enthuse about the research she is about to begin with Captain Kirk? "We intend to examine the optic fundi of a large number of patients suffering from trench fever."

As a surgeon, Isabella is in the minority. However much she may be longing to discuss the vexed questions of her discipline – which combination of antiseptics is most effective in bathing and irrigating wounds, for example, and how to protect the skin from these powerful compounds in this hot climate – most of the others have had little opportunity to undertake any surgery since their student days. For that matter, relatively few of the patients they are caring for at the moment are surgical. The official reports divide the cases into the sick, who will

rarely need surgery, and the wounded, who may.

In one group of figures, the wounded of 1916–17 make up less than 4 per cent of more than 24,000 patients, and little St Ignatius is taking care of a third of that 4 per cent, leaving even fewer surgical cases for the other hospitals – and for the other women. Isabella may justifiably feel left out: her professional concerns are quite different from those of the women around her.

Not that she is the only one who is isolated. Edith Martin is still directing her attention to the mental health of the soldiers. May Thorne has been addressing her energies to the health of women and military families out here, but whatever their discipline, all these lady doctors have one thing in common. As the shop talk wanes, the teacups empty and they wonder whether they should go back to their lodgings or stay for gin and tonics, the conversation veers to some of the matters which are beginning to irritate every single one of them.

"The passport is in the clothes," one of them says, as they compare bitter experiences of being refused entry to this or that event and having to stand, watching the men with whom they work each day entering freely simply because of their uniform.

"Clothes we are not entitled to wear," someone adds, echoing the disillusionment they are all beginning to feel.

"All our efforts to look the part did no good. Even when we stick ourselves in khaki, the whole world knows it is not real."

"Yes. Every Tom, Dick and Harry can see it's not the ticket."

"It means nobody has any obligation to salute us, and there's not a bally thing we can do about it if they don't."

The voices reach a cacophony as each woman expresses her own particular lament about how, not only has this or that private or NCO failed to salute her but insult has frequently been added to injury.

"At the very least, they should stand up and doff their hats! In civilian life such a gesture would be common courtesy, yet here many of the rank and file are downright insolent. One frequently receives neither a salute nor the raising of a hat."

"Sometimes I've gone onto the ward and received a mere mumbled, 'Good morning.'"

There is general agreement that the officers are more considerate and respectful, but they can all point to an increasing expectation amongst the officers in charge of the hospitals.

"The other day my Commanding Officer ordered me to wear something lighter for the evening in the Mess, so I was forced to do my evening ward round dressed for all the world as if I was a little girl off to a party! It was quite ridiculous! You should've seen the nurses tittering – it did no good at all for the dignity of medical womanhood. We've always said that even if the army is ambivalent about us, we regard ourselves as being fully under its rules and regulations, but does that really include obeying such undignified orders from the CO?"

And the conversation drifts to what it is appropriate to wear, to the best tailors in Valletta, and time goes by, and it is nearly midnight, and they murmur again about poor Dr Tate, dear Isobel, before hiring *carrozin* to get back to their lodgings, not knowing that within twenty-four hours the Germans will begin their campaign of unrestricted U-boat warfare.

SECTION 7

A HOSPITAL CONCERT, MAY 8, 1917
DEDICATED TO A VOICE

She will wish her pure strings to be mute—
Heal us, alone, by thy voice!
We are weak—with an arm, or a foot,
'Tented,' or bound, to no choice;
Ours are the bandaged eyes,
A-search for the Singer's face—
Denials, through darkness, arise,
Pierce it with sound, for a space:
> *O Singer of Life—so, of pain!*
> *Sing 'Vita'--thy 'Vita'--again and again*

Ah! those were old words, that we've read—
'O Sempre Amore'—that stirred;
And Love's for us lads, sick in bed,
And Love is the wounded's last word;
And a warmth drew in from the street,
And we slipped to an English June,
And England and Italy meet,
And touch the same chord of Love's tune:
> *O Singer of Love—lift from pain!*
> *Sing thy 'Sempre Amore'—again and again!*

Then he sank to an under key—
'O Pena'!—O Pain! is it not?
And we fell to a blind reverie—
For we've had our pain, God wot!
We were back in the fever and ache,
Or peered in a pal's dead face,

Or were feeling the lift and the shake,
And the moan in us down to the Base;
> *O Singer—though sweetest—of pain!*
> *Sing 'Pena'—thy 'Pena'—again and again*

Then he wrought us—passionate—loud—
'Guerra, ah Guerra'!—is it War?
For our slack frames stiffened them proud,
And the men, we were once, we saw—
Over and on to a Leader's sign,
Tightening their teeth on wild breath,
Spilling their blood like the reddest wine,
While they staked for winning or death!—
> *O Singer of madness and pain!*
> *Sing 'Guerra'—'thy Guerra'—again and again!*

The ward empties to shuffle and drill—
All but two bedridden rows;
But he's made eyes,—the dryest—to fill,
He's breathed all our souls to new glows;
And a pale face, still in a trance—
Is away to the glory of things;
And the crutches tap tap to a prance;
While a voice to the hollowness clings—
> *O Vita dolce, si sovente amara!*
> *O Sempre Amore—Pena e Guerra!—*

Valletta, May 10th, 1917   F.D.B.

1

As I walk back through the side streets, I reflect. I may not yet have unearthed any link to the beads, but the details of Isabella's life here are, slowly, threading colour onto the bare warp of her story – and I am getting impatient to weave in a simple poem printed on a flimsy piece of pink paper. I ought to wait – it is dated May 1917 – yet back in my room I find myself digging it out and letting my eyes trace the flourishes and loops of the words Isabella has scrawled directly above the verses: "'<u>Salvati</u>." St. Ignatius'. Inexpressive, opaque, they are still so much more than she usually writes. I glance at the poem's title, *A Hospital Concert, May 8 1917, Dedicated to a Voice*. Instantly, I am in St Ignatius, blanching at the poet's carefully chosen words.

Of course I should have known – there are enough photographs – but I simply assumed that Isabella was treating legs, arms and torsos. It never crossed my mind that she would have to deal with blindness too. Hesitantly, I glance at the swathed heads of her patients. Could the poet himself, F.D.B., be one of these men? They can hear the orderlies clattering chairs into rows, but they cannot tell whether their friends are among the patients shuffling in from other wards. They do not know that the staff are squeezing into every corner of the room, but one of them twists his head towards the sound as Isabella props herself beside his bed. She leans to reassure him and I try to digest what this poem is revealing – Granny-who-loved-silver-hairbrushes is not only sorting out macerated limbs but trying to save these men's eyes, patch up their faces, and help them begin their terrifying adjustment to life without sight. For the first time, the disjunction between the elderly grandmother I knew and this young Isabella, hits me, but a sudden silence interrupts my thoughts. A man in evening dress is taking his place at the front. He opens his mouth and the blind no longer need explanation.

Washed in the cascading notes of *Sempre Amore*, bodies relax and hands creep towards pockets that cradle photographs of wives, children, mothers. Well, most hands do, but here and there I spot the clenched jaws of men refusing to meet their own gaze – the jilted, who have learned that *amore* is rarely *sempre*, and the deeply maimed, who know for sure that nobody will ever *amore* the bodies they themselves detest.

Modulating his key, the singer moves on. *Pena*, pain – he cannot be British, he is tackling it head-on. The muscles of the men's faces are tightening as each one revisits his own suffering – the fever and pain; the agonising, jolting journeys; and, worst of all, F.D.B. reminds me, the faces of dead pals …

"Sing it again," they all murmur, "sing it again."

The final note of the song fades and I let my eyes return to Isabella. Ever since she went to France, she has been looking after men whose physical pain she cannot soothe with powerful twenty-first-century analgesics, men whose fevers linger on, unbroken by antibiotics, men whose emotional pain is fathoms deeper than I would ever dare to dive, and I know for absolute certain that I will never truly grasp her story, however hard I try.

But even as I accept my inevitable defeat, the voice is continuing. Masterful, this singer knows his power, he knows the needs of these men. He has brought them to these depths but he does not plan to leave them here. In wisdom, he stiffens his tune. Loudly and passionately, *Guerra* – War – his voice reverberates against the hard stone walls, his words resound through the building. And in each bed, on each chair, the men draw themselves back up, proud soldiers once more.

As the last note resounds, triumphant, even the weakest try to march as they shuffle back to their wards. Only the bed-ridden remain, snatching for echoes of the 'Voice'. And me. I do not want to leave F.D.B.'s verses. I do not want to lose touch with the terrible reality faced by Isabella and these men, her charges.

But gradually I do emerge from the singer's spell. And I begin to question. What was so special about this particular concert? Who is this 'Voice', who inspired F.D.B. to pen a poem that Isabella will keep forever? Heading back to the *Daily Malta Chronicle*, I scroll through the early days of May in the hope of enlightenment. May 11th, I read, 'Musical treat at St Elmo Hospital'. A performance in one hospital will almost certainly be repeated at another, so I glance through the article. St Elmo, apparently, set up an ornately decorated stage in the courtyard. Various dignitaries – the leaders of the British Red Cross, several chaplains, and many 'well-known' people from Valletta – joined the patients and staff for the performance. It sounds so much more elaborate than F.D.B's description of St Ignatius' concert that I am about to give up when I spot the words 'Signor Salvatore Salvati.'

Salvati! Exactly what Isabella wrote – '"Salvati." St. Ignatius'! I start again, this time studying the whole account much more carefully. The concert was arranged by Chevalier Lancelotti, the impresario who runs the Theatre Royal. Patriotically, the programme stuck to works by composers from the Allied nations. After a few introductory pieces, Signor Bascetta played some Elgar on the violin 'with charm and sympathy', and the cellist, Signor Battista, gave 'a most devotional rendering of Mascheroni's *Ave Maria*.' Then came Signor Salvatore Salvati, 'the popular tenor'. He was, the *Chronicle* records, given a 'great reception', and he sang *Mignon* by Thomas and the duet from *Les Pecheurs de Perles* before joining Signorina de Frate in Tosti's *L'Ultima Canzone*. In response to prolonged applause, he gave *La Donna è mobile* from *Rigoletto* as an encore.

So now I know. The 'Voice' is a tenor, his first name is Salvatore, and he is popular. But surely not popular enough to be online? A quick google proves me wrong – an Italian just three years older than Isabella, he has been performing in Italy and South America since 1908. I click a video link. An old record spins. A needle descends. The picture shifts to the rotating centre of the disc. I close my eyes. In moments the very 'Voice' that sang in St Ignatius, the 'Voice' that moved both F.D.B. and Isabella, fills my room. But when my eyes flick open, I hit pause.

A man I recognise is filling the screen – well, I am fairly certain that I recognise him. Hurrying through Isabella's photos, I dig out a three-quarter length portrait of a man, his hands in his pockets, a watch chain draped across his slightly portly stomach. Isabella's daughter told me she thought he was an Italian doctor on whom her mother had 'had a crush', but is he? Zooming in, I check his face against the image on the video: thick hair combed straight back from a large forehead, closely

312

spaced eyes, a slightly bulbous nose. There can be no doubt about it – Isabella's supposed 'crush' is not an Italian doctor, he is an Italian tenor.

And now that I have zoomed in, I cannot avoid the four words that stand out from the Italian in one corner of Isabella's photograph: 'Miss Stenhouse ... Salvatore Salvati.' Quickly, I rummage through Isabella's treasures, certain that amongst them lies something else in Italian. Here – it looks like a business card. I turn it over. Yes! Once again it is from Salvati: 'Salvatore Salvati, Milano, Piazza Risorgimento, 3'.

What exactly, has Salvati written on this card? Why did he send it? Is Isabella indulging in some female version of the notorious male propensity to fall for actresses and haunt stage doors? My brother comes to the rescue.

"On the photograph, Signor Salvati has written: 'To the 'gentile' doctor Miss Stenhouse. In memory. Salvatore Salvati.' Gentile is hard to translate. It means kind or dear, but not in a romantic sense," he emails.

But if it is not 'love', what is happening between the two of them? Why should Salvati carry any memories of her, or is he just being polite to an over-enthusiastic fan?

"The business card makes it clear," my brother explains, "Salvati has written:

19/6 (Valletta)
6D Strada Cavaliere
Dear Signorina
I am sorry to tell you that tomorrow, Wednesday, I can't give you your lesson at 7 because I have to sing in a con-

cert for the British Red Cross. I will expect you instead on
Thursday at 7, and hope that will be convenient to you.
Forgive me, but it is not my fault.
With best wishes
S. Salvati."

This is far more puzzling than a romance. I have an address, a date, and a motive, but I need an explanation: why on earth should Isabella Stenhouse, army surgeon at St Ignatius Hospital, be taking singing lessons from a famous Italian tenor?

2

Since it is a fine day, I make my way to Salvati's lodging on *Strada Cavaliere*, Cavalier Street, by boat. The modern ferries between Sliema and Valletta may not be as elegant as the tall-funnelled vessels of a century ago, but they follow exactly the same route across the harbour. When the little ship docks, I am as utterly dwarfed by the sheer walls of Valletta as Isabella is on June 21st 1917. Like her, I climb the side streets beneath shabby wooden balconies draped with rows of washing. I pass small shops and clamber up steps and over cobbles. If I got rid of the parked cars, and swapped the mopeds and tourists for goats, priests and old ladies in *faldettas*, I would be treading exactly the Valletta that Isabella treads.

But why is she coming here? She is far too busy. I am certain that if she is not in theatre, she is preparing patients for surgery, and if she is not doing that, she is on the never-ending task of changing dressings. It is not the gas gangrene which was so lethal in France that worries her, but the particular infections which thrive in Malta's sweaty heat – suture abscesses for example. To prevent them, each wound needs regular disinfection. I can see her gripping the offending member firmly and dousing the wound with the stinging chemicals, thoroughly inured to the writhing, grimacing and even cursing, of the leg, arm, or torso that she is trying to mend. Maybe she is even hardened to the excruciating pain she has to inflict on faces and eyes. Once she is satisfied no bacterium has a chance of breeding, she reviews what she has exposed and decides how to pack the wound before she applies the fresh dressing.

Not that her work is then over. Oh no. Heading for the X-ray room, she joins the gowned figures standing round the table. The clamour of machinery prevents all conversation and the anaesthetist has to gesture for the radiographer to fire up the apparatus. As the din increases, the innards of the sleeping man on the table start to glow. The strange, green light reaches up to Isabella's face as she extracts the bullet, or piece of shrapnel, or whatever other strange foreign body has been causing trouble – the dangerous procedure that I did not understand when she was in France, and that caused such ructions with Triqueneaux.

But even that is not all. Once a week, her twenty-four hours as Orderly Officer come round and she is tied to the hospital. Accompanied by an NCO who booms out "Shun, Orderly Officer!" as she enters each room, she has to inspect the kitchens and wards. And when that is done? She has scores of other duties of which I know nothing. But with Salvati's message clearly stating, 'Your lesson', I have been forced back to the evidence. And its hard facts have exposed the truth – my knowledge of Isabella's workload is way out-of-date.

I guess it is because I jumped into the poem too early, but only now do I discover that the number of patients has continued to fall since Christmas. Many of those who remain are suffering from intransigent wounds and their healing depends more on time and patience than constant medical intervention. By the time February's glorious weather arrived, the wards had quietened enough for the staff to up their jaunting. They had rambled through exotic spring flowers, or travelled out to

Hagar Kim, Dingli or Mellieha. Yet each day, the waters that they could see from every point of the island were becoming more sinister.

Back in November, the *Britannic* and the *Braemar Castle* had foundered when they travelled into minefields designed to sink whatever ship passed by. The Germans had not been deliberately flouting international law by targeting hospital ships. But at the beginning of February, that changed. The new policy of unrestricted submarine warfare means that the enemy now regards British hospital ships as legitimate targets. Even before the end of March, their U-boats had successfully torpedoed two hospital ships, the *Asturias* and the *Gloucester Castle*. And as transporting patients to Malta had become more dangerous, I read how the mood on the island had become increasingly anxious. But on 2nd April, amidst a flurry of rumours that all the medical staff were about to be transferred to Salonika, joyful news had arrived – the USA had joined the war against Germany. Not that the jubilation had lasted long. Only five days later, the Germans had tried to bomb the Maltese dockyards – and they would have succeeded if their airplane had not caught fire over Italy.

Lord Methuen had given instructions to ensure the island was ready for the next attack. Six blasts from the siren in the docks were to warn everybody that an enemy aircraft was approaching. From that moment, electricity and gas supplies would be cut, church bells were to cease their ringing, boats and vehicles were to extinguish their lights and everybody was to wait inside.

But in the midst of the apprehension had come fresh hope – the Japanese navy had arrived. The reinforcements had been honoured with a big reception outside the Governor's palace in Valletta, and everyone had felt a little safer as they watched the flotilla leader and the eight or so Japanese destroyers coming in and out of the harbour, protecting them and the vital supplies. But the optimism had not lasted long – food prices had started rising. Bread is now costing three times as much as it did before, meat three and a half times, and sugar four times. The poor of Malta had been the ones to suffer first and the men working in the docks had come out on strike. On top of that, three more hospital ships had gone down, the *Salta* on 10th April, and both the *Lanfranc* and the *Donegal* on the 17th. Women and children, even military women, had been temporarily forbidden to leave the island.

At the top of Old Bakery Street, just before I reach Cavalier Street, I pause and look back. From here, it is as though somebody has dissected a slice out of the city and exposed its very structure. The contours roll down and up and down again all the way to the sea. It had been the end of April when the long-expected announcement had come. Five general hospitals were to be transferred to Salonika. The tented hospitals – St. Patrick's, St. Paul's and St. David's – were closed down, as were the big hospitals at Spinola and Floriana. Already, the women doctors who had been working at Spinola have travelled to Salonika as part of the 64th General Hospital, and another large group is preparing to leave at the start of July.

I look again at the sea. In all, 2,543 men had travelled across it in April, but in May only 603 cases were sent over and this month, June, only 37 new patients will arrive on the island. Yet St Ignatius has remained open and Isabella is not being sent to Salonika. With most of her patients having been in the hospital for long enough for their treatment to be well under way, it is safe for her to leave them in their beds and walk through these narrow streets to *Strada Cavaliere* for singing lessons with Signor Salvati.

Turning, I face the street itself – St John's Cavalier stolidly ancient opposite the short row of houses. I can see now how Isabella has time for lessons but I still fail to understand why she wants them. At some point, in an action that could be considered almost brazen, Isabella must have approached the renowned Signor Salvati and requested tuition. Even more bizarrely, he had said, "Yes."

Bemused, my mind drifts to a strange advertisement I noticed in the *Chronicle*:

Lost (Thursday) two songs near Floriana. Finder please return to Miss Hodgkinson, St George's.

As I try and think of every possible way in which Miss Hodgkinson could have lost a song – forgetting the words, losing a record, mixing up the tune … the penny slowly drops, and I am back beside the piano in John's Place, realising what I have forgotten. They need sheet music. With no radio or television and only a limited selection of 78 rpm gramophone records, sheet music is the only way to keep up to date with the newest songs. Isabella and her sisters are not only being trained to perform: like everyone else, they are being taught that it is their moral obligation to share even the tiniest shreds of their talent. And in wartime Malta in 1917, Isabella is eager to improve her skills.

So at 7pm on 21st June, she goes into No. 6, Signor Salvati's lodgings, perhaps already knowing where and what she wants to perform. But as I prepare for her scales and arpeggios to echo round the high stone walls, a warning bell starts ringing in my head. For weeks now, the *Chronicle* has been running advertisements for Chevalier Lancelotti's 25th Annual Grand Concert, Signor Salvati being its main attraction. The bell in my head is telling me that that concert is today – but surely Signor Salvati cannot have re-arranged Isabella's lesson to clash with the time he is meant to be performing in Chevalier Lancelotti's concert? I must be wrong.

But no. Double-checking every announcement against the days of the week in 1917 confirms that 21st June is a Thursday, exactly as specified by Signor Salvati in his new arrangements for Isabella's lesson, and simultaneously exactly as specified by the newspaper as the day of the big concert. Then I spot it. Two hours. Isabella's lesson begins at 7pm. The concert does not begin until 9pm. Isabella will be singing here with the ever-professional Signor Salvati at 7pm, and by 9pm he will be perfectly ready for curtain up at the Theatre Royal a few streets away. Solved!

But as I leave Cavalier Street, I feel more than a little dissatisfied. I may have worked out the logistics, but have I really got to the heart of the matter? Sixty-six years is a such a very long time to keep a message that merely rearranges the time of a singing lesson. Especially when Isabella has kept so little else from her war. There has to be more to it than a love of music. Maybe she really did have a crush on Signor Salvati, but I wonder. Could it have less to do with romance and more to do with Signor Salvati's singing? Perhaps his voice somehow released the pent-up emotions which Isabella herself never expressed.

But I have to leave my unanswerable speculations. I have reached what remains of the Theatre Royal after the Germans bombed it in 1942, and must seat myself. From the Chronicle I know exactly how this Annual Grand Concert will proceed and I follow it through the various solos and comic pieces of skilled amateurs, the star turns by Salvati and the other professionals, to its finale – a hilarious Anglo-French sketch entitled *English as she is spoke*. When it is time for the National Anthem, I stand with the audience, but I do not join them to descend the steps and make my way home. Next month, Isabella will be back here for Signor Salvati's farewell concert. Again, it will begin at 9 o'clock, but the weather will be sultry, and she will need her fan.

Letting the *Chronicle* carry me forwards to 23rd July, I watch the eager music-lovers settling back into their seats for Salvati's final treat. Life here is getting tougher. There have been scares about supplies of food and petrol. There have been exhortations to husband resources. The bakers have been accused of tampering with the flour and producing low quality bread. They have fought back by blaming the army for the sub-standard flour. Indeed, it is becoming clear that worries about the supply of food were as much the reason for the closure of the hospitals as the problem of transporting patients. Now though, even providing water is becoming so difficult that everybody, including the hospitals, is being ordered to hold back. When Isabella arrives here, she is coming from a day struggling to maintain standards of hygiene and sterility without the security of a reliable water supply. Thankfully for her, tonight's proceedings will be eminently successful – at least that is what the *Chronicle* will report on 31st July. That is the day after her thirtieth birthday. It is also the first anniversary of Beth's death.

SECTION 8

Isabella has been using her medical instruments here for near-ly a year now, but there has been no trace of a prisoner. Yet I have discovered that prisoners of war were held on Malta, and Joe has offered to drive me to their camp at Fort Verdala. Despite his long architectural career, he has never been there – he did not even know the history of the place. Which fits with my research. The use of Malta for the detention of prisoners of war is couched in such terms as 'Malta's dark secret,' and 'History's missing link.' Website copies website with such sentences as, 'This highly secretive operation by the British,' and, 'The British used Malta as a huge concentration camp.' Joe pulls into an empty plot opposite Fort Verdala's ornate gateway, reputedly the oldest part of the long defensive wall which allowed the British to establish several prison camps near here. They housed thousands of prisoners from most of the enemy nations – Germany, Austria, Hungary, Bulgaria, Turkey and Greece. Thankfully, the assurance by the experts at the V&A that the beads must have been the gift of an officer has limited my options. Isabella's donor can only have been held here in Verdala, where all officers were housed.

No gate blocks the entrance, so Joe and I walk straight through the tunnel in the fortified walls towards the buildings we can see beyond. Built as barracks in the 1850s, they are now used as houses, and the clutter of daily life is everywhere – cars, road signs, washing lines. Joe takes himself off to explore, but I dig out the book which is my treasure trove for this place. The moment I try to match up the first of the old photographs, I find myself slipping back to autumn 1917. Newly arrived German prisoners are standing on the spot where a play area stood. Weary nags replace the brightly coloured springy horses which had been awaiting their toddling riders. Innumerable wooden crates bury the parked cars. A heap of kit bags swallows up a Catholic shrine and its life-sized praying statue.

When I look up, I can see the armed guards on the roofs of the houses. Security here was quite relaxed in the early days of the war, but it has been much tighter since two prisoners managed to escape in the spring of 1916. Now, the guards are scrutinising every movement and the new arrivals are staring back, anxious-faced. They have had a long journey to get here, so they already know about being under guard and in enemy hands. But at the moment they are just waiting. This place is already crowded. It was built to house 350 soldiers, but now nearly 650 prisoners are having to squeeze in. Washing facilities are limited. No space remains for reading rooms, or any sort of church, chapel or mosque. The British have to make sure they abide by international conventions regarding the internment of enemy prisoners, so to improve conditions a little, they have levelled a space just outside the gate. They planned it as a skittle alley, but the prisoners have turned it into a garden.

The heat is sweltering, but there will be no relief for these newcomers at dusk when they are locked up. Many of the rooms are stuffy. Last year, some of the prisoners noticed that a hospital ship in the harbour was lying extraordinarily low in the water. Believing that she must be carrying heavy military equipment – a blatant violation of the laws of war – they had somehow relayed their observation back to Germany. The British had vehemently denied the charge, but to prevent any further spying, they have boarded up the windows.

Slipping to another day, another photograph, I walk to the other end of the complex. A small orchestra is seated beneath a trio of German flags. Two violin players are concentrating on the score, their bows energetic. A man with a cap is playing the flute. A mustachioed clarinet player is waiting, intently counting bars for the moment when he needs to bring his instrument to his mouth. I sense the air filling with the German music that Chevalier Lancelotti rejected. The audience is seated at small tables nearby, but there are not enough chairs to go round – some of them are having to make do with camping stools. It would look like a pleasant afternoon in the Mediterranean sun if I did not know that all these men are prisoners who will not see freedom until the war is over.

Could one of them be the man who gave Isabella her beads? Their clothing is varied, like the population of this prison. At the start of the war, Verdala was used to intern enemy aliens. Germans, Austrians and Turks from as far away as Egypt have been held here ever since August 1914, more than three years. Those enemy aliens will be the men wearing civilian clothes. They almost outnumber the men in uniform, but since I need a military man, I ignore them.

The first non-civilians to arrive here were apparently the crew of the German cruiser, SMS *Emden*. For several months in the autumn of 1914 she had carried out notoriously daring raids across the Indian Ocean. They had caused so much destruction and terror that people like the scientist Ernest Rutherford, who had been in Australia when the war broke out, had been forbidden to return to Britain while the *Emden* remained at large. Come November, she was finally defeated, her crew were captured and they were shipped to Malta, where the other prisoners welcomed them as heroes. Her officers are held here in Verdala, and I study the naval uniforms. I have always imagined Isabella receiving her beads from a soldier, but could they come from one of these dashing sailors? It would be very romantic ... But I hesitate. At the start of the war, these naval officers were already on duty in South-east Asia. When they left their wives, fiancées and girl-friends, there was no need to hurry any romantic talisman into their pockets. Reluctantly, I dismiss them. They are as unlikely to have given Isabella her beads as the enemy aliens.

But there are plenty of soldiers in this audience, still dressed proudly in their uniforms. Relatively large numbers of Germans captured during both the Sinai and the East Africa campaigns have arrived in Malta during the summer and autumn this year, 1917. The East African officers' uniforms have dramatic slouch hats, but, more importantly, they have large pockets. They have plenty of space for beads. Suddenly my eyes are jumping from pocket to pocket, wondering what each one hides. There may be precious mementoes, like the beads, in every single one of these men's pockets. Their owners will perhaps draw them out occasionally – not too often, that would be too hard, but once in a while, in a quiet moment, they perhaps allow themselves the heart-rending joy of sitting and remembering their girl, or their wife, or their children.

With that idea, the enormity of what it would mean to give such a treasure away suddenly hits me. Could a man really give away his treasured link with his home, with his beloved? Can Isabella's beads really have been the gift of a prisoner of war? Awed, I cast my eye over the sheer number of men in this place, men with memories, interrupted lives, grief and frustration. Will I ever be able to identify precisely which of them gave Isabella her beads? Already by September 1916, 23,142 able-bodied Germans were held by the British. The National Archives in Kew firmly state that they hold no lists of prisoners of war, although their papers include a range of requests from prisoners in Malta for news of wives or families, or for financial assistance from home or for exchange on health grounds. Somebody has advised me to contact the archives of the USA, who as a neutral power, supervised the camps until they entered the war, or of Switzerland, who took over after that, but the thought is so daunting that I have merely filed it. It is as if I am trying to locate one particularly unique bead among more than 23,142, and I do not even know if I would recognise that bead if it was staring me in the face.

Somewhat depressed, I walk back to the other end of the compound. There is one last scene to watch. A huge group of prisoners is standing in the courtyard looking up at the photographer, for all the world like twenty-first century guests at a wedding. Diaries and letters from other prison camps are full of the detainees' bitterness at being robbed of their youth, of their longing for a past that will never return, and of intense sexual frustration. They write of endless inspections and the unvarying monotony of the routine, and of being trapped in the company of people with whom they would never choose to mix.

I survey the Verdala men. How do they avoid going crazy, stuck in here day after day, year after year, under the constant control of the guards, never knowing when, how or if it will end? The book explains. In between all the roll-calls and restrictions, the prisoners are printing a magazine in German which pokes fun at their British captors. They have turned to educating one another, and to handicrafts – painting and making models, carving in wood and stone. They even set up exhibitions of their work. Back in the museum in Valletta, beside the torpedo that the *Laburnum* brought in, lie felt slippers made out of a hat, a cardboard relief map of the straits of the Bosphorus and a walking stick carved with little pictures, all made by prisoners of war.

But what happens when one of these men becomes ill? So long as Isabella's prisoner is stuck here in rude health, there will be no call for her to treat him, no gratitude will grow, and no beads will change hands. The book gives me hope. Apparently a prison doctor visits the camp every day, but for more serious complaints the men are sent to hospital.

"Which hospital?" I want to yell, as the paragraphs wind slowly on.

'Cottonera Hospital,' the words, at last, reveal – and I start to panic.

If Cottonera is the routine, how is Isabella, busy at St Ignatius six miles away, going to treat one of these prisoners? And why would the authorities send one stray patient over to St Ignatius when Cottonera sits right on Verdala's doorstep? Are none of the prisoners from here going to come under Isabella's care after all? Have I been completely wrong about the link between this place and the beads? My heart sinking, I plod towards the gate. The prison buildings of Verdala slump back into twenty-first century homes. As Joe drives me away, I try hard not to give in to despair.

2

Back in my accommodation, I decide I need to revisit my sources and check my ideas closely. I start with Isabella's army papers. The first line reads: 'Embarked for Malta 12.8.16.' The next line is equally bald: 'Egypt 4.5.18'.

Thanks largely to Walter's website and the *Daily Malta Chronicle*, I have roughly threaded Isabella's story up to the summer of 1917, but now I need to find the weft that will carry the tale on to next May.

All Isabella's own collection offers is a lightweight silver box with 'Malta 1917' scratched into its top. Whatever Isabella used it for, she used it well – all that remains of the orange silk lining is a series of parallel threads. But does it really tell me anything about her time in Malta? Perhaps it will be a Christmas present in December, but it might just as easily have been a birthday present in July, or a farewell gift from a friend at any time of the year.

Needing more definitive sources, I click up documents I copied from the archive of the Medical Women's Federation. On September 15th 1917, Constance Astley Meer, one of the women who travelled out with Isabella, writes home reporting that the contracts of most of the women doctors have been renewed, and that Surgeon General Yarr, the Director of Medical Services for Malta, has declared the medical women to be 'a great success' – I can almost hear the satisfied echoes of the lady doctors' voices as they talk the matter over in the Club.

"What else would you expect from such a marvellous group of women?"

"After all, we've proved our abilities every one of the last thirty years!"

As I read on, I discover that the army has been so satisfied with the work of the lady doctors here that it has started to employ female medical officers at home. Simultaneously, other sources reveal that the reduction in bed numbers that began when hospitals were closed and moved to Salonika has continued. Isabella and the remaining staff watch the tents coming down at Tigne', St George's, Imtarfa, Cottonera and St Andrew's. They can no longer send convalescents to the camps at Mellieha and All Souls, for they too have closed, as have the hospitals of Bavière, Hamrun and the Blue Sisters' Convent.

By the end of August only 5,465 hospital beds remain, and that includes the beds needed by convalescents and men waiting to leave the island, who require very little medical attention. About half the doctors, half the nurses and half the supporting RAMC staff have been sent elsewhere. The 'Wounded in Malta' column has disappeared from the *Chronicle*. There are eulogies and retrospectives about Malta's response to the emergency, and analyses of how the race was run. Lord Methuen will soon be commenting, "I am glad I came to Malta, if it was only to help the country in the organization of these hospitals." The work is winding down, so why has Isabella chosen to be one of the few women doctors, only twenty or so, who stay here?

"Why are you so sure she remains?" Walter emails.

"To start with," I reply, "there is the small matter of her army record. Why should I suspect it of being incomplete when the records of other women spell out their service in Salonika, their transfers back home or the resignation of their contracts? But it is not just that. On the back of the photograph of Isabella sitting beside the tree at St Ignatius, she has written 'September 1917'. That's two months after her annual contract came up for renewal in July. Since she is still with the Army in Malta in September, she must have chosen to renew."

But Walter has a point. Across the war zone Isabella could find many other places in far greater need of her assistance. Not for the first time, I wonder whether it is the needs of her family that are holding her back. When I check Ena's Red Cross record, I find that she, too, is choosing to stay in Malta. Again, why? VADs are needed elsewhere just as much as doctors. Could Mother be the real issue?

I recently noticed that in one photo Janet has swapped her deep black collar for something paler. Delving into the etiquette of mourning dress, I discovered that she would only do that after the first anniversary of the death – in other words she is still in Malta in August 1917. Maybe it is the dangerous seas that are keeping her here, but there are pressing reasons for her to go home. Back in Britain, Frank has joined up, and Jan, heavily pregnant with their second child, has returned to John's Place. With plenty of ships carrying medical staff away from the island, I cannot help wondering if Janet's horror at Beth's death is overriding the maternal instinct that would send her rushing to her youngest daughter's side. It almost seems as if nothing can lure her back into the house where her beloved Beth died.

But if Mother has stayed in Malta, Isabella and Ena must stay too. Not that they have no work to do. Carrying on here may be less glamorous than enduring the hardships of Salonika, but the patients who remain still require proper care. Pioneering surgery is being undertaken at St Elmo hospital. The American, Dr Sarah White, will assist the consultant in a groundbreaking operation to remove a bullet from Trooper Robert Martin's heart by inserting forceps through his right ventricle. In the hospital on Manoel Island, Dr Prudence Gaffikin will be undertaking some important heart work with Sir Arthur Garrod which will be published in the medical journals. Being half-marooned in the middle of a Mediterranean Sea dominated by German U-boats is not necessarily a bad professional choice.

Not that there is any specific mention of the work at St Ignatius, but then it is a small hospital, and it never has been much mentioned. Some sources admit they have no idea when it closes, while others mention 1919, but one source reports its conversion into a mental hospital in September 1917, the very month to which Isabella has dated the small photograph of herself on the steps of St Ignatius. Could it be that the picture is not merely some chance moment captured for eternity, but the record of a finale, documented by somebody's little Kodak?

More crucially, if St Ignatius is about to become a mental hospital, where will the army send their surgeon, Dr Stenhouse? Only two of the remaining hospitals specialise in surgery – St Elmo at the tip of Valletta, and Cottonera. As I read the word 'Cottonera', I wonder if I dare let my hopes rise. If, just if, Isabella were to be transferred to Cottonera, might she find herself treating prisoners of war after all? Could the beads be back in the frame? My mind wants to gallop ahead of the evidence and work out how the prisoner would actually present her with the beads, but it is, as yet, a ridiculously speculative idea and I force myself to leave it in favour of the safer ground of the archive of the Medical Women's Federation with its definitive letters, memoranda and articles.

There may be very few medical women left here, but one of them, May Thorne, has a reputation for caring for her colleagues. I can see her keeping the cohort together, rallying them in their roles and making sure they support one another. I picture Isabella among the little crowd of women who gather at the dock to wave goodbye to Constance Astley Meer, Helen Greene and Edith Guest one November day. They wave until they are sure their handkerchiefs are no longer visible from the deck, and then turn, sombrely, to leave the dock.

"We seem to bid farewell to somebody almost every fortnight at the moment."

"Do you wonder? When we hear of the casualties from the summer campaigns in France who are now languishing in hospitals throughout England?"

"Naturally. I understand why people go. Daily I ask myself whether I should follow suit, but there is work here that needs doing. We can't all leave and shut up shop."

"Constance, Helen and Edith have not gone for good – they're only going on leave."

"Officially, yes, but we all know that's not their real game. They're going to try and bully the War Office into giving them a transfer. And they're sure to get the home postings they want, just like so many of the others. We'll be waving them off again soon enough."

But when the three women return, they bring dramatically unexpected news.

"I beg your pardon, did you say you're being posted to Egypt?"

"Yes, Egypt."

"They didn't offer you posts at home?"

"No. Very politely they said that since we'd done so well in Malta, would we be prepared to go to Egypt?"

"How did you reply?"

"We're in the army. We're under orders. Naturally we said we would go wherever we were sent."

So on 17th December, Isabella and the others again make their way to the dock and wave the trio off, but this time the women are heading for Alexandria, not London. They are part of yet another experiment by the army. Constance, Edith and Helen are to be the first female medical officers to work with the RAMC in Egypt.

Isabella and her colleagues are left behind to prepare for a very frugal Christmas. Not only is food in short supply, but the Italian government has been reluctant to issue passports, so Chevalier Lancelotti has been having difficulty recruiting performers.

3

Systematically, I decode the archaic handwriting from the MWF archive and gradually become aware that the raw materials of a story are gathering themselves on my computer, a story that matters desperately to the women doctors. It begins with an order issued over in Salonika in October 1917. The order declares that the medical women are no longer to count as officers for the purposes of censorship.

To my untrained eyes, it is so obscure that I would ignore it but for the fact that the papers in the archive keep coming back to this matter of censorship in Salonika. Slowly, between grappling with the unfamiliar military protocol and gasping at some of the lady doctors' sentiments, I begin to understand the outrage that floods from the documents.

"You mean to say that we can no longer censor our own letters? We'll have to pass them to the officers with whom we work each day?"

"Yes. They'll have to read and censor every word we want to post. They'll be completely *au fait* with our most private business."

But this personal indignity is far from the harshest effect of the order. It has also stripped the women of the responsibility which every medical officer normally bears – the censorship of his or her own patients' letters.

"How can we be expected to carry out the medical officer's job of maintaining hospital discipline when the powers that be trumpet their distrust for us in this blatant fashion?"

"Yes, the less intelligent men already find it hard to remember that we hold exactly the same authority over them as the male doctors. The fact that we are no longer censoring post will only increase their suspicion that we are not as good as the men."

"And this comes after a year in which the authorities have time and again expressed their satisfaction with our work!"

The discussion goes broader as they ruminate on the wider implications of the new command.

"There are people who say we should never have agreed to come out here without rank or uniform, but the need was said to be so desperate."

"Exactly – it was too much to expect the army to change things all at once."

"The medical men themselves have accepted us. I can't recall a single complaint."

"This new order is sure to deter other medical women from joining up. I mean, who would choose to work under such an odious order?"

Their righteous indignation carries me right to the heart of how serving with the army is working out for the women doctors, but I have to read warily. I cannot afford to let a good story entice me into something which does not affect Isabella. Does she even know about the issue? The women in Salonika can hardly be mailing their complaints about the censorship order to their colleagues back in Malta.

I read on, until I come across a particularly fierce and articulate argument presented by Dr Katherine Waring, one of the women who sailed out with Isabella in 1916. Dr Waring had been sent to Salonika in July 1917, but by January 1918 she has returned home. That much is a fact, but while Dr Waring declares that she has parted company from the army after refusing to renew her contract under the present conditions, the army records that she was invalided home after a bout of dysentery. Are these contradictions, falsehoods? Or opposing facets of the same bead, spun by the speakers to reflect themselves in the best light and to throw the other side's argument into question? Whatever the truth of the matter, now that Dr Waring is no longer serving with the army, she is free to speak, and immediately I find she has provided me with the evidence I needed. Isabella does know about the issue. She is fully aware of what is going on.

Right from the start of her tirade, Dr Waring emphasises that the censorship issue has merely brought to the fore the 'invidious position' in which the medical women have been placed ever since they began working with the RAMC. She is, she declares, speaking not only for the women doctors working in Salonika, but also for those serving in Malta. Her words do not merely give me permission to explore the story – they command me to examine it in all its detail and work out how it weaves into Isabella's own tale.

Walter warned me about Isabella's contract. Now, time, experience and the move from Malta have allowed mild grumbles to mature into vociferous complaints. In London, Dr Waring's protest on behalf of her silenced former colleagues is so effective that the men of the BMA approach the MWF, offering to cooperate in any action the Federation feels is required. The

MWF canvasses its members, and letters and appeals cataloguing complaint after complaint flood in from women working with the Army across the UK and abroad.

So what, exactly, is happening in Malta, for Isabella? In the club in Valletta, I can see the conversation starting with the problem of travel.

"It is so undignified! If we cross to Sicily on the mail boat, it is the unqualified VADs who will travel up through Italy with the officers in first class, while we, having neither uniform nor rank, will have to take our place in third class with the rank and file. And we have all seen what that does for discipline!"

"The Italians are so wary of women travelling in civilian dress that I have heard of lady doctors being smuggled between platforms to avoid officials."

"I have heard of others being plied with scraps of uniform just to get them through."

"Not having uniform is driving the girls in Salonika mad. It means they have to carry many more garments, which the army laundries then refuse to wash because they are not uniform."

"But the whole problem is more serious than the travel and uniform, isn't it? Do you recall the dreadful way in which that ear specialist was treated? The man she took over from had been receiving the usual half a crown a day for his services, but the scoundrel kept drawing it when he left, even though he'd gone back to being an ordinary Medical Officer! The woman who replaced him received nothing at all for her skills."

"There was an eye specialist too, wasn't there? Didn't the man who was sent to help her take the full half crown while she did most of the work?"

"Specialist or not, I find myself getting daily more irritated. However long we stay with the army, however many years' experience we bring to a post, we have no commissions, which means we will always rank lower than the most newly recruited and inexperienced male doctor, simply because he is a man and we are women."

"Very true. By now, after over a year with the RAMC, we should all be captains, but the lowliest new medical man is given the rank of Lieutenant so he immediately out-ranks us, even if we have been practising for years and he is fresh out of college."

From HQ in London, the MWF asks whether uniform would solve the problem, and from across the war zone, even from Constance far away in Egypt, comes the resounding reply, "No!" Uniform without 'the proper status' would be worse than useless. Yet in March 1918, I read how the army, while still refusing to give the medical women commissions and rank, at last grants them the right to wear uniform. They have ended up with exactly what they regarded as 'worse than useless' – uniform with neither rank nor commission.

Their dress is to be similar to that worn by the ladies of the new Women's Army Auxiliary Corps. They will be entitled to wear RAMC buttons and badges, but not the Sam Browne belts which only commissioned officers are entitled to wear. Giving with one hand and taking with the other, the army warns the women that they will have no extra outfit grant to help them purchase their new kit. "You had something last autumn," it grumbles, "that will have to do."

At this point, I draw out another document from Isabella's archive, one of the invitations she must have received every year to confirm her entry in the Medical Directory. This particular letter will arrive after her death in 1983, sixty-five years after this discussion. One of the positions she is asked to confirm is that she worked as 'Capt. RAMC 1916–19'. Her daughter affirms that yes, Isabella was a Captain.

"But," I protest, "she can't have been. The army categorically refused to give the women doctors any rank at all. None of them were lieutenants, let alone captains. Isabella can't be the only one who was made a captain."

Her daughter is insistent and this letter from the 1980s backs her up. Clearly, I will have to carry on searching until I find out when and how the medical women receive these longed-for commissions, but with the arrival of spring 1918, it is time for Isabella to leave Malta. In a photograph, she is seated on a boat deck accompanied by three ship's officers, a grumpy looking fellow in khaki and two other women, '*Kaiser i Hind*, Empress of India', declares the back of the picture.

"The background looks like Valletta," says Walter.

A quick check reveals that the *Kaiser* is a super-speedy liner requisitioned by the government. By 1918 she is being used on the route between Marseilles and Alexandria.

Ena has already gone home – she left for England at the end of February and has been posted to a hospital in Reading. In the absence of any other evidence, I have to assume that Mother and Auntie have also gone back to Britain – perhaps Mother is already ensconced in Hampshire, as she will be in August. So why is Isabella not heading home too?

Could she have heard from the women who are already working in Egypt? Constance and Helen's letters to London tell of being posted to Sinai. They report how Lady Allenby, the Commander-in-chief's wife, had gone into raptures about their departure for the desert, "All Egypt stood on tiptoe to see you pass."

Out in Sinai, they had found themselves working under a very sympathetic Colonel, "Why, his own wife is a doctor!" He had entrusted them with convoys of up to 350 a day, and five other women from Malta had joined them. Together, they had been given responsibility for all the routine work – surgical, medical, eyes, ears, X-rays and so forth. The patients had flooded in and the hospital had grown to 2,000 beds. They had expected to move on to the Holy Land, but instead the hospital itself has been transferred to Salonika while they have been retained in Egypt. At present they are working in Cairo.

I look back at Isabella in the photograph. With tales like those ringing in her head, she may be as keen as mustard to work in Egypt, but while the women beside her are standing, she is perching on some seat. While they are military in skirts, jackets, ties and hats, she is not. Their uniform dutifully and properly resembles that of the WAAC, but Isabella is elegant in a turban style hat, open-necked blouse and a skirt and jacket which are clearly not the khaki of the other women's prescribed uniform. They are taking full advantage of their new rights, while Isabella, very definitely, is not.

4

With Isabella leaving Malta, it is time for me too, to leave, but as the plane takes off, I am gripped by an uneasy sense of disappointment. Yes, I have found out a reasonable amount about Isabella's life on the island and with the army, but I expected to find out more about the beads – maybe not the prisoner's precise identity, at least some clue as to where they came from.

Now the only lead I have will involve scouring the archives of the USA and Switzerland to see if any records remain of their supervision of WWI British prisoner of war camps. And why should such documents, even if they exist, provide the answer? The only thing which would provide a definite lead would be a list of doctors' names matched to the health records of the prisoners. But such a register would almost certainly record the senior officer's name, not Isabella's. Those beads! After tantalising me for years they are still resisting my efforts!

But back home, the heavy strand captivates me once more. It is so intricate – higher quality and more awe-inspiring than I remembered. Construction-wise, it is very similar to the V&A's *sautoir*, but design-wise the two are poles apart. Between each motif, the maker of Isabella's beads has split the weft to string the warp into five even strands, creating little decorative linking sections only a single bead wide. The museum's Viennese necklace has none of these appealing fiddly bits. Instead a bold chevron pattern runs smoothly along the piece. Its creator must have calculated in advance exactly what he or she wanted, then followed the template right to the final bead. The design is so elegant that it makes Isabella's beads look almost higgledlypiggledy. They display almost no hint of any overall strategy or pattern. Apart from centimetres, nothing would be lost if the strand simply stopped after any one of its motifs. It is almost as if the weaver set up the loom and experimented his or her way along, asking at the end of each motif, "What shall I do next?"

But who could that weaver have been? Surely a sophisticated German or Austrian jeweller like the creator of the V&A's *sautoir* would not have indulged in such playfulness. Could the stylish, craft-loving, secessionist girl have made them herself? Maybe the memento her lover snatched was home-made. In fact, she could have been emulating something she had seen worn by her social superiors, in which case – the inconvenient truth dawns on me – in which case, her man, Isabella's prisoner, need not have been an officer and my search is thrown right open – almost any German is now a potential bead donor. As if to confirm my hunch, an elegant French *sautoir* pops up online, all black and silver. It has the same fiddly bits as Isabella's string of beads, but its solid sections are gracefully symmetrical diamond designs. I may admire Isabella's *sautoir*, but it is completely outclassed by these chic museum specimens.

Flummoxed, I click aimlessly, drifting from one dead end to another. Time has long since vanished before a fresh combination of search terms, like an archaeologist's new tool, uncovers an entirely unexpected thread. Soon, a whole group of objects is assembled on my screen. Each one is constructed from Bohemian glass beads, and, incredibly, each one was made by men interned in British prisoner of war camps during the First World War.

OK, most of them are beaded crochet snakes. OK, the websites say they were made by Turkish prisoners, but here at last are prisoners of war who can get their hands on large numbers of glass beads and know how to thread them. Is it time to revisit my ideas about Isabella's beads? To confront my double doubts as to whether any prisoner could ever bring himself to give up his precious talisman, and where and how Isabella could have met him?

The photographs show that the beaded crochet snakes are intricate, colourful and painstakingly made. A snake that is five feet long is said to have been two years in the making. An online rumour suggests that the longest stretches for a full eighteen feet. I learn that Turkish prisoners were working with beads well before 1914. It was more than a way of filling the dreary days. The little objects they made could be sent home as tokens of affection, or sold for pocket money. The snake is a traditional Turkish symbol for good luck, so once the war began, it was snakes that the prisoners crocheted wherever they were interned. Passing allied soldiers bought them as souvenirs, and the prisoners used the money they earned to buy extra tobacco and coffee.

And the place most famous for its beaded snakes? Egypt, where more than 70,000 prisoners of war were held. Not only that, in Egypt the British were so concerned that the unfortunate men in their care did not 'go dotty', that the army itself provided the supplies for crafts.

With Isabella herself about to arrive in Egypt, this all looks oh-so tempting. But is it a blind alley? These snakes often have harsher and brasher colours than the subtle hues of Isabella's beads. They are made with a crochet hook, not woven on a loom. Can there be any possible connection? Then I come across some delicate pink frames, and websites assuring me that loomed items were also made. Would it be arrogant to re-visit the possibility that the prisoner himself wove the beads when the experts at the V&A ruled out the idea? In despera-tion, I contact the leading expert on beadwork by prisoners of war, Adele Recklies in New York.

"The problem with art experts explaining about beadwork is that they don't do beadwork, and they often have no clue what they are talking about," she replies, debunking the authority of the V&A in one scathing statement. "I wouldn't put too much faith in their opinion that it is German Secessionist in style. Basically they are just saying that it was done in the style of the times."

She explains how the narrow geometry of the loom con-strains the designs, "There are certain logical patterns that oc-cur and these can be seen in the motifs of the piece. Frankly, you could look at the Greek key panel and say that it was in-spired by Turkish sock patterns if you didn't know that the Greek key is a common design element."

Every word she says magnifies my already overwhelming sense that a prisoner could have made Isabella's beads. I find myself tempted to picture, not a craft-loving girl, but the pris-oner himself gathering a handful of beads and setting up his loom. Tracing out a grid in the Egyptian sand, he draws cir-cles and scrubs out crosses until he comes up with a pattern for his first motif. Letting the piece grow section by section, he challenges himself to dream up ever more combinations and permutations that will fit within the constraints of his ten warp threads. But I must not let this vision grip me as truth. Apart from the ringing words of the experts at the Victoria and Albert, the beaded objects I have found online were made by Turkish prisoners, and I am looking for a German.

Then Adele reminds me that, "Beadwork in many forms was a popular female pastime in the Victorian and Edwardian eras, so the German prisoners were at least familiar with the practice."

And there were plenty of Germans imprisoned in Egypt …

I am coming dangerously close to believing my own hypothesis. I am going to have to do the thing I have been dreading ever since I started to follow Isabella – I am going to have to go to Egypt. Apart from its incomprehensible language, Egypt is where rebellions happen, terrorism flourishes and Westerners are vulnerable. In justification of my reluctance to go there, I have persuaded myself that the Egyptians will long since have obliterated all trace of their colonial masters, that I have no leads to follow up in any archives, and that even if I did have, I would never find them since I cannot read Arabic. But I know it is a fudge, it is cowardice and the time has come. To solve the mystery of Isabella and her beads, I will have to go to Egypt. I log on, add airline tickets and two hotels to my shopping cart, and press 'Buy.'

5

When the coach to Heathrow breaks down at 1am before it even leaves my local bus station, my hopes soar. This will be my excuse! I will miss the plane and claim the journey back on insurance. But I am out of luck. A few hours later I find myself taking off for Egypt and immediately I am glad, for Isabella's story starts replaying itself beneath me. There are the white cliffs of Dover, the English Channel where so many hospital ships were sunk, the bloody battlefields of northern France.

May 1918 is not a good time for the British in France. The 3rd of March treaty between Germany and the new revolutionary government of Russia has allowed thousands of enemy troops to arrive here from the Eastern front, and the German army has been advancing rapidly towards Paris. American troops have arrived in Europe, but they are still in training, they are not yet ready to fight. I try to imagine the terror of hearing that the Germans have a gun which can shell Paris. It has even destroyed a church and killed the worshippers, but in no time the plane has crossed the Alps and is heading towards the Adriatic.

Even further south, Isabella too is en route for Egypt. The *Kaiser i Hind* is known as a charmed ship. She is so speedy that she has escaped from German U-boats five lucky times, most recently only week or so ago. She was steaming west across the Mediterranean with 3,000 troops and 500 crew on board when her engine room and stokehold were hit. Thankfully, the torpedo failed to explode, but to celebrate her good fortune, the dent left by the weapon has been painted green. This is her first voyage since the incident.

Three other women doctors are travelling with Isabella. The oldest, 44-year-old Margaret Dobson, is an eye specialist who has been serving at Valletta Military Hospital. She has been compiling a superb series of drawings of the ocular pathology she is coming across while on service. The other two, Margaret McEnery and Margaret Stewart, are roughly the same age as Isabella. Until last summer, they had been working in Malta, but they were then posted to Salonika, the place this plane is approaching.

The minute landscape beneath me is breathtakingly beautiful and the illogicality hits me. On a fine sunny May morning in the twenty-first century, it seems bizarre beyond imagining that there should be fighting, let alone that British, Indian, Anzac and Canadian troops should be fighting down there, so far away from home. I know there are strategic reasons for the campaign that military minds could readily explain, but in a sweep of the plane, the region is gone, and all I can see is the sea.

The *Kaiser* is only one of many British ships criss-crossing the Mediterranean this May. The Turks have not yet been defeated, but Jerusalem was captured last December, 1917, so thousands of allied troops are being shipped from Egypt to France in a desperate attempt to stem the German advance against Paris. That, perhaps, is why the *Kaiser* was so heavily laden last month. Like most of the other ships, on this return journey, she will dock in Alexandria, but my plane crosses the coast and carries on inland, above a dirty desert haze that washes everything pale brown. Miles later, Cairo appears, its regular rectangles and upward-stretching buildings disturbing the flat acres of the desert.

The moment I knew I was going to come here, I knew what I had to do. I bought tiny glass beads as small as the *sautoir's* originals. I sourced linen thread to match its warp and weft. I designed motifs nine beads wide like the motifs on my grandmother's string of beads. I overcame my dislike of the tedious business of catching the fiddly little things, and started to savour the whole process of weaving. Like Isabella's story, the new string of beads is almost complete, but not quite. It is still bound to the loom, little pots of tiny beads sitting beside it in my case. I am going to investigate what Isabella sees in Cairo before I make a pilgrimage to Alexandria. There, as I complete the weaving of this new strand, I hope to solve forever the mystery of Isabella's string of beads.

Why Alexandria? Family tradition never hinted as to where in Egypt Isabella might have served so, back in London, my whoop of joy had echoed all across the silent desks of the Wellcome Library when I spotted Isabella's name on a list of the lady doctors serving in Egypt with the RAMC in June 1918. Fifteen of the women, including Constance Astley Meer, Helen Greene and Edith Guest, were in Cairo, while Isabella and seventeen others were stationed in Alexandria.

It is Cairo, a cosmopolitan city with the allure of the East, the fascination of the pyramids and the excitement of the recent archaeological finds, that is the must-see destination for the British serving in Egypt. This June 1918, the Egyptian Expeditionary Force is so depleted by the departure of its troops to France, that a new campaign against the Turks will have to wait until reinforcements arrive from India. In the meantime, work is slack and staff can take leave. At one time or another, everybody gets themselves here. Can Isabella come immediately? Perhaps not, but she will be here soon, and she will follow the advice she is given and travel with someone else, perhaps one of the other lady doctors.

Wartime hotel prices have been fixed for the military, bringing places unaffordable before the war, with luxuriously comfortable rooms, excellent food and proper baths within the budgets of ordinary RAMC staff such as my grandmother and her friend, but this time neither they nor I can stay in the old British favourite, Shepheards. By 1918 it is HQ for the allied forces, and by the twenty-first century, the building is undergoing refurbishment. Isabella is forced to stay at the equally delightful Continental, but I cannot join her. By the twenty-first century, it has been disused and derelict for forty years.

My only chance of achieving an experience anything like hers has been to book into the Mena House Hotel, out by the pyramids in Giza. During the Gallipoli campaign, it served as an Australian military hospital, and now the jaunting British regard it as the very best place to take refreshments before and after touring the pyramids. Isabella is certain to visit.

But when the taxi delivers me to the hotel entrance, it feels as if I have landed on some alien planet. A liveried doorman takes my suitcase into the hotel lobby. A porter insists on carrying it to my room. Gritting my teeth, I follow, reminding myself that being served is very much a part of Isabella's world. She has always had servants, not in huge numbers, but they have always been there. She has always known how to order somebody to do something, how to accept little courtesies. Like the other women around her, she regards such marks of respect as her due. A security guard nods to me as I pass his booth. If you are used to such attentions, as the lady doctors are, you will feel their absence, and if they are deliberately neglected by men under your care who are choosing not to know better, you will feel it, as the women doctors do, very keenly indeed. I scrabble for a tip as the porter ushers me into my room, and close the door with a sigh. I am still very, very far from putting myself in Isabella's shoes.

In the morning, my guide is Olaa, twenty-seven years old and beautifully swathed in modest Muslim dress. As she guides me through the beeping Cairo traffic to the Egyptian Museum, I warn her that although I want to see the place because the building was opened in 1902 and the antiquities fascinated the visiting British, nothing discovered since 1919 interests me because Isabella could not have seen it. Expertly, Olaa explains about kings and sarcophagi, coffins, mummification and the countless deities of the different kingdoms of ancient Egypt, but my attention drifts. I keep imagining Isabella and her companion looking at these same exhibits, and wanting to know who is guiding them. Some officer who has followed the news of the excavations, devoured the countless books published on the matter and added the knowledge of Egyptian civilisation to his existing knowledge of ancient Greece and Rome? Or an archaeologist, enticed from some corner in the hotel, and crustily – or is it flamboyantly – expounding on the marvels he has unearthed?

Soon, reluctantly, I have to follow Olaa upstairs to the Tut-ankhamun section. King Tut will not be discovered until 1922, so there is no chance that Isabella will see these treasures, but I pretend to listen patiently. Until I notice a small photograph of a beaded object in one corner of a large poster.

Completely distracted, I have an excuse when Olaa wishes to talk to a fellow-guide. Taking off, I discover a whole glass case filled with items made from a glorious assortment of beads – turquoise, white, rusty red and green. But every single bead is far too large. I glance towards the next cabinet, 'Goods returned from the Metropolitan Museum in New York'. Suddenly I see them. 'My' beads. Tiny glass beads lying loose in a plastic pot, just like the beads in my suitcase. Each one is round. Each one is royal blue. Each one has tumbled loose. The thread that wove them into a 'something' that served a very particular elaborate and religious purpose in King Tut's royal tomb has long since decayed, but I am transfixed. Loose beads from centuries ago? Beads that have rolled free from their story? These little round scraps of blue are worth far more to me than any world-famous golden mask. They are treasure indeed.

6

For lunch, Olaa picks up something Egyptian from a fast food shop, but eating falafel in a radio-polluted Cairo traffic jam makes it hard to re-inhabit the military world in which Isabella lives, however many European-style buildings we dawdle past. I wish I had asked to visit Groppi's. Before the war, Swiss M. Groppi was famed for his sumptuous pastries and croissants, his superb chocolates and ice cream smothered in crême Chantilly. Whether or not he will be able to conjure his magic today, it is to his Tea Garden that I have to imagine Isabella and her companion going. Constance, Edith and Helen are waiting for them. Immediately, the girls from Alexandria can see that the three older doctors have donned khaki. An officer's tunic sits neatly over their white or khaki blouses. Brown shoes and stockings are visible beneath their khaki skirts, and before the younger women have even seated themselves, the trio are off.

"The heat does make it rather hard to keep the collars looking crisp."

"We wear a Sam Browne when we are on orderly duty. I know the order from London didn't specify that, but the Director of Medical Services out here has permitted it."

"I wish he'd do something about the hats. Some of the young ones wear the most dreadful service caps," Helen looks pointedly at Isabella and the young woman beside her, "it makes them look so cheap. One of the Colonels said he thought they looked like Apaches. All their hair and even their whole head is swallowed by their silly caps. They look such frights!"

"We stick with these sun-helmets," Edith gestures to their

solar topees, "and swap them for panamas or khaki felt in the winter."

"I'd like to see those youngsters in neat little forage caps," Helen glares again at the visitors from Alexandria.

"Of course, as you know, the whole get-up is not compulsory," Constance comforts them. "It is partly a copy of what the WAACs wear, but the DMS out here has modified it somewhat."

Edith and Helen continue their diatribe. "Some of the girls in the other hospitals choose not to wear it, but they look so untidy!"

"I can't understand why they refuse. How do they manage to travel anywhere? When I was in mufti I found it extraordinarily difficult to persuade the authorities that I was an official personage with permission to travel, but my uniform serves as its own passport. Everyone is now sweetness and light and I sail through. And of course now we are in uniform we actually receive the reduced fares that soldiers and sisters have always been granted and which we should have been awarded months ago."

"Personally, I see our uniform making the biggest difference on the wards. I find the patients very much more inclined to treat me as an officer."

At last Isabella's companion manages to chip in, "The other day common courtesy led a man to stand up as I walked past. His sergeant promptly told him to sit down because, "He need not stand for 'that'." He did not even dignify me by calling me 'a lady doctor' or even 'her,' he called me, 'That'."

The three older women exchange glances. According to the letters they have written to the MWF, Alexandria is not on 'lines of communication', so the only way to find out what is happening up there is when they meet the medical women from Alexandria when they turn up in Cairo like this.

"In Cairo we have been accepted into every mess."

"Most of us in Alexandria have been allowed to join our officers' mess. It is just that particular hospital," Isabella reassures them.

"The medical officers taunt us because we have no rank," continues Isabella's companion, "they say it would be infra dig for them to sit down with us because we are even lower than the NCOs."

"Why here, most of the MOs, even the colonels, express their surprise that after all the work we have done, we are still denied military status and commissions," Constance sympathises, "We certainly need to be commissioned as proper officers – for our patients' sake as much as for our own. Uniforms without commissions are not enough when one has to maintain discipline over as many as 130 men."

Nothing can stop them now, and I imagine Isabella and her friend nodding in agreement, recognising the truth of the arguments from their own bitter experience.

"The fact that we have no rank makes both men and officers look down on us. It is quite contrary to the principle the medical profession has always stuck to: that no one section should ever be considered inferior to another."

"'Equal pay for equal work' has been the hallmark of the profession ever since we gained the right to qualify. Here, we receive the same mess allowance as the men, but they receive 2/6 a day for doing specialist work that is denied to us."

"But it's not just specialist work, is it? I come back again and again to the fact that we are senior in service to many of the men here, but every single one of them, however young and inexperienced, ranks above us. Even if, God forbid, the war continues and we find ourselves staying here for another ten years, any youngster who has not yet started his training will still take precedence over us."

This is familiar territory, but, cut off from communication, what Isabella and her friend want to know is whether any progress is being made – what has happened since they boarded the *Kaiser i Hind* in May.

"I hear that the government is to be approached about the whole matter," declares Constance, "I have written to the Medical Women's Federation, impressing on them how urgent the problem is. We cannot wait any longer. Who knows when this war will end? The matter must be addressed immediately."

Edith and Helen are nodding, "We have both added our penny-pieces."

"Our Colonel says it's going to take concerted action by the BMA as well as the MWF," Constance continues. "The male doctors found it difficult enough to secure their position after the South African War. Apparently Sir Alfred Keogh is in favour of granting us commissions, but doesn't himself have the power to do it. It's a matter for the War Office and parliament."

"We are pressing them to discourage any new women from coming out," declares Edith. "We can put pressure on the powers that be by refusing to renew our contracts unless we are granted commissions, but that will have no effect if our places are readily taken by newcomers who haven't realised the gravity of the situation."

Edith will be as good as her word. She will refuse to renew her contract and will arrive home in August. After that, she will never again work for the army but Constance and Helen will stay in Egypt until May 1919. None of them know that in London, the President of the MWF, inundated with anguished letters about the conditions, has already warned the War Office to expect a mass exodus if something is not done promptly to ease the situation. She is working closely with the BMA. She is corresponding with members of parliament. She is seeking the advice of the various suffrage societies about the best tactics for timing questions in the House. The campaign is underway.

The traffic disperses, and I, like Isabella and her companion, at last reach the Great Pyramid for a final spot of sight-seeing. By way of explanation, Olaa starts to scratch a diagram in the sand, but apart from noting that this is exactly what I imagined the prisoner doing, I am not concentrating. Time and history are eliding. Descriptions written by the British wartime visitors still apply. Look at the oranges – they all talk about oranges. And that group of tourists scrambling up the foot of the pyramid, they are Tommies swarming up to arrange themselves for photographs and enjoy the scene beneath them. And the camels – around them should be clustered not tourists, but officers and nurses. The camel handlers themselves are so weathered that they might almost be the descendants of the Arabs who robbed the Pharoahs' tombs not long after they were built.

As they plead for passengers, the wheedling voices of trinket salesmen get louder. Hands dangle plastic pyramids and tawdry sphinxes before my face.

Shooing the men away, Olaa deposits me safely back at Mena House. Taking tea in the very building where Isabella and her friends will, eventually, order their own tea, I imagine them clambering onto the awkward saddles of the camels. Security hedges mean I cannot see them riding round the Great Pyramid, jolting out towards the desert and wending their way back past the Sphinx, but when they arrive here, their unsecured view will be of the Great Pyramid surrounded by mile upon mile of desert.

7

Speeding along the new desert road to Alexandria, I pass irrigation projects and concrete buildings that Isabella cannot see, pigeon lofts and mosques almost identical to those she passes on her train journey northwards. But then come factories and industrial complexes, and the car has slowed to a crawl before it eventually draws up at the Metropole Hotel.

Inside, baksheeshs and check-in negotiated, an elegant woman leads me to the lift. We squeeze inside. She reaches to close the outer iron railings. Concertinas the inner gates shut. Presses 4. This is an Isabella-style lift. We jolt upwards through an antique marble stairway, past the open door of the Versailles room, the *deuzième étage*, the *troisième étage*, and creak to a stop at *quatrième* – French that fits with the cosmopolitan Alexandria I have visited in books.

I am in luck – this place is as historic as I had hoped. I wanted somewhere Isabella might have been, somewhere that would give me a sense of Alexandria as it used to be. The receptionist unlocks room 421. It is dark. Even when she flicks on the light it remains dim. She leaves me. I walk to the window and tweak the red damask curtains, gingerly finger apart grey nets rigid with dirt. Next come shutters. I tug. They refuse to open. The car is on its way back to Cairo. I am alone, in the dark, in Alexandria. If I do not brave going out now, I never will. Packing my bag with very little, I risk the teeming exterior.

Within one block, I am glad I have done it. Nobody has so much as glanced at me. So much for being the focus of attention, the target of beggars, traders and worse. I start walking along the front trying to decide which buildings Isabella sees. Some are clearly Art Deco, so must have appeared since she was here, but there are a lot I cannot place. The famous library of Alexandria is nearby, so I head there. Is it the sixteenth archive I will have visited during the course of this research? In the fifth different country?

"Do you have anything about the British in Egypt during the First World War?" I ask at reception. From the top of the building to the bottom, librarians check their catalogues. But my presumption proves correct – they hold not a single document. By way of consolation, they suggest I visit the library's exhibition of old photos of Alexandria, "You'll have to be quick, we are closing soon."

Hurriedly, I rush into the exhibition and begin photo-surfing. Matching dates to styles, I study buildings I have heard of, ignore the rest and move on as slowly as compatible with the place's imminent closing time and my extreme distaste for the idea of a night in the library. Even at this speed though, I can see that it would take a mass of research to disentangle Isabella's Alexandria, and I already know that that research would be tricky.

At the start of the Gallipoli campaign in 1915, hospitals were set up in Egypt just as efficiently and extensively as in Malta. As casualty numbers fluctuated, they were expanded, closed and shifted around in exactly the same way as the Maltese military hospitals. But the records of what happened here seem to be even scantier than the records of events in Malta and with no Walter having been interested enough to create a website, and

Isabella herself having left no tantalising clue-comments, I am having to be selective. I already know that, as a surgeon, she will be operating, changing dressings and battling infections. I need to focus on the differences – what British military life is like in Egypt, how the struggles of the women doctors are affecting her, and, of course, I want to solve the mystery of the beads. This is my last chance: if I do not solve it here, I never will.

With the minutes vanishing fast, I arm myself with the exhibition's juiciest morsels to guide my investigations. Here is E.M. Forster, a military nurse in the city during the war, commenting that, *'If one could judge Alexandria by her gardens, one would do nothing but praise.'* That would suit Isabella, I think, as security rounds the corner and turns me out.

Out among the shoppers, I am the only European on the street. Gorgeously clad muslim ladies are seeking pins for their headscarves. Shirt-sleeved Arab gentlemen are seated at pavement cafés. The whole scene is so thoroughly eastern that it is hard to believe that a century ago Alexandria was reputed to be more European than Arab. This very road was lined by Western-style shops that were patronised by elegant French and Italian ladies, British nurses and soldiers – and Isabella.

8

Up in my darkened room, I move all the lights to one corner. I read again my notes about prisoners of war, unpack my loom, dig out my little containers of glass beads and begin to weave.

First I spear a cream bead, another cream, a royal blue, and three more creams with my needle. A blue resists my attempts to catch it, but at last it and two more creams join the first six beads. I slide these chosen nine onto the weft thread that trails from the needle and ease them all the way to the loom, where the warp threads still grip the beads I wove at home.

Firmly, I press my nine new beads upwards until each one is wedged tight between two of the ten warp threads. Now I have to wrap the weft thread up around the warp before thrusting the needle back through the nine new beads, locking them in place. That is the tricky part. The holes of the beads are small and the least misalignment stops my needle getting through. Sometimes the warp threads go slack or the needle gets bent and it takes me many minutes to re-tension the warps, or to bend the needle back into shape, but I suppose the man who wove Isabella's beads faced the same snags.

There, I have caught myself saying, "The man who wove Isabella's beads." Since my email exchange with Adele, my thoughts have crystallised. I have rejected the opinion of the experts in the V&A that no prisoner could have made Isabella's beads. I have discarded my long-held dream of the beads reaching the war-zone after a gloriously romantic evening in Germany. I am convinced that Isabella's beads were not only given to her, but also woven, by a prisoner of war.

Not that I yet know exactly who that prisoner was. Isabella specified a German, and her prisoner cannot have come up with a piece of jewellery so similar to what was being worn in the capital cities of Europe unless he knew about *sautoirs*, unless he was reproducing something he had seen, but there are a million possible scenarios.

Did he perhaps, thankful for Isabella's medical skills, look round the prison camp to see what he could make for her, notice the beads the Turks were using in their section of the camp, and decide to try his hand at reproducing something he remembered. Perhaps he worked out how to manage the loom, then designed different motifs and colour combinations for each section in a systematic, and very Teutonic, fashion?

Or did he describe what he wanted to one of the Turks and commission the Ottoman to carry out his scheme? And if I am correct that Isabella's string of beads has been made with a full knowledge of European *sautoirs*, he must have been a man who had the social status to move in *sautoir*-wearing circles. Am I back to looking for an officer? Although now I come to think of it, he could have been a servant, or a well-to-do civilian. Isabella said, "Prisoner of war," after all. She did not say, "Soldier."

Glancing back at the pattern I have drawn for this section, I fumble with the cream and blue beads. It is easy to lose count and make the motif too long or too short.

Just up the coast from this dark room, at Sidi Bishr, is a prisoner of war camp. There used to be two in Alexandria, but the one at Ras-el-Tin was closed down in 1917. Since then all the prisoners have been held at Sidi Bishr. The camp houses about 5,000. There are Turks from the campaigns in Sinai and Palestine, Germans from the East African and Palestinian campaigns, and German and Austrian civilians brought in from the streets of Alexandria right at the start of the war, civilians who had until then been living happily alongside the British, French, Greeks and Italians as part of the cosmopolitan melting pot that was Alexandria. I jab hard to get the weft thread back between a row of beads.

Up here behind these heavy curtains and shutters, I feel cut off, but in a few rows time, I will finish this weaving and leave the room. Isabella's prisoner cannot go anywhere when he completes her string of beads. This final motif is meant to represent him. A male symbol, a royal blue arrow attached to a royal blue circle on a cream background, it mirrors the female symbol I have used to signify Isabella at the other end of the strand. I have just reached the arrow head, where I have three blues to lay correctly between the creams. These weavings need thousands of beads – over 200 for just one motif – but the whole process has been much faster than my original attempt to mimic Isabella's *sautoir*. The prisoner will not need as long as I thought. And if I can weave in this gloomy light, he should have no problem out in the Egyptian sunlight.

At the end of the motif, I release the warp threads from the loom. One by one, I weave them securely into the weft. These beads are not meant to come loose – yet. Laying it on the bed, I survey the result. The motifs tell a story.

At one end lies Isabella, a gold female symbol against a pale pink background. At the other end is a man, the male symbol I have just completed.

She comes from Scotland, so there is a saltire, white diagonals against deep blue. He is German, so there are the black, white and red stripes of the flag the Germans are using during this war.

She trains as a doctor, so there is a stethoscope, rubber red against silvery blue. His story turns dark as war demands that men kill and maim, so I have woven a gun, iron black against the innocent blue sky.

Their stories collide right in the middle. The man is taken prisoner and needs a doctor. Isabella can heal him, so the Asclepian snake of the RAMC coils round its rod, brown and green against golden desert sand. The boundaries of gender and enmity which fascinated me right from the start have been crossed. Boy has met girl, the scene is set for Isabella to receive her beads.

But I need more details. Exactly how have these two met? Logically, only recent captives will be suffering from raw war wounds. Prisoners who have been held for longer will require surgery only for the after-effects of intransigent wounds, or for the normal afflictions of being human – appendicitis, hernias, cancers, accidents. Sidi Bishr has its own doctor, its own infirmary and even its own operating theatre. And since a woman is not going to be appointed doctor to prisoners starved of female company, the only way for this particular prisoner to receive treatment from Isabella is for him to develop a condition far too serious for treatment within the camp, a condition so serious that he has to be sent to one of the hospitals in Alexandria – the one in which Isabella happens to be working.

9

Laying the beads safely ready for the morning, I descend to the Versailles room for dinner. This hotel glories in being an archaic time-capsule, so it takes no imagination to step back a century to when it was built. I order my meal beneath a high ceiling bedecked with original, ornate, gilded plaster shapes. The only things it lacks are the whirring fans. Beside me, slightly tattered panels of rich red damask line the smoke-dirtied cream walls. No table is set for fewer than six, but the room is almost empty, and as the *maître de hotel* places a plastic bottle of mineral water beside me, I wonder if there is anything more depressing than faded, empty glory. What this place needs is a few enthusiastic British officers with their girls – lady doctors as well as nurses. It needs a few potted palms and a full orchestra instead of a smarmy man with a feeble keyboard. There should be the laughter of arrogantly loud British voices grabbing the moment.

Yet when I return for breakfast, the gloom is gone, the curtains are open, the sea is glittering and I have a pilgrimage to make. Since the six lanes of speeding traffic refuse to morph into British army vehicles and horse-drawn locals, I simply join the work-bound Alexandrians hurrying along the Corniche. Twenty hot minutes later, I find myself out by Fort Qaitby on the harbour bar, surveying a sunny morning sea.

In 1918 Alexandria is one of the largest ports in the Mediterranean, the arrival and departure point for most of the British military staff in Egypt. To the west, Isabella can see a stream of naval vessels, transports and hospital ships slipping in and out of the harbour. Her *Kaiser* was luckier than the troopship *Aragon*, which was torpedoed about 10 miles off-shore just after Christmas 1917. Six VADs and more than six hundred others lost their lives in that disaster, but today the sea is sparkling and innocent – not even the cruise ships and container vessels that at present use the port are disturbing the skyline.

On my way back, I watch Alexandria curling round the Eastern Bay. The British love driving along this coast. Cadging a lift in an army car or hopping into the tram seats specially reserved for Europeans, they pass sumptuous mansions with well-tended gardens on their way to the cinema at San Stefano, or the casino at Ramleh, or the beaches that lie to the east of the city. Not that I can see any of these beauties. Like Sliema, Isabella's Alexandria has been buried beneath concrete and tourism. But the sea remains. I try to conjure my grandmother promenading here with her friends, watching the fishermen as I do, but instead of the T-shirts and jeans worn by the swarthy men I am passing, Isabella's fishermen wear red tarbooshes and loose white robes.

The final three places I need to reach are not tourist attractions. The hotel receptionist checks my route against the map, then sends the bellman out to negotiate the price of a taxi. Through the hotel door I watch one yellow and black cab moving off, the driver shaking his head with a completely legible, 'never-heard-of-that-one-mate' expression on his face. The bemused bellman phones the receptionist and there is much to-ing and fro-ing before a driver, at last, nods his head. I am ushered into the vehicle, the door shuts, and I am bowling through the un-known streets of Alexandria in a rickety bee-striped Lada.

Does this driver understand English? I try out a few, timid sentences, but in no time we are laughing in despair and re-sorting to communication by gestures alone. If I pointed at a map, he could take me to all sorts of interesting British haunts: Pompey's Pillar – that is a good picnic spot; Nouzha Gardens, where a band plays; Antoniadis gardens. The list goes on, but my pilgrimage takes me to none of these. Instead, we are start-ing at the Alexandria Sporting Club.

For Isabella it is the centre of the social scene, a vital life line. Yet today, the moment the taxi draws up, we hit a problem. I am not a member and the security guards refuse to let us in. Through the window I can see the plush green, irrigated lawn. When the British play golf here in 1918, they have to make do with 'greens' pressed out of hard brown sand. For the right tip, the 'native' caddy will reserve an officer the same set of clubs week after week. From my seat in the back of the taxi, this place hardly looks big enough for a golf course, let alone for the ten-nis courts, polo ground, hockey pitch and horse-racing track that the British have constructed here.

I glance at the guards. This taxi driver may not speak my language, but he is doing exactly what I need – keeping se-curity talking and buying me a few minutes. Across the lawn, there is a pure white club house far too new to be the one that Isabella uses. Hers has British officers coming and going with their rackets and golf clubs, teacups, cocktails and girls. With-out the club, claim the voices of the time, life would be dull indeed. Every officer, they write, including nurses and VADs, is allowed to join the club.

Suddenly I wonder. Does 'officers' include Isabella? With the anomalous position of the women doctors, are the medical ladies accepted here? Or is Isabella, like me, banned from this place?

I dredge up the memory of one of the few remaining photographs in her archive. Tugging at the brim of her panama hat to shield her eyes from the sun, she and another woman are on board a ship with four male companions. One, I have been told, is a member of the RAMC, another an officer from an Irish regiment, and the remaining pair are naval lieutenants, so Isabella is most definitely socialising with officers on board that ship. But does that mean she is allowed to socialise with them here in this club? An important detail gives me hope: taking advantage of her new rights, Isabella is at last wearing military uniform with RAMC badges. The woman beside her is wearing another variation on the same theme. Anybody can see that they are military doctors, and there must be a good chance that their new outfits are serving as the passports they have needed for so long.

A lurch lands my thoughts back in the taxi. The engine is starting up but another feature of the photograph means that I no longer mind that the driver has lost the argument. Isabella and her friends may be merrily lined up beside the railings of a ship, but between them and the photographer thrusts a gun, the mouth of its barrel just visible to the left of the picture. It is all very well to talk of golf and polo, tennis and tea, but that is not why any of them are here – they still have a war to win. Over the summer of 1918, reinforcements arrive from India, and by September the Egyptian Expeditionary Force is once more ready to fight. The time for socialising is past.

Hurtling along highways and flying round floral roundabouts it is not long before bilingual signs warn me that we are nearing the second stop of my pilgrimage. Letting myself out of the cab, I raise five fingers three times to tell the driver how long I will be, and walk through an entrance that resembles a miniature fort. The thick walls create the same isolating silence as at Pieta. The grassy pathways offer the same verdant stillness as the cemeteries in France. Before me rises the Cross of Sacrifice, the tall stone cross with its bronze sword that stands protectively above the graves in all but the smallest of the cemeteries where the British dead of the First World War lie buried. This is the place that the other taxi drivers did not know, Hadra, the British military cemetery.

I have read that, during the First World War, Alexandria houses several General Hospitals, as well as separate units for officers and for Indian troops. Orders dictate that severe wounds, whether inflicted by torpedoes or acquired in land battles, are not to be treated here but are simply to be patched up for safe transport to England – in other words, the very cases that Isabella has been tending in France and Malta are to be sent home.

What is her new role? Well, she must be continuing the struggle against infectious diseases of all sorts – everyone has to. She must be treading the excruciatingly hard stone floors of the hospital buildings and enduring their scorching summer heat – she cannot avoid them. She may be working in the torrid, tented hospitals. Perhaps she is doing night duties – night duties that sound remarkably like Saturday evenings in twenty-first-century casualty departments – drunken Irishmen, the victims of fights, inebriated Lancashire miners and policemen turning up at the same moment as suspected cases of appendicitis. But even though I have no evidence of precisely what she is doing, nor exactly where she is working, this cemetery gives me certainty. It was created when the previous cemetery ran out of space in 1916, so, if one of Isabella's British patients dies, he will definitely be buried somewhere here, among these horrifically familiar rows of tombstones.

Only a few paces into a row of graves, one of the headstones demands my attention: 'Private W.E. Terry, Royal Army Medical Corps, 1st November 1918, Age 21.' It is the date that gets me. After the long wait to build up the size of the Egyptian Expeditionary Force, General Allenby finally leads his troops into battle against Turkish forces near Megiddo on 19th September 1918. He follows victory there by capturing Damascus, and then, on 26th October, Aleppo. These defeats are not the Turks' only problems and, as October wears on, they send emissaries seeking the suspension of hostilities. An armistice comes into effect on 31st October, exactly one day before Private Terry dies.

I have visited so many war cemeteries by now that I had imagined this visit would be easy but it is the reverse – it is the hardest yet. Look at the flowers at the foot of Private Terry's tombstone. They are everlastings, but he has not lasted for ever. He has not even lasted his allotted three score years and ten. He has died just 24 hours after the hostilities in this part of the world have ended. I know he was probably not killed by rogue Turks flouting the ceasefire. I know it was probably some long infectious disease which happened to reach its awful climax on 1st November, but that does not change the fact that a young man who could have had a rich life has died, and that that death has taken place at precisely the moment when the risk of death in battle, in this part of the world at least, has ended for good.

Only a few days after Private Terry's death the final, big Armistice of the war is signed. At 11 o'clock on the 11th day of the 11th month every gun falls silent. In Alexandria, it is apparently almost night-time before the news gets through, but when it does, the streets fill with revellers, all the many nationalities of this cosmopolitan city singing and celebrating in their own languages, a glorious cacophony of sound.

Somewhere, Isabella too enters into the spirit of the festivities and breathes the same collective sigh of relief, but these rows of graves make it painfully obvious that the end of the war is not the end of her work here. As I walk along the rows of stones, I can see the deaths mounting up through November and December. Many of these graves hold the bodies of young men who have been killed not by the Turks, but by Spanish flu, the lethal virus that targets the young and fit. In Syria, the disease had hit General Allenby's expeditionary force very severely. Men reportedly died like flies, with more than half of them being out of action by the time they marched into Damascus.

Solemnly, I walk along the rows, trying to picture the horror of how these soldiers collapsed, exhausted and shivering, as their lungs filled rapidly with fluid and their faces became blue. It happened unbelievably fast, I have read, but it was best when they gave up quickly, coughing up bloodstained sputum. If they were unlucky, they lingered on until their faces turned brown, their feet black and a savage pneumonia hit. After their deaths, these influenza victims were hurriedly laid beside the other fatalities of the day in whatever space was left in the mortuary.

Grave after grave rams home the truth that Isabella's life here is far more than a social whirl at the club. It is far more than a series of debates and arguments with the War Office about rank and recognition. Only the medical profession has any chance of, somehow, defeating this particular deadly enemy, and Isabella is a member of that profession.

By the end of December, the *Egyptian Gazette* is reporting that the number of deaths caused by influenza is going down in Alexandria, but the rows of tombs here tell me that Isabella is still fighting for lives as 1919 dawns and spring approaches. Bending, I read the inscription '15th May 1919'. That is after Isabella has gone home – her army record states that she arrives back in Britain in early April 1919. But the graves do not stop filling. Some have dates as late as July.

Quietened by the tragedy of it all, I turn and walk back to the taxi. This place has touched me in much the same way as the graveyard in Frévent and F.D.B.'s poem. However much Isabella may be enjoying sight-seeing and social life, her mission here never stops being deadly serious.

10

Subdued, I confirm the final destination of this pilgrimage to the driver, "The beach at Sidi Bishr." Off he swerves down back street after side street until we are swooping east along the road to Ramleh that the British so love. I have unearthed many aspects of the mystery of Isabella and her string of beads, and now, as the final, solemn act of my quest, I want to commemorate the man who started it all. I want to bury my new story beads in the sand where his prison camp stood, where, I believe, he wove her beads. The story of Isabella and her prisoner of war will take its place in the canon of the many tales hidden beneath the sand of Egypt.

Towering modern buildings hide the spot where the prison camp at Sidi Bishr is said to have been constructed – a healthy site on the sea shore where the sand dunes created a miniature landscape of hillocks and valleys dotted with palm trees. In 1917, delegates of the International Red Cross visited to inspect the conditions under which Turkish prisoners were being held. Their report is so full of praise that the word 'whitewash' comes to mind – like so many of the reports from that era, it would never be issued in the twenty-first century. The accommodation, the bedding, the way in which the prisoners were given a budget on which to cater for themselves, the clothing and the extras which they could order from Alexandria – everything was excellent. Well, the rain did leak into a few buildings but, *'the extreme rarity of such an occurrence makes it of no importance.'* The water supply, the levels of hygiene, the medical care and the rates of sickness and death – none of them attracted the Inspectors' criticism, and when it came to pay, correspondence, recreation, religion and amusements, the only grievance they logged was the complaint by imprisoned officers that they were not allowed to go into Alexandria or to visit their wives who were interned in Cairo. Not that my scepticism means that the Inspectors' observations were untrue. Other reports describe how some of the British officers in charge of prisoner of war camps cared deeply about their charges, and the sheer number of creative pastimes indulged in by the prisoners in British hands shows that the thought given to the men's welfare went well beyond keeping them dry and fed.

Doubling back, the driver manoeuvres the taxi onto the same side of the carriageway as the sea and draws in. Hesitantly, I get out. How can I reach the beach? With massive concrete buildings smothering every spot of land on the other side of this road, the beach is as near as I can hope to get to the sand of Sidi Bishr prisoner of war camp, as near as I will get to where I believe Isabella's own string of beads was woven. Avoiding the slick operator beside the first opening, I walk back to a humbler looking option.

"How much to go on the sand, I don't want an umbrella or a chair," I say, "I'll only be here for a moment."

The young man hesitates, pretends to understand, then mumbles, "LE7."

Fending off young boys who want me to relax in a recliner or take up residence under one of their umbrellas, I make my way past deserted tables to the equally deserted sand. I am the sole object of the lads' interest and I march stolidly onward, refusing eye contact and declining every incomprehensible offer with a shake of the head. How am I to carry out this solemn finale to my long tracing of Isabella's prisoner with a crowd of young Egyptians hawk-eyed at my every move? I wanted time to muse. Before leaving home, I had once again struck lucky online. A detailed account of a man who was held here, Christoph Nagel, had suddenly appeared on-screen. To my utter amazement, he was a jeweller. Glancing at the boys, I force myself to ponder Christoph …

Some of the prisoners are housed in solidly constructed buildings with timber frames and brick partitions, but Christoph lives in a tent. A photograph shows him and his brothers nattily dressed in jackets and bow ties beside their prison home, an iron bedstead visible through the opening in the canvas. The records make it clear that its many layers protect him neither from the freezing cold of winter, nor from the burning heat of summer – he is always either far too hot, or shivering with cold. I can see him getting up. It is his turn on canteen duty.

Each group of prisoners is responsible for its own catering – the authorities reason that if the captives get familiar food, they will complain less. The men for whom Christoph will be preparing breakfast are, like him and his brothers, civilians. He is only a few miles away from his boyhood home, but – he stomps across to the mess – he can never visit. He is only a few miles away from the jewellery shop where he took an apprenticeship after leaving school, but – he gives a surly nod to the other men on duty with him – he can no longer design jewellery and place precious stones in intricate settings for the ladies of the city. He is Austrian. Would he have liked to leave his gems and join an army? Nobody asked him.

The summons for roll call resounds through the camp. How many years is it now? Three? Four? With every day the same, it is easy to lose track of time. Three years of wasted youth. Three years of being unable to get on with setting up his own business. Three years of being unable to find a wife. Three wasted years!

He follows the other men outside, blinking in the brightness. The British do not force them into hard labour, which is good, but he hates them. It is not that they treat them particularly badly, apart from these roll calls. It is time that makes him hate them. This awareness of the things he could have done, and the things he cannot, refuses to leave him. On top of that is the constant weight of having nothing worth doing in the seconds, minutes, hours, days, months and years that he now has to live through. It is a killer!

From his place in the line, he looks across at one of the older Austrians. A year or three ago he carved old Hans a chess set to fill time. It had been a good job. He had done it well. Nothing to be ashamed of there. A couple of the other fellows had wanted sets and he had obliged, but it had become tedious.

He glances surreptitiously towards his tent. Now he has another challenge. He is determined to learn English. Then he will be in a position to get even with these detestable British who have deprived him of life. The dictionary he is using is lying neatly on the shelf beside his bed. Of course he does not work at it every moment. He joins in with the activities the others organise – the concerts, the sports, the dramas. Joining in is part of the struggle not to sink into the deepest of glooms, not to let the British win. With just watching the weeks go by being enough to drive anyone insane, it is best to join in, not to ostracise yourself from the people you have been forced to live with. But, he wriggles his fingers, at heart he is a craftsman. Give him back his jewels!

I look left and right along the sands. Where can I most easily bury the beads? With these boys on my heels, the chief parameter is speed and the avoidance of too much intrusion. The security police would not like what I am trying to do, and their English is poor. If I had to explain, they would not understand.

Determinedly, I walk westwards, trying to turn my attention to how Isabella will react when angry young Christoph turns up on her ward. Most of the accounts from nurses seconded to care for enemy prisoners veer from initial horror – "Do I really have to help save this man for the Kaiser's army?" – to the gentle realisation that each one of these 'enemies' is a human being tossed about by the chaos of war just as much as she is herself. A German suffers with his pain just as much as a British Tommy does. A German longs to be back home just as much as every other patient in her hospital, every soldier on every front.

I can almost hear Christoph's clumsy attempts to communicate with the orderlies and nurses, but Isabella spent a year in Germany. She can talk to him as easily as his friends or family – although it perhaps feels strange to be letting her tongue twist its way round the harsh consonants and distinctive vowels of his language now, after all the havoc his nation and its allies have wrought. But she is a doctor, it is her duty to heal. There is no doubt that she will go up to his bedside and make sure that he is given the best possible treatment.

Kneeling down on the sand, I begin digging to commemorate their meeting, looking around nonchalantly in an attempt to disguise the fact that I am trying to dig an invisibly deep hole very quickly with only my bare left hand. Are my little followers watching? I risk flicking out the beads. Something has definitely excited them – they are chattering like Egyptian magpies. They are not budging though – they are still a few metres away. I scrape on, trying desperately to make my hollow less shallow.

Perhaps Christoph faces a long recovery. When the nurses jolly him into action, maybe he remembers the Turks working with their beads, and decides to go back to his old trade and fill a few hours by making something beautiful for the lady doctor. Or does he return to camp dreaming of his few, blissful days of hospital semi-freedom and his strange conversations with that lady doctor? She may have been British, but without her he might not be alive, however much there are moments when he wishes he was not. Using his newly broken English he demands beads, thread, loom and needles from his captors, and after he has once more helped with yet another meal, and stood through yet another roll-call, he works out the design for the next motif. And maybe, in the late afternoon, the feeling that he has got to get out overwhelms him. Much as it galls him with home so nearby, he makes his promise not to escape, and follows the guards outside the camp onto the beach where he played as a boy.

The word 'taxi' reaches me from the boys' conversation. My camera is in my right hand now and I am taking pictures as I dig. Did they say, "Driver"? With my left hand I begin to scoop the sand back over the beads. The boys are pointing. I click the shutter furiously. The beads are almost covered but the youngsters' chatter is getting more and more agitated. With one last flourish the beads vanish and I manage a final snap before I stand up, wondering what on earth has been happening.

Mustering as much dignity as I can after such a clandestine procedure, I saunter back to the entrance. There, I find the driver lounging against a fence, contentedly bantering with another group of boys over a cigarette. When he sees me, he stubs it out, ready to go. The boys offer me a towel. My feet are sandy, but I am desperate now to leave. Sand can wait. Struggling into my shoes and socks, I scramble back into the Lada.

11

The car whisks me back towards the Metropole. I managed it! I buried the beads! Mission has been accomplished. OK, it did not go quite as I had wanted, but when do things ever go to plan? 'Sometime' came and I followed the call. The crossing of the barriers of gender and enmity has taken me utterly by surprise. It has been so very far from the romance I have always imagined. Christoph may not have been the particular prisoner who gave Isabella her beads, but the real donor is far more likely to have thought and felt as he did than to have been the matinée idol I have pictured all these years. Yet far from being disappointed, I am satisfied. It makes sense. It is as if I at last understand the treasures in the Flower Press box. Now, perhaps, they will let me rest.

Beneath the hotel is a tempting patisserie and, since Alexandria is still as famous for its cafés as when M. Groppi began his career here, I push open the smoked glass door. Its warm brown fug hits me. Tables small and large are filled with Egyptians taking lunch, with groups smoking shisha pipes. Every notice is in Arabic, as is the conversation that sings through the air. A disparaging waiter grunts me to a seat and I examine the menu. In honour of M. Groppi's famous croissants, I keep my order simple. While I wait, I study the wall in front of me. Three dancers in harem pants and curve-toed sandals cavort amongst gyrating, Art Nouveau swirls that endorse the café's website name: www.trianon1905.com. Could Isabella have come here? Refusing even to contemplate the intrusive question, I immerse myself in a novel – the time for research and imagination is past.

On the flight northwards, I cannot take my eyes off the green Nile meandering through the brown desert, but once the desert becomes the sea, I revert to my book. The habit of tracing Isabella is dying hard and I have ended up with *Daughters of Mars*, Thomas Keneally's novel about Australian nurses serving in the First World War. I left the girls on a hospital ship boarding casualties from Gallipoli, but within a few pages they are back in Alexandria. Where will Keneally place them?

'The palm court at the Metropole,' I read.

"The Metropole? The very place I have just stayed? Oh, please, Mr Keneally, don't send them there! Please don't let them into the very place that seemed so ripe for a visit from Isabella! Not now – not when I thought I'd finished, not when I've just relaxed my rule of never, ever reading fiction about the First World War for fear of being tempted into inaccuracy."

The urge is too powerful. I let myself slip back to yesterday's croissant and the Art Nouveau dancers. The painting does not change, but the soft sofas where two Egyptian *effendi* were discussing business morphs into an empty Edwardian restaurant table with two chairs. The piped eastern music fades as musicians wearing *tarbooshes* and dinner jackets bend their bows to a waltz. Beside the palms, khaki-clad officers are seated in groups. Demurely dressed nurses sit nearby. A waiter wearing a smart white western jacket over his long eastern robes is showing a couple to the empty table. Heads are turning as this particular officer passes, acknowledging the odd acquaintance. The waiter pulls out a chair for his girl. A large brimmed hat screens her face, but the sling which supports her arm focuses my attention, and when she smiles I know exactly who she is.

The officer accompanying her turns to call for the waiter, the twist of his body revealing his medals and badges, the same medals and badges that attracted Walter Bonnici and David Jones to the very last of Isabella's war photographs. They had no eyes for my grandmother, standing pretty in a peplum top beside the object of their interest.

"The red tabs on his lapels and the lion and crown on his forage cap show that he is a staff officer. And he's wearing a Military Cross – he must have been very brave. Do you know who he is?"

Of course I know who he is. He is my grandfather, Captain Hubert Samuel Lane. Walter and David's observations simply confirm the family tradition that he served on General Allenby's staff. Now, I watch him passing Isabella the sugar, a solicitous expression on his face. Reputedly, he admitted to taking part in the brouhaha which erupted when Allenby's mess was informed that a woman would be joining them.

"And not just any woman – a female doctor!" I can almost hear the grumpy barking, the precise echo of the battle narrated in the papers of the Medical Women's Federation, the embodiment of the prejudice the women doctors are facing.

But there must have been a first time, a particular day when Isabella braved opening the mess door to join Allenby's men. My mind insists on replaying the scene in the film *Lawrence of Arabia* when Allenby's officers stop their game of billiards to stare as Lawrence, dressed in flowing robes, shepherds a parched Arab boy to the bar. Was Isabella's first entrance as dramatic as that? And when did it take place?

Was Miss Stenhouse on tenterhooks as Captain Lane set off with General Allenby and the Egyptian Expeditionary Force in September? Was it his name she was looking for on the casualty lists as she followed the force's progress through Megiddo and the other cities? Did her heart miss a beat when news reached the medical community in Alexandria that Spanish flu was devastating the British more effectively than were the Turks? Perhaps not. In fact-checking mode, I find that it was only some weeks after the Armistice, on 26th November 1918, that the whole division, including General Allenby's staff, arrived in Alexandria.

As I look across at my grandparents, I cannot tell if Isabella has succeeded in charming the whole mess, but she has certainly charmed Hubert. He is a widower. His wife died in childbirth in 1913. Originally a cavalryman, he is also the proud owner of two horses.

"But you can't ride Dinkums," he is reported to have told Isabella. "He'd be far too much for you."

"Oh no he wouldn't," she is said to have retorted.

The debate must have continued, because a well-worn family tale records that the day came when the pair of them headed out for the desert with Isabella firmly mounted on Dinkums. All went well until the thunder – a sudden clap out of nowhere. Startled, Dinkums threw Isabella. As she landed hard on the firm sand, her arm broke.

Sceptical, I check the weather statistics. Is there any chance that this story contains even a shred of truth? Are there ever storms in Egypt that could have given Isabella a broken arm? Not in Cairo, the statistics suggest, but storms are common around Alexandria in the winter.

Then, if March counts as winter, perhaps there is some truth in the old tale. Maybe it is the desert ride and the broken arm that lie hidden behind the final, bald sentences of Isabella's army record:

Arrived from Egypt 4.4.19. Granted six weeks sick leave to 7.5.19 (from date of embarkation) on a/c injury received (not on duty) in Egypt.

"She always told me that it was when Hubert's kind blue eyes gazed down at her as she lay on the sand that she fell in love," relates Isabella's daughter, while Isabella's daughter-in-law comments more pragmatically, "That arm troubled her for the rest of her life."

Opposite me in the Metropole, Isabella's sling tells me she will soon be shipped home. Somehow, Hubert must stand out from all the other officers she has met over the last four years.

If it is a spur-of-the-moment, end-of-the-war romance, I am part of the evidence that it will work. Hubert, the insurance man with no degree who has made it to Allenby's staff, and Isabella, the determined woman doctor, will get married at St Giles' Cathedral in Edinburgh on 14th October 1919. In the newspaper announcement of their wedding they will go against tradition and define themselves not by their parents, but by their achievements. Hubert will be 'Captain H.S. Lane, M.C, The London Irish Rifles,' and Isabella will be 'Isabel Stenhouse, M.B., CH. B. Edin.' They will get married from a house in Great King Street, Edinburgh, rather than the old family home, for 9 John's Place will be sold. From now until she dies in 1952, Janet's home will be with Isabella and Hubert.

Will Jan make it to the wedding? I suspect she will. After a year with the RAMC, in September 1918 Frank signed up as a Captain with the Australian Imperial Force. He will be shipped back to Australia in August. When he is settled, Jan will take their sons out to join him, but that is the last her family will see of her, for in giving birth to another child in 1921, she will die. Isabella will commemorate her by the name she chooses for her daughter – Alison Janetta, but nobody will make any effort to remember Beth.

And Isabella's career? She will carry on working. Like most of the other women doctors who have pushed the boundaries, learned new skills and served their nation during this war, she will find herself rewarded not with the surgical posts for which she is now well-qualified, but by being shunted back into the avenues traditionally acceptable for lady doctors – women, children and public health. As Hubert's career guides where they live, she will take posts working for the Maternal and Infant Welfare centres in Poplar, and at the all-women-run Elizabeth Garrett Anderson Hospital in Bloomsbury. She will follow those by working for Newcastle-upon-Tyne & Durham

Council. Wherever she goes, she will keep up her membership of the MWF, for there are still many battles to fight.

And what about that posthumous invitation from the Medical Directory to confirm that she served as a Captain with the RAMC from 1916–19? While she is still on sick leave with her broken arm, Winston Churchill, the Secretary of State for War, will send a disparaging letter to the MWF dismissing the claims of the women doctors that they should receive rank and commissions. Not one of the women doctors who have been attached to the RAMC during this war will be entitled to style themselves 'Captain', but Isabella is not the only one who will go ahead and claim the rank anyway.

Walter looks through the Medical Directory and comes across one here and another there who effectively says, "I deserved this so I'm jolly well going to take the credit for what I did." Isabella will tell her family that she was a captain, and they will believe her. Other women will do the same, and the myth will build, but these military titles are as phoney as the uniforms the women gave themselves when they first sailed with the army in 1916. Reluctantly, the MWF will decide that they will never win the case in the aftermath of this war and will defer the battle until the next war.

Opposite me, Hubert is paying the bill. Isabella's broken arm has ended her war, but this war is by no means over. Back in Sidi Bishr, men are still waiting to go home. In Hadra, the grave diggers are still preparing new graves.

Epilogue

Isabella is seated on her pale green settee, the July sunshine filtering through the long net curtains. Before her lies a large cube-shaped parcel. Around the room I, and her other nine grandchildren, wait with varying degrees of restlessness.

"Open it, Granny. Open it," somebody urges.

Reaching out a wrinkled hand, she starts to peel away the sticky tape. Soon, the paper is removed and every eye in the room is staring at her birthday present. Enquiringly, she looks towards her son, David.

He takes her hand, "It is a tape-recorder, Mother."

"We want you to record your memories," explains Alison, her daughter, putting her arm around Isabella's thin shoulders.

We youngsters know Ena – she is watching the spectacle from the armchair by the fire. We remember Hubert, even though he died when we were small. David and Alison remember Janet, the grandmother who lived with them all through their childhood, but none of us remembers Jan. None of us remembers Beth. None of us remembers the First World War. Even if we grandchildren do not yet understand, David and Alison know that this eighty-year-old lady, their Mother, our Granny, did something unusual.

"Please try, Mother," they beg.

Out of the fullness of the heart, the mouth speaks, says the proverb, but when it comes to war, I now know that the heart can be too full. It has seen, heard, touched and felt matters far beyond the pitiful smallness of words. It can ache with memories too potent to unlock. At the age of eighty, sixteen years before her death, Isabella chooses to ignore that tape-recorder and to continue her silence.

Author's Note

This book records my quest to unearth and retell a true story. It began with the thrill of research, when unexpected documents appeared from cyberspace and helpful archivists produced trophies from their vaults. But as my computer filled with files and data swirled around my mind, I faced a new problem: how on earth was I to thread this surfeit into an accurate history of Isabella Stenhouse, her war and her beads? I found myself an unwilling curator – every detail I decided to leave out shaped the story and its accuracy just as effectively as the particulars I chose to include.

To complicate matters, I wanted to weave behind the facts, to understand what my grandmother saw and felt. But how could I bring her experiences to life when she left so few rumours and such a tiny written archive? Fiction was not an option – her story was far too unusual for that. That is when I began travelling and risking letting scenes come alive – and my inner storyteller loved it. But it was hard. With every painstaking sentence, I understood why biographies fill up with 'might haves', 'could haves' and 'would haves'.

My scientific side reacted fiercely, "How dare you describe those scenes? However much they make Isabella's life more vivid, what about certainty? How can you be sure?"

The storyteller fought back just as ferociously, "One more 'fact' here, one new piece of information there and the whole tentative edifice deduced from your so-called-certainty would tumble." That shut the scientist up – it had seen such collapses many times.

The storyteller danced a victory jig – it knew it would make mistakes, but it also firmly believed that stories and scenes got far closer to the heart of any matter than an agglomeration of facts dosed liberally with caveats. But even as its jig ended, it flagged up another danger, "What if the instruments in the Flower Press box are false leads?"

That got me worried. Suppose I have ended up highlighting threads my grandmother would have ignored? What if I have missed gems she would have included? I certainly feel nearer to understanding what she lived through than when I began my quest, and I very much hope that she would recognise the tale that I have woven, but exactly how close I am to the story she chose never to tell – that is a mystery that will always remain.

ACKNOWLEDGEMENTS

My research would not have been possible without the help of a diversity of experts. A trio of officers – Colonel W Bonnici L/ RAMC (Retd), Lt Col (Retd) David Ashton Jones TD and Major Lizzie Hunt, RAMC BM BCh MA(Oxon) MRCPsych primed me on the Royal Army Medical Corps. Drs Danielle Huckle, Caroline Murray, Meg and Kate Dillon helped me understand what it means to be a woman doctor. Paul Atterbury, Adele Recklies, Alexander Wilson, Graham Best, Isla Cruikshank, Peter and Jennie Barrow, Joe Cacchia and Irene Townsley gave me the benefit of their specialist knowledge.

The write-up would have defeated me but for the encourage-ment of professional writers Horatio Clare, Ivy Alvarez, Patrick Dillon and Frankie Bailey of The Literary Consultancy as well as Bern, Marc, Jeremy and Griff – the poets of Chapter 11.

Super-special thanks go to Kate Strudwick – without you I would neither have started nor finished this quest. Equally special thanks go to Lila Haines and Walter Bonnici – you both know what you have done, and that without you, this book would not exist. And to Tracy Pallant – without you I would never have made it through that long midway section.

And to my long-suffering, endlessly patient family, who are by now heartily sick of Isabella – here's to the future!

One other acknowledgement: Isabella and the women who signed up with the RAMC were not the only women doctors who served in WWI. Significant numbers of medical women served with the Scottish Women's Hospitals, the Women's Hospital Corps and other smaller units.

Copyrights and permissions

The photograph on p.43 is reproduced by courtesy of Lothian Health Services Archive, Edinburgh University Library: P/PL1/C/062
The photograph on p.89 is reproduced by courtesy of the Imperial War Museum, who have also given permission to use material from Mrs Doughty-Wylie's diaries.
Material from the archive of the Medical Women's Federation is by courtesy of the Federation.

Sources

Information has come from across the globe, in particular

from the Women's Library, the Imperial War Museum, the Wellcome Library, the Liddle Collection, the National Library of Scotland and the British Library, but also from numerous other libraries and archives in the UK, France, Malta and Egypt as well as across the internet – but most notably from Penylan Library in Cardiff.

Key information has derived from Isabel Hutton's autobiography, *Memories of a Doctor in War and Peace*; Mrs Doughty-Wylie's diary; Colonel Walter Bonnici's website www.malta-ramc.com and the archive of the Medical Women's Federation.

A FEW OF THE BOOKS:

Brittain, V. (2011) Testament of Youth. Virago Press Edition. London: Virago Press

Brittain, V. (1982) Chronicle of Youth: War Diary 1913–1917. Charnwood Edition

Callus, L. ed. (2014) The Salter Album. Rabat: National Archives of Malta

Crofton, E. (2013) Angels of Mercy, A Women's Hospital on the Western Front 1914–18. Reprinted Edinburgh: Birlinn

Cushing, H. (1936) From a Surgeon's Journal 1915–18. Boston: Little Brown and Company

Englund, P. (2011) The Beauty and the Sorrow. London: Profile Books

Hutton, I. (1960) Memories of a Doctor in War and Peace. London: Heinemann

Ismail, A. (2011) Alexandria was our destiny: based on the memories of Marie-Luise Nagel. Alexandria, Egypt: Bibliotheca Alexandrina

Macdonald, L. (1993) The Roses of No Man's Land. London: Penguin

Mackinnon, A. (2012) Malta, Nurse of the Mediterranean. Reprint edition. Forgotten Books

Macpherson, W.G. (1921) Medical Services; General History. HMSO

Marlow, J. (1999) The Virago Book of Women and the Great War. London: Virago Press

Martin, A.A. (1915) A Surgeon in Khaki. Edward Arnold

Navarro, A. (1917) The Scottish Women's Hospital at the French Abbey of Royaumont. London: Allen and Unwin

Powell, A. (2009) Women in the War Zone: Hospital Service in World War One. Gloucestershire: The History Press

Recklies, A. (2006) Bead Crochet Snakes. New York: Reckless Beading Press

Roberts, A. (2007) Crème de la Crème: Girls' Schools of Edinburgh. Glasgow: Steve Savage Publishers

Thompson, P. (1992) The Edwardians 2nd Edition. London: Routledge

Tubby, A.H. (1920) A Consulting Surgeon in the Near East. London: Christophers

Whitehead, I.R. (2013) Doctors in the Great War. Barnsley: Pen and Sword Military

Want more details?

Get in touch via:

Website: www.katrinakirkwood.org

Twitter: @kkstories

Blog: http://isabellaandthestringofbeads.blogspot.co.uk

Lightning Source UK Ltd.
Milton Keynes UK
UKOW05f2253260117
292949UK00009B/226/P